P9-ASI-654

Teaching Flaubert's
Madame Bovary

Approaches to Teaching World Literature

Joseph Gibaldi, series editor

For a complete listing of titles,
see the last pages of this book.

Approaches to
Teaching Flaubert's
Madame Bovary

Edited by

Laurence M. Porter

and

Eugene F. Gray

The Modern Language Association of America
New York   1995

Library of Congress Cataloging-in-Publication Data

Approaches to teaching Flaubert's Madame Bovary / edited by Laurence
    M. Porter and Eugene F. Gray.
        p.   cm. — (Approaches to teaching world literature ; 53)
    Includes bibliographical references and index.
    ISBN 0-87352-729-1 (cloth) ISBN 0-87352-730-5 (pbk.)
    1. Flaubert, Gustave, 1821–1880. Madame Bovary. 2. Flaubert,
Gustave, 1821–1880—Study and teaching. I. Porter, Laurence M.,
1936–   . II. Gray, Eugene F., 1936–   . III. Series.
PQ2246.M3A66   1995
843'.8—dc20   95-13050

Cover illustration of the paperback edition: Gustave Courbet, *Lady in Riding Habit*
(*L'Amazone*). Oil on canvas. The Metropolitan Museum of Art. Bequest of Mrs. H. O.
Havemeyer, 1929. The H. O. Havemeyer Collection. (29.100.59). All rights reserved.
The Metropolitan Museum of Art.

Set in Caledonia and Bodoni. Printed on recycled paper
Published by The Modern Language Association of America
10 Astor Place, New York, New York 10003-6981

For
Carole

CONTENTS

PREFACE TO THE SERIES

In *The Art of Teaching* Gilbert Highet wrote, "Bad teaching wastes a great deal of effort, and spoils many lives which might have been full of energy and happiness." All too many teachers have failed in their work, Highet argued, simply "because they have not thought about it." We hope that the Approaches to Teaching World Literature series, sponsored by the Modern Language Association's Publications Committee, will not only improve the craft—as well as the art—of teaching but also encourage serious and continuing discussion of the aims and methods of teaching literature.

The principal objective of the series is to collect within each volume different points of view on teaching a specific literary work, a literary tradition, or a writer widely taught at the undergraduate level. The preparation of each volume begins with a wide-ranging survey of instructors, thus enabling us to include in the volume the philosophies and approaches, thoughts and methods of scores of experienced teachers. The result is a sourcebook of material, information, and ideas on teaching the subject of the volume to undergraduates.

The series is intended to serve nonspecialists as well as specialists, inexperienced as well as experienced teachers, graduate students who wish to learn effective ways of teaching as well as senior professors who wish to compare their own approaches with the approaches of colleagues in other schools. Of course, no volume in the series can ever substitute for erudition, intelligence, creativity, and sensitivity in teaching. We hope merely that each book will point readers in useful directions; at most each will offer only a first step in the long journey to successful teaching.

Joseph Gibaldi
Series Editor

PREFACE TO THE VOLUME

Arguably the greatest novel of nineteenth-century France, *Madame Bovary* is widely taught in required general education courses in world literature and Western civilization and in French or Romance literature in translation, as well as in the traditional introduction to literature required by English departments for prospective majors, in comparative literature courses, and in courses on European intellectual history and on the novel as a genre. *Madame Bovary* raises key issues in human relations, ethics, and social justice, as well as problems concerning the use and misuse of language, novelistic structure, tone, and figurative expression in literature.

If you believe as we do that the primary goal of literary studies is to teach students to read and write—to enable them to understand others and to empower them to express themselves as effectively as possible—then *Madame Bovary* offers an ideal combination of accessibility and sophistication. The simple main plot of fantasy, frustration, adultery, profligacy, and self-destruction can readily be grasped by students. Yet Flaubert's practice of withholding authorial commentary and his use of symbolic objects and of irony make the novel more complex than it appears at first glance. Aided by leading questions, students can experience the satisfaction of independently discovering the novel's structures of symmetry and progression and its pervasive undercurrents of mockery and pessimism. Its strong element of bourgeois critique remains pertinent to our own capitalist society, motivated by consumerism and profit. Since most students have not encountered the novel in other forms (excerpts, television, or film) before they read it in college, their experience of it will be unencumbered by competing versions.

To aid instructors, we have sought essays that tease out the two opposing strands of the work: the particular and the general. The core of the action is a bad relationship without communication. Everyone has experienced such relationships. Classes can thus examine the interaction of the couples—Emma and Charles, Emma and Rodolphe, Emma and Léon—in ways that make it pertinent to students of diverse backgrounds and sexual orientations by examining universals in interpersonal dynamics, such as triangulation, self-deception, narcissistic mirroring, and codependency. All these concepts can be simply illustrated with examples from daily experience.

Teachers can generate lively classroom debates by asking students to take sides in evaluating the status of the heroine herself within her society. Does Emma Bovary remain a "Don Quixote in skirts" throughout the novel, or does she eventually become disillusioned with her Romantic ideals? Although snared in the same web of mediocrity that binds everyone else, is Emma more sensitive than those around her? Or is she victimized mainly by her selfishness and gullibility? Flaubert's sensitive treatment of his heroine raises still-urgent issues concerning the education of women and their social role, inviting discussion of the novel from a feminist perspective. *Madame Bovary* makes clear (though this point is often overlooked) that Emma possesses certain talents, yet she received the traditional convent education, designed to produce an agreeable companion, wife, and mother. No other prospects were open to her in her circumscribed world.

Essential to preparing a feminist discussion of the novel is background concerning the manifold constraints imposed on women in nineteenth-century France (and until the late 1970s): they were disenfranchised, regarded legally in many ways as minors, and limited to the career choices of servant, housewife, nun, or prostitute. Yearning for independence, Emma Bovary, ironically, is prevented by her acculturation from imagining any solution other than to vest her aspirations in males. She has made little progress beyond Cinderella and Sleeping Beauty, except in her use of theft and lies to carve out a limited, precarious, and short-lived autonomy. Today's female students tend to believe that the feminist battles were fought and won a generation ago; they may not always recognize that they, too, can become victims of social inequity. Teachers can bring out the continuity of oppressive gender polarization from Emma's time to the present by using resources like Ruth Gordon's *Adam's Rib*, Carol Gilligan's *In a Different Voice*, Alicia Ostriker's *Stealing the Language*, and Sandra M. Gilbert and Susan Gubar's *The Madwoman in the Attic*. We hope that this MLA volume will help normalize such an approach, making instructors more comfortable with it and presenting feminism as a form of humanism that frees everyone.

At the same time, of course, teachers must help students realize that Emma is no heroine. She is a histrionic, self-centered person who fails to master the developmental tasks of achieving the capacity for intimacy and for generativity (in Erik H. Erikson's sense: the ability to take care of other people and of things). She is the target of almost continuous irony owing to her debased interpretation of Romanticism, a congeries of ideas that Flaubert both cherished and deplored. Instructors who prefer an aesthetic approach and who believe that literature classes should not be used to examine social values can study the novel's irony to help students apprehend the central literary phenomenon of figuration, of discourse that ostensibly says one thing but means something else as well. To have students locate instances of irony and of comedy in the text enhances their sensitivity to tone, always a difficult concept to convey, while focusing their efforts on a small, manageable segment of the novel that nevertheless can generate an overarching thematic discussion.

In his depiction of society, Flaubert is a great comic moralist whose virtuosity has often gone unrecognized. One outstanding example, which students should be encouraged to examine critically, is whether the pharmacist Homais should be dismissed as a harmless buffoon, ultimately indistinguishable from his adversary in debate, l'abbé Bournisien, or whether he stands at the center of Flaubert's analysis of what can go wrong in a modern society, illustrating the dangers of the misuse or abuse of technology. His crucial role in the disastrous clubfoot operation on Hippolyte and his paralegal practice of medicine provide a focus for questions of medical ethics, a subject increasingly taught in college programs. Does Homais merely reincarnate the classical *alazon*, or does he represent a debased, destructive form of the notion of progress (the great Enlightenment ideal forms the philosophic basis of the founding of both the French and the American republics) contributing indirectly but profoundly to Emma's downfall and death?

Teaching Flaubert also provides a valuable access to training in the art of the realistic novel, by far the most popular literary genre in undergraduate courses. To recognize the new descriptive dimension Flaubert added to literature, one need only compare his settings to the vague landscapes of Romanticism. Yet he also frees these settings from the clutter of episodic expert observers and from the rhetoric of material-moral correspondence that pervade the fiction of Balzac. From the stylistic point of view, Flaubert's influence on later writers has been enormous; he often is called the father of the modern novel. Manuals for aspiring novelists (such as Macauley and Lanning's *Technique in Fiction*) openly recommend many of his techniques.

Close reading allows students the satisfaction of discovering for themselves the symbolic value of descriptions; effective starting points are the famous set pieces presenting Charles's schoolboy cap and Emma's wedding cake. They may also note recurring descriptions that signal change, such as those of the greyhound Djali and the plaster statue of a priest. From such discussions students can be led to infer Flaubert's views on the absence of guiding values, a materialistic emphasis on quantity rather than quality, and the resulting corruption of society. More important, students who have learned to read critically will become less vulnerable to exploitation supported by others' unscrupulous use of language.

Just as a focus on relationship pathology in the couple can show students the links between the drama of *Madame Bovary* and their own experience, so a focus on the relationships between the business and professional person and his (we use the gender-specific term advisedly) clients in the novel helps students recognize Flaubert's satire by pointing to enduring ethical issues. A general discussion concerning what we understand by unethical practices in business and in medicine will better prepare students to understand how the fates of Emma, Charles, Hippolyte, the blind man, and little Berthe illustrate Flaubert's somber general view of his society. The famous seduction scene at the agricultural fair draws a clear parallel between economic and sexual exploitation, while Emma's assumption of a "masculine" role near the end of the novel (taking over the power of attorney from Charles and making Léon her "mistress" more than she is his) broadens the issue of exploitation from its usual gender-based mode to a consideration of a more general interaction of power with dependency.

In recent years, the acuity of Flaubert's social awareness has been much at issue. But most agree that *Madame Bovary* exposes the corruption of taste and the vitiation of traditional guiding myths (such as the sanctity of the family, the probity of the small tradesman, the transforming power of religious faith, and the moral superiority of the Romantic idealist) during the Second Empire period. Teachers should highlight these myths at the outset and then ask students to look for ways in which Flaubert undermines them. He questioned them so keenly that he and his publisher were prosecuted for having offended against public morals.

Since students encounter few examples of satire in standard curricula (or since instructors of beginning courses tend to avoid teaching literary works as satire because of the topical baggage that full understanding often requires) and since students often experience difficulty in recognizing the comic in sophisticated literature, *Madame Bovary* can serve a valuable purpose in enriching their understanding of comic or satiric literature in general, regardless of which label an individual instructor prefers to place on the novel. Flaubert's novel can thus be readily integrated into a course that includes such later authors as Gabriel García Márquez, Günter Grass, Joseph Heller, George Orwell, Kurt Vonnegut, and Tom Wolfe.

In the context of cultural history, *Madame Bovary* again serves well to provoke discussions related to our own times. The rapid expansion of primary schooling and literacy in the 1830s (at the onset of the revolution, only one quarter of France's inhabitants were first-language speakers of standard French), coupled with the development of inexpensive printing technology, gave rise to a spate of serialized novels that provided a vehicle for disseminating publicity so as to create a demand for the consumer goods of the industrial revolution. The production of these popular fictions led to a widespread propagation of Romantic ideas in a diluted, popularized form. Flaubert was one of the earliest authors to depict the debasement of language through the use of clichés and propagandistic and commercial texts. In an age when many media bombard us daily with advertising and political campaigns, the question of the use and abuse of language is crucial. The electronic revolution of the late twentieth century has reached an even broader public than the readers of serialized novels in Flaubert's day, since television requires neither literacy nor the creative participation of the viewer (whereas the "hot" medium of print does require such participation). In different ways, both Flaubert's novel and television force us to confront the questions What should we read? and Why should we read at all?

For more sophisticated student groups, these questions may be recast in the form of the debate concerning Flaubert's postmodernism. To what extent do his celebrated represented discourse (free indirect style) and indeterminacy (a simple example: there are three Mme Bovarys in *Madame Bovary*) contribute to a subtler, more profound understanding of human consciousness, and to what extent do they foreshadow the breakdown of the concept of a unified, purposeful humanistic self in the era of deconstruction? Here again, an initial exploration of students' definitions of selfhood and identity can relate *Madame Bovary* to almost any course in the humanities.

Finally, the ironic and satiric thrust of *Madame Bovary* allows the instructor to situate the novel in the broad current of oppositional narratives. Any text, as Roland Barthes observed, must be an oppositional text to emerge as a separate entity. But in its time, *Madame Bovary* was read as particularly subversive, provoking a storm of protest from critics who deplored the absence of morally inspiring characters. Teachers can stimulate lively classroom debate by asking whether fiction should affirm or question accepted values or be neutral. What is "redeeming social value" (*Madame Bovary* was extensively censored in its first publication in *La revue de Paris*), and is it legitimate to expect such value of literature? Can art find a viable middle ground between "radical chic" and conformity?

We are indebted to the Modern Language Association for suggesting and sponsoring this volume; to Michigan State University, its College of Arts and Letters, and its Department of Romance and Classical Languages for facilitating our work; to our late mentors, René Jasinski and Robert J. Niess, who first introduced us to the serious study of Flaubert; and to Benjamin F. Bart, who often guided and encouraged our early projects on that author.

Laurence M. Porter
Eugene F. Gray
Michigan State University
East Lansing

Part One

MATERIALS

Editions and Translations

French Editions

Nearly two-thirds of the survey respondents who teach *Madame Bovary* in French use the Garnier-Flammarion edition, whose 1986 version (the one used for quotations in this volume unless otherwise noted) reproduces the 1873 Charpentier edition, preceded by a chronology and preface by Bernard Ajac. Several teachers praised the quality of the introduction and the inclusion of the lawyers' and judge's speeches from Flaubert's trial for subverting public morals. Nearly all the remaining respondents use either the Classiques Garnier or the Folio edition. Regarding all three editions, their reasonable cost for students is the major consideration. One-tenth of the respondents use excerpts in French, relying either on the Classiques Larousse abridgement or on the Leggewie anthology of French literature.

English Editions

More than half the respondents teach *Madame Bovary* in French only, one-eighth teach the novel only in English, and one-third teach it in both languages. Half of those who teach it in English use the Norton Critical Editions volume, "a substantially new translation by Paul de Man" based on the version by Eleanor Marx Aveling, Karl Marx's daughter. (All quotations are from this edition unless otherwise noted.) De Man includes early scenarios and scenes, sixteen critical essays, and three letters by Flaubert, plus a selected bibliography. Several respondents praised the selection of criticism, but those who commented on this edition are evenly divided regarding the merits of the translation. It does contain a number of errors. Published in 1965, moreover, this edition is now far out of date. Norton is preparing a new version with a different translation. The other respondents are evenly divided in their preferences among the translations by Alan Russell (Viking Penguin), by Francis Steegmuller (Random House's Modern College Library), and by Lowell Bair (Bantam Classics). The World's Classics edition (Oxford University Press), translated by Gerard Manley Hopkins and edited by Terence Cave, does not yet seem well known, but it merits a trial. Two teachers praised the Bantam version as being more accurate than Steegmuller's and less stilted than de Man and Aveling's. Those who teach excerpts in English rely either on the *Norton Anthology of World Masterpieces* (Mack et al.) or, in one instance, on *Literature: The Human Experience* (Abcarian and Klotz).

Courses and Course Designs

Respondents have chosen to teach *Madame Bovary* for unsurprising reasons: its status as a classic, its aesthetic merits, and its representativeness of the French realist period in literature. That two respondents identify the novel as typical of the transition between Romanticism and realism while two others find it typical of the transition between realism and modernism attests to its "universality." Dean de la Motte, in his survey response, calls it the "starkest and most complex depiction of the frustrated desire that dominates French and European fiction."

Sixty percent of the respondents work in foreign language departments; twenty percent are teachers of English; the remainder are scattered among departments such as comparative literature, humanities, and philosophy. Half the respondents teach *Madame Bovary* to French majors, sixty percent of them teach in upper-division courses, and nearly two-thirds teach the work in an elective course. Among the most unusual course titles are Society and the Individual in the Modern European Novel; Irony; The Portrayal of Women in Literature; Psychoanalysis and Literature; The Novel; and Fictions of Love. Overarching topics include female suicide, the relation between love and death, the quest archetype, the ironic distance between desire and language, and Flaubert as a precursor of the style and techniques of the modern novel.

When asked which other disciplines they combine with the study of literature, instructors most often mention history (twenty percent), followed by psychology, art history, sociology, social history, and feminism (fifteen down to ten percent in the order given). Only one-eighth of respondents describe their critical stance with a single label; two teachers are applying the theories of René Girard, and one each the theories of Jacques Derrida, Jacques Lacan, and Tony Tanner. Twenty percent identify their approach as close reading (which, pace our respondents, is not a critical method), and fifteen percent avow being eclectic. Fifteen percent each identify themselves as feminist, narratological, and psychological critics, although, as the bibliography of works cited at the end of this volume attests, no one mentioned specific works by critics espousing either object-relations or Lacanian theory (other than Lacan), two highly fashionable schools in psychoanalytically oriented literary criticism. Only ten percent call themselves poststructuralists; apparently, that wave has passed its crest.

Regarding the practical problems of reaching students (an issue addressed in this volume both indirectly, by Benjamin Bart, and directly, by Ross Chambers), our respondents are unanimous. Overwhelmingly, the greatest problems confronting students are their difficulty in recognizing and appreciating Flaubert's irony, their difficulty in distinguishing between the viewpoints of the protagonist and the narrator, their tendency to be blinded by either sympathy with or distaste for Emma, and their insensitivity to the nuances of

Flaubert's style. These issues are interrelated, and they patently preoccupy many of our contributors in the classroom. The restraints placed on women in the nineteenth century are unfamiliar to students; many of them wonder why Emma doesn't simply obtain a divorce (illegal in France from 1816 to 1884). Finally, the sheer length of the novel and the richness of its vocabulary are a problem for many.

Suggested techniques used to help students appreciate the novel include having them try to write entries for Emma's diary or to give her advice (exacerbating the problems mentioned just above), helping them visualize the era through watching a film version of the novel, and, most commonly, showing students—from either a sociohistorical or an individualistic perspective, depending on the temperament of the instructor—how they, like Emma, are self-deceived, how they flee reality and take refuge in fantasy, and how they are deluded by a culture that mediates desire through advertising and through the media in general. "Students are living this novel every waking day of their lives," Andrew McKenna observes, "and it is amusing and fruitful to send them out to look for images and advertisements and programs that continue Emma's sentimental education." As Lauren Pinzka concludes, "Flaubert speaks of our inability to think beyond the limits of our education and language; of the rampant materialism, addiction, and greed of modern society; of false spirituality; of compulsive sexual gratification—in sum, of the mediocrity of modern life and the inability to express ourselves in words that are but products of our mass culture. He dramatizes the waste of women's potential and the triumph of the shallow and pretentious."

In terms of specific readings, course designs that include *Madame Bovary* appear to follow one of six major patterns. (1) Instructors contrast *Madame Bovary* with "Un coeur simple" (egotism versus selfless devotion) or with *Salammbô* (the everyday versus the exotic). (2) Instructors include Flaubert's novel in a series that exemplifies realism and naturalism in nineteenth-century France and that, predictably, includes Balzac's *Le Père Goriot*, Stendhal's *Le rouge et le noir*, and Zola's *Germinal*. (3) Instructors teach *Madame Bovary* together with other novels treating adultery, such as Tolstoy's *Anna Karenina* and William Dean Howells's *A Modern Instance*. (4) Instructors include Flaubert's novel in a course involving works on the subjugation and oppression of women, notably Sand's *Indiana* or *Mauprat*, adding at times Duras's *Le ravissement de Lol V. Stein*, Zola's *L'assommoir* or *Nana*, Balzac's *La Cousine Bette* or *La femme de trente ans*, Shakespeare's *Hamlet*, Richardson's *Clarissa*, Ibsen's *Hedda Gabler* or *A Doll House*, Dumas fils's *La dame aux camélias*, Diderot's *La religieuse*, James's *The Portrait of a Lady*, Norris's *MacTeague*, Maupassant's *Une vie*, or Tennessee Williams's *The Glass Menagerie*. (5) *Madame Bovary* is at times also included in a course on the pathology of love relationships, including such works as Goethe's *The Sorrows of Young Werther* (his *Elective Affinities*, not mentioned, would also provide an effective counterpart), Proust's *La prisonnière*, Robbe-Grillet's *La jalousie*, a version of the legend of Phaedra, or Mérimée's "La Vénus d'Ille." (6) Finally, Flaubert's novel may be integrated into a course treating divine discontent, overreaching, and self-deception, involving works such as Dante's *Inferno*, Goethe's *Faust 1*, or—by way of contrast—a version of the heroic woman at odds with society in some version of the myth of Antigone. Obviously, many of the works listed above could be used in more than one of the syllabi mentioned.

Recommended Readings

Background Materials

Instructors can find annotated bibliographies of Flaubert criticism in Eugene Gray and Laurence Porter and in Porter and a nearly comprehensive listing, without commentary, in David Colwell's four-volume work. Otto Klapp's *Bibliographie der französischen Literaturwissenschaft*, appearing annually since 1960 as early as October following the year covered, remains the best source for updating bibliography, including dissertations and book reviews. The *MLA Bibliography*, complete, appears in book form and on CD-ROM; *The Year's Work in Modern Language Studies* has annotations but is hopelessly belated, spotty, quirky, and biased.

Gordon Wright's classic *France in Modern Times* is the most widely used historical source, readily accessible to both students and teachers. The chapters headed "The Varieties of History" sketch the major divergent interpretations of each period since around 1760. A truly broad-gauged introduction to the Western world in Flaubert's day may be found in Asa Briggs's *The Nineteenth Century*. Other recommended background works include Cesar Grana's *Bohemian versus Bourgeois*, F. W. J. Hemmings's three books, Claude Pichois's overview of literary history, Michel Raimond's and Martin Seymour-Smith's surveys of the novel, and Eugen Weber's and Theodore Zeldin's social histories. Overviews of the realist movement in George Joseph Becker and Bernard Weinberg (140–41, 159–76) should also prove useful for both students and their teachers.

Regarding Flaubert himself, the works most often mentioned are selections from Flaubert's correspondence. In addition to those letters reproduced in the Norton edition of *Madame Bovary*, English translations may be found in Francis Steegmuller's edition of *The Letters of Gustave Flaubert*. Instructors can find further guidance in making selections by consulting Charles Carlut's *La correspondance de Flaubert* and Geneviève Bollème's *Extraits de la correspondance*. A compendium of satiric targets may be found in Flaubert's *Dictionnaire des idées reçues*, edited by Lea Caminiti, also available in a masterly translation with a penetrating introduction by Jacques Barzun as *The Dictionary of Accepted*

Ideas. Benjamin Bart's is the leading biography of Flaubert, although those by Herbert Lottman, Enid Starkie, and Steegmuller—along with the relevant sections of Maxime Du Camp's *Souvenirs littéraires* (1882–83; see vol. 1, chs. 7, 9–14; vol. 2, chs. 21, 25, 28–30)—each have one or two advocates. Steegmuller's is, in our opinion, the most readable and accessible for undergraduates. Moreover, it offers generous extracts from Flaubert's letters; the later editions incorporate advances in scholarship; and Steegmuller's appendix contains a translation of the second scenario for *Madame Bovary*. For iconography, see the *Album Flaubert* (Bruneau and Ducourneau).

Background works not by Flaubert, in order of how often they were mentioned, include Gérard Genette's groundbreaking essays on narratology, which our respondents recommend supplementing with works by William Martin, Gerald Prince (*Dictionary*, *Narratology*, and *Narrative as Theme*), and Lawrence Rothfield. Also, regarding censorship under the Third Empire, see the first two chapters of Dominick LaCapra's Madame Bovary *on Trial*. Finally, two respondents mentioned André Lagarde and Laurent Michard's history of French literature.

General Introductions

The opening chapters of Victor Brombert's *Flaubert par lui-même* richly characterize Flaubert's imagination. Brombert's *The Novels of Flaubert*, an often-cited, lucid study, was mentioned by many respondents. Works by Eric Gans, Rosemary Lloyd, Maurice Nadeau, Charles-Augustin Sainte-Beuve, Albert Thibaudet, and Anthony Thorlby each were recommended by at least one or two respondents as introductions for advanced students, as was Sartre's *L'idiot de la famille*—now available in English, although the first volume should be used with caution because it contains numerous errors in translation. The fourth volume, intended as an exegesis of *Madame Bovary*, never appeared during Sartre's lifetime, although his notes for it were published in volume 3 of the revised edition (663–812).

Critical Studies

Helpful collections of major essays are available in de Man's Norton edition and in the compilations by Raymonde Debray-Genette, by Laurence Porter, and by Naomi Schor and Henry Majewski. The critics most often mentioned were Jonathan Culler (over one-quarter of the respondents use him) and then Erich Auerbach (accessible to students), Tony Tanner, and Mario Vargas Llosa in that order (ten to twenty percent of respondents). Also mentioned on two or more questionnaires were Baudelaire, Roland Barthes, Leo Bersani, Stirling Haig, Georges Poulet, Jean-Pierre Richard, and Richard Terdiman.

The Instructor's Library

Our respondents rarely mentioned whether particular books are more appropriate for students or for teachers. Nevertheless, some specialized research tools that deserve mention, in addition to the bibliographies, include Jean Bruneau's Pléiade edition of the *Correspondance* (vol. 3, covering 1859–68, appeared in 1991), Claudine Gothot-Mersch's edition of *Madame Bovary*, and three editions of the *Œuvres complètes*: Bernard Masson's, which is convenient because compact; Maurice Bardèche's, unusually complete but textually unreliable; and Maurice Nadeau's, in a small format containing all the essentials. For stylistic, thematic, and genetic studies, respondents recommended the concordance by Charles Carlut, Pierre Dubé, and Raymond Dugan; studies of manuscript variants in the agricultural fair (the most widely taught scene, judging from the questionnaires) by Jeanne Goldin (Flaubert's *Les comices*) and in Gothot-Mersch's edition as well as her *La genèse de* Madame Bovary; and the chapter by John Porter Houston, which clearly situates Flaubert's style in its historical context. In addition we suggest Charles Bruneau and Albert Thibaudet, whereas Gustave Lanson, Ferdinand Brunetière, and Alf Lombard provide useful insights into typical nineteenth-century aspects of Flaubert's style. On the thorny question of free indirect style, Charles Bally and Stephen Ullmann each furnish useful *mises au point*, and Gérard Strauch gives a detailed historical overview. Finally, the unmentioned Larousse *Grand dictionnaire universel du dix-neuvième siècle* is a mine of information about the period (see, e.g., the article "Officier de santé").

Aids to Teaching

Few aids were mentioned, although the essays in this volume by Mary Donaldson-Evans (film) and by William Nelles (symbols in the visual arts and in literature) offer a rich repertory of examples with suggestions for their classroom use. More than one-tenth of the respondents said they use slides of nineteenth-century French painting; the same number show the Vincente Minnelli film. We editors recommend taking a few minutes to contrast baroque with Romantic music; the instructor could simply play it in the background as a prelude to class. Kenneth Clark's video on Romanticism in his *Civilisation* series (pt. 12, "The Fallacies of Hope") has been used by more than one instructor, particularly in general humanities and culture courses. And finally, in the 1991 French film version, Claude Chabrol attempts to provide a faithful rendering of the novel, often incorporating Flaubert's text into the dialogue and narrative.

Part Two

APPROACHES

Introduction

The essays in this volume illustrate the diversity of approaches to Flaubert's novel yet do not exhaust the possibilities; indeed, no single volume could. In his opening essay, Benjamin Bart provides an overview of the novel, placing it within the development of Romanticism.

Lilian Furst presents the social situation in which Emma finds herself in nineteenth-century France. Edward Ahearn adopts a sociohistorical approach, suggesting links with the revolution of 1848, examining the issue of antagonism between the city and the countryside, and showing how desire and sexuality are inextricably tied to social and economic concerns.

Susan Wolf provides a feminist reading of the text, while Lauren Pinzka adopts a Lacanian point of view, stressing the centrality in everyone's existence of psychoanalytic issues like gender, family dynamics, and sexuality.

Several approaches are formal in nature. Dean de la Motte examines the different facets of the character Emma: the tragic, the romantic, the realist, the modernist. William Nelles examines the important question of symbolism in the novel, in particular the symbolism of the horse. Michal Peled Ginsburg shows how the formal aspects of the novel, in particular the ways in which characters are seen, make *Madame Bovary* a good choice for a course on the novel. Beryl Schlossman points out the importance of grammatical categories in studying Flaubert's style. Michael Issacharoff examines the comic and ironic aspects of *Madame Bovary*. Gerald Prince analyzes in detail the novel's narrative structure.

Dorothy Kelly attempts to enable her students to take pleasure in the paradoxes of the text, to help them appreciate the beauty and complexity of the writing, and to bring them to question their assumptions about the way language relates to reality. James Winchell begins his teaching of the novel with the premise that the concerns and objections raised by today's students are valid responses perfectly in keeping with the most compelling and problematic locus of meaning treated by the novel itself. Andrew McKenna looks at desire and its representation in the novel.

Mary Donaldson-Evans explains how the film versions of *Madame Bovary* are helpful to the appreciation of Flaubert's text. Monika Brown shows how *Madame Bovary* would fit in a Great Books or World Literature course based on the topic of realism. Carol de Dobay Rifelj suggests ways in which writing assignments may stimulate both rewriting and rereading of the novel.

William Berg and Laurey Martin propose creative techniques and tactics for reading the novel based on two principles: first, seeing textual elements not as isolated data but in terms of their relations with other elements of the text and, second, formulating questions, since the reading of literature is an active process of questioning the text. Ross Chambers analyzes Emma Bovary's dilemma in terms of the dilemma of reading.

Note In the essays that follow, parenthetical page references follow translations, providing page numbers first for the French and then for the English. In block quotations, the numbers for the French text follow the French; those for the English text follow the translation. Unless otherwise noted, all quotations from the French text are taken from the Garnier-Flammarion volume, edited by Bernard Ajac (1986); quotations from the English text are taken from the Norton edition, translated by Eleanor Marx Aveling and Paul de Man (1965).

Teaching *Madame Bovary* in a Humanities Course

Benjamin F. Bart

In a humanities course, it is useful to begin by identifying for students where *Madame Bovary* stands in the development of Romanticism. Flaubert was born in 1821 as high Romanticism was about to sweep over France. He grew up with not only the movement's great contributions but also the standard claptrap that it invited young people, then as now, to admire. Like Romantic heroes, he slept with a dagger under his pillow. But as he matured, he came to realize the dangers inherent in this worldview. He never ceased to be a Romantic, but now he knew better, and his view while writing *Madame Bovary* may better be thought of as anti-Romanticism: he was both possessed by it and aware that it was a false doctrine.

Let me suggest a general account of Romanticism. In one of the standard dichotomies that dog and enliven the modern world, we are constantly faced with the opposition between ourselves and "externality," the world in which we are situated. I suggest that Romanticism, for our purpose, depends on the Romantic's decision that when the individual and the world of externality come into conflict the individual must seek to triumph, so as to give ever freer rein to what most marks the character as an individual. Since human reason is widely shared by most individuals, Romantic individualism tends to concentrate on what most differentiates a particular character from all others: that character's emotions. When these emotions come vigorously into play, the individual will almost inevitably find externality in opposition. To submit seems a tawdry end; to offer fruitless combat makes up the principal burden of Romantic tragedy. *Madame Bovary* may readily be taught from this approach. I emphasize from the outset that finding Emma wrong, as Flaubert does, does not mean that Yonville is right. This double-edged satire has been called Flaubert's binocular vision. Students may need assistance to realize that Flaubert wishes them not only to understand why Emma acts and feels as she does but also to know that she is wrong in doing so.

The rigid socioeconomic barriers of nineteenth-century France also should be explained to students. Emma rejects her background as the daughter of a relatively improvident farmer. But her convent school was already far above her level, and she will always lack the polish, the manners, the savoir faire, and the wealth of those from higher social levels. She will naturally wish to rise (don't all American students assume that such an ascension is always possible?), but in nineteenth-century France it would have been nearly impossible. Hence her dreams and desires make her a willing victim to a man who could fool her into believing he shared them—in order to share her bed.

Emma wishes to mold Yonville nearer to her own desire or to rise above it, albeit only clandestinely, but she faces nearly insuperable odds, which will ultimately destroy her. Where according to Greek tradition the gods and fate direct humanity, Flaubert turns to the modern concept of psychological determinism to explain Emma. Emma believes what she believes and strives as she does because of who she is. When students have finished the book, the instructor may fruitfully encourage them to question whether a novel based on probabilities can embody the grandeur we associate with tragedy, with humankind in the confrontation of its ineluctable limitations and hence its destiny.

Necessarily, then, Flaubert seeks to make Emma's character entirely clear in his chapter on her early years in the convent school (1.6). He then derives all her behavior from that history. We see her in typically Romantic fashion, already insistent on perverting externality to match her dreams. Her character will not vary from this principle; she is to that extent psychologically determined. When, at her end, neither of her lovers will rescue her from her financial plight, then, like Flaubert's contemporary Baudelaire, she would rather abandon a world "in which action is not the sister of our dreams" (Baudelaire, "Le reniement" 115).

Every action in the novel has been more than adequately anticipated, but students may miss the essential guideposts Flaubert places along the way. At the end of part 1, chapter 5, Emma has been married long enough to wonder exactly what her romantic books meant by words such as *happiness, passion,* and *intoxication.* Chapter 1, part 6, explains where and how Emma obtained these ideas. It opens with a paragraph referring to Bernardin de Saint-Pierre's *Paul et Virginie,* now almost unknown, but the tone of Flaubert's paragraph will reveal what he intends: "[Emma] had dreamed about the little bamboo hut, the black man Domingo, the dog Fido, but above all the gentle friendship of some good little brother" (94; 24–25; trans. mine) who would get you anything you want. Emma will always long for the thrill of exoticism and for such a compliant companion.

The remainder of the chapter also deserves close attention. Emma discovers religion but promptly perverts it into a mystical and above all a sensual emotion. Students should be invited to compare and contrast Emma's self-serving religiosity with other, more profound depictions of religion.

In nature, Emma seeks the drama, spectacle, and contrast: wild tempests, greenery among ruins, and the like, a typically Romantic view. And then the key analytic sentence: "She had to be able to get from things a sort of personal profit, and she rejected as totally useless everything which did not contribute to the immediate consumption of her heart" (96; 26; trans. mine).

A fundamental problem appears in this context and should be discussed, either here or at some equally clear moment in the book. Flaubert's analytic sentences, such as the above, are rare; he felt that authors are most powerful when they do not tell but instead show the reader the points they wish to make. Hence students must usually infer these points on their own: this famous dogma of his is usually referred to as the command to writers "Show, don't tell." The power of this approach is such that most careful authors since his day have accepted it, but the burden and the problems it imposes on students deserve to be emphasized.

In this chapter Flaubert next moves to the disastrous effects upon young people of reading about romantic love. When readers are too young yet to have truly experienced the emotion, they feel they already know all about it. So when they experience the real phenomenon, they are already jaded and disabused, unable to make anything of real, experienced emotions, which seem unacceptably quiet, even dull.

Emma learns about love from the bad romantic novels she reads in the convent. Like such romances today, they concentrate on what the heroine wants and invent improbable male characters who will live solely to satisfy the dreams of silly romantic girls. From here to the end of the novel, the story will almost run itself, for Emma's character has been defined. She is already displaying what later critics have called Bovarysm, the practice of imagining life as more perfect than it can be and then being bored or angry and rejecting it. Instructors might ask students whether this attitude in fact characterizes some of their friends and, if so, how they assess it.

In part 1, chapter 7, students learn with Emma that her dreams of marriage are not being realized and watch her romantic—but futile—efforts to incorporate "passion" in her life. Charles was never going to be the ideal lover she sought; no one could be. Indeed, she was unlikely ever to find a man nearer to her desires, for she was only a farm girl and dreamed of a noble lover. And despite her view of him, Charles is always good and kind. It is one of the by-products of romantic notions of love that the good in a real husband or lover must always fall short of a woman's dreams. If only she had had better luck, Emma imagines, life would now be different.

Part 1, chapter 8, describes the ball at Vaubyessard, an experience that will have fatal consequences for Emma. Careful readers will have a clear view of what is actually transpiring, but Emma misunderstands most of what she sees (the drooling old duke who had "slept in the bed of queens" [109; 35]) and hence imagines that she is seeing her fantasy world come to life. For months thereafter she dreams of returning to the château.

Part 2 opens with chapters describing the new town, Yonville, and the arrival of the Bovarys there. Flaubert felt that the author in his novel should be like God in his universe, "present everywhere but visible nowhere" (*Correspondance*, ed. Bruneau, 2: 204). Flaubert does not often emphasize the irony in his own voice (*voice* here, one should explain, refers to moments when the author openly writes his own views of the matter he is discussing). He prefers to let the reader discover his irony.

At the inn, we meet most of the characters who will play roles in the rest of the novel, and for the most part we sense their shallowness and pretentiousness—although Flaubert will never so label them. In the conversation between Emma and Léon, the two callow Romantics exchange many of the romantic clichés of the day and are in full and delicious agreement, for each finds in the other confirmation of the validity of his or her private romantic dreams in opposition to commonly accepted views of externality. But their remarks—for instance, on the beauties of Switzerland—conceal Flaubert's irony: neither of his speakers has ever been there.

Flaubert develops the affair between Emma and Léon slowly. Neither of them has enough sophistication to carry the affair boldly forward. This reticence allows Flaubert to display a Romantic in a platonic love affair: nothing but frustration could ensue. Should students admire their virtue or mock their lack of worldly knowledge?

The more Emma takes pleasure in the company of Léon, the more irritated she becomes with Charles. But Flaubert arranges matters so that we see only her view of Charles. Hence, we rarely pause to inquire whether Charles is not really better than she thinks and Léon less attractive than she imagines him; that is, Emma has typically substituted her private and romantic views for the more sober reality before her.

Then Emma discovers that Léon must love her, but she makes no move to invite him to possess her. Significantly, though without overt comment from Flaubert, the merchant Lheureux visits her the next day to offer his wares; she need be in no hurry to pay him. It is only when we have finished the novel and discovered Lheureux's role in her financial ruin that we may reflect on this juxtaposition of her love life, her love of luxury she learned from her novels, and her financial irresponsibility.

Flaubert must persuade us that Emma could not escape the trap he has laid for her. He must show us that none of the safeguards society places around marriage could restrain her: not friends, Church, or other limitations. Of course, Emma can have no friends in Yonville. But what of the Church, we may ask, which had been for centuries one of society's bulwarks of morality? Students should note the significance of the disastrous visit Emma pays to the priest Bournisien. That that simple man could not understand her leads to a ridiculous scene between them; but had Bournisien been a better priest, he would not be settled for life in Yonville. The Church cannot help Emma.

Léon finds himself in despair over his fruitless love for Emma and the tedium of life in Yonville. He leaves, and only after his departure does she permit herself to think openly about how much she desired him and to know that she wants a lover.

Flaubert must also arrange a fully consummated love affair for Emma. He elects to examine two sides of the matter. In a first liaison, Emma is completely dominated by her lover; in a second (and final) one, she dominates him.

Rodolphe, her first lover, is knowledgeable about women and admires Emma's attractive figure (instructors may ask students to note this and other indications of Emma's powerful sexual attraction). She is, he sees, "gaping after love like a carp on the kitchen table after water" (196; 93). The ugly simile characterizes the man. Flaubert will play off Emma's romantic dreams of a man who will love her soul against Rodolphe's desire for sex, which Rodolphe will mask in her terms. His prior experience has already taught him the language.

Yonville hosts an agricultural fair, one of the famous scenes in the novel. Rodolphe uses it to carry out his seduction (2.8). Note Flaubert's use of ironic contrast to mock the speaker, the inhabitants of Yonville, the farmers, the bourgeois, and above all Homais, the pharmacist. The seduction scene, which accompanies this mockery, is one of Flaubert's best. Outdoors there is the absurd speech of the government official, full of clichés, pomposity, and mixed metaphors, while upstairs, indoors, Rodolphe carefully offers as real all the Romantic clichés that he well knows Emma longs to hear. Like Léon, Rodolphe appears to be offering Emma external validation for her dreams of love. But Rodolphe's are only fraudulent elements in his seduction of her. Externality has not in fact been replaced by Emma's desires.

While the precise idiocies Rodolphe uses might not persuade a young woman today, they have been replaced by others no less foolish. When students read this scene, teachers may assign the exercise of transposing its phrasings into those of our day and noting the way in which the speeches inside and outdoors correspond ironically. Flaubert closes this farcical scene with one of the few paragraphs expressing esteem for a character, the awarding of a prize to a simple peasant woman for fifty years of faithful service on a farm. Students may be asked to comment on the meaning of this apparently unrelated detail, for again ironic contrast carries the message.

Rodolphe suggests horseback riding to improve Emma's health, offering to lend her a horse and to accompany her. His seduction during the horseback ride merits close study. It is built on Flaubert's awareness that there is much about love that cannot be put into words, yet he must find a means to express what is happening. Here and later, he makes a description of nature incarnate the emotions of his characters, especially Emma's. It is a Romantic device put to use by a realist.

As she rides, Emma feels herself freed from all the normal safeguards in her life. The riders climb a high hill and look down on Yonville from above. She reflects that it has never seemed so small. Gradually, the surrounding nature envelops them till they become part of it. Only then does Rodolphe close in on his prey. Upon her return to her home she exults, but not because Rodolphe was such a wonderful man. Rather, she exclaims to herself, "I have a lover! a lover!" (229; 117). And—under the influence of her readings—she feels she has now joined the host of famous women lovers. Here the instructor may point out that Romantic literature has claimed another victim, who, like all romantics, believes that her private vision of the world is now being vindicated against those who do not sense the primacy of individual emotions in conflict with externality.

Through the long clubfoot episode (2.11), Emma seeks to raise Charles in her esteem as a counter to Rodolphe, but Charles's failure throws her into Rodolphe's arms more ardently than ever before. Students can study how Rodolphe dominates Emma entirely. But in the long run he has to disengage himself. Repetition is dulling his pleasure.

Here, Flaubert treats one of the great problems of Romanticism: the relation between the words lovers (or any people) use when speaking to each other and what they are really feeling. Flaubert was always keenly aware of the age-old problem of how words mean and what they can mean. It is illuminating to introduce students to the problem of the relation between words and the external world, which one branch of modernist criticism holds to be a dichotomy. Flaubert discusses at length why Rodolphe does not, cannot, believe the words of passion that Emma uses to describe her adoration for him. Flaubert even specifically says in his own voice that no words can really correspond to such levels of feeling, a point that modernist criticism has seized upon. But a few pages later Flaubert does indeed display for his readers what the two lovers could feel, in the famous moonlight scene (2.12), through his description of the rising moon. It is one of the most successful scenes in the novel and tackles head-on the modern philosophical problem of human communication by reminding the reader that we communicate in many ways, some of which may even displace words entirely, as in this scene.

Nevertheless, Rodolphe still desires to break off the affair. In his letter to Emma he blames "fate" (271; 146), a convenient word that recurs several times in the novel. Students should watch for it. Is Rodolphe's departure inevitable, as Flaubert seems to suggest, or, as Emma feels repeatedly, has she once again had bad luck in choosing her men? Emma falls dangerously ill for many months.

At this time, Charles, needing money to care for Emma, also discovers Lheureux as a source for loans. In a probabilistic novel, such moves are indispensable. At the same time, Emma wishes to return to the Catholic faith of her childhood. But, true to her nature, she perverts her foolish readings and, in the end, does not find salvation there.

To help in his wife's convalescence, Charles escorts Emma to the opera in Rouen. There Emma once again meets Léon, now a more mature, less naive man. She arranges to have her husband urge her to remain in Rouen one further night. Again, students can weigh the probability of these events as Flaubert presents them.

In this relationship, Emma, who was completely subordinate to Rodolphe, now dominates her weak lover. To understand what Flaubert is saying about Emma's misunderstanding of love (one still present today), we should recall that romantic love does exist for Flaubert (evident in the moonlight scene), but he believes that it must not be perverted. Emma has been perverting all her emotional responses ever since attending convent school.

Emma and Léon visit the Cathedral of Rouen in an entertaining scene of delightful irony and then depart for their long ride in the hackney cab, another of the novel's great scenes. It is one of the funniest seduction scenes in literature and certainly one of the most chaste. The chasteness of the account is in itself revealing, for Flaubert felt that the words of literature must be chaste, so as not to limit the possibilities for voluptuousness in the imagination of the reader. Most later authors have rejected this view. Was Flaubert right?

Emma finds an excuse to return to Rouen for three whole days with Léon. Students should study how the basic fallacy of their position must destroy the relationship. This scene is a slow, careful analysis of why Emma cannot in fact know romantic love, for "she had to gain some personal profit from things" (96; 26), as Flaubert phrased it in the convent chapter. At the start, each moment is bliss; then they explore more-experienced forms of lovemaking (always chastely phrased), till finally they find in each other little more than boredom and a wild desire to revive the affair. The account reflects a dismal view of love, one that students can productively place beside other accounts of romantic love. Floods of money are indispensable to the tawdry concept of love that Emma nurtures. Hence Flaubert follows the ways in which Lheureux involves her ever more deeply in his schemes.

Students may explore how Emma's false understanding of romantic love must necessarily destroy what she and Léon do have. Since their emotions are neither entirely real nor at all profound, each must deceive the other about her or his true sentiments, and both must seek ever higher levels of physical enjoyment to make up for what they lack emotionally. Both routes lead ultimately to disappointment, and toward the end both lovers are in fact tired of the affair. But as always, Flaubert will decline to spell out this disenchantment, preferring to show it and leave it to the reader to understand, as Emma comes to dreaming once again of another man who would be perfect. In part 3, chapter 6, Flaubert examines her self-deception by having Emma sit outside her former convent school and recall her dreams of long ago. The instructor may invite students to examine whether her dissatisfaction seems inevitable, for Flaubert believed that he had made it so.

At length Emma realizes, to her discouragement, that she has "found again in adultery all the platitudes of marriage" (364; 211). (In most editions, either French or translated, "this adultery" appears. Fearing the censor, Flaubert changed his original wording to this form to lessen the scope of his statement. Students might be asked to evaluate the two versions.)

Flaubert combines his two themes—the bourgeois reduction of all values to money and the inevitable failure of romantic love—when Lheureux sells Emma out for her debts. Now both Emma's dreams have come to their fated culmination. Students may usefully explore the implications of this result, which Flaubert sought to make at least probabilistic.

In a general humanities course, it is illuminating to ask whether Emma's suicide is tragic. It is certainly deeply sad, and Flaubert shows his sympathy in his description of Emma's horrible death agony. Moreover, Flaubert has made her despair inevitable, for he has constantly noted that Emma was completely lost in the toils of Lheureux.

But sadness is not tragedy, and *pathos* is the word Flaubert applied to this novel. Is it the case that Emma lacks all grandeur and is simply wrong from the start, though, to her credit, she has both the determination and the courage to drive through to the fated and fatal conclusion? The contrast between pathos and tragedy may be useful to draw out with students. They may be asked if Emma's sad fate is what we really understand tragedy to mean and then, further, whether other writers can achieve tragedy in a modern bourgeois society.

Emma Bovary:
The Angel Gone Astray

Lilian R. Furst

Emma Bovary is, by profession, a housewife. She has a husband, a daughter, and a home to look after. Although Charles Bovary is a mere public health officer (not quite as well trained as a registered nurse) and not a real physician and although even physicians in mid-nineteenth-century rural France had a less lofty status and income than do doctors in the United States today, Emma would nevertheless, in her position, be expected to maintain certain standards. Her failure to fill her normative role—indeed, her contempt for it—was almost as shocking to readers of her time as her adulteries were.

For middle-class women such as Emma, marriage and motherhood were virtually the only honorable options since no career opportunities existed then, and those who failed to marry had little or no choice but to become governesses, a demeaning and unsatisfying position in society. The education of girls was directed toward domesticity and submissiveness. Bonnie G. Smith, in her informative study of nineteenth-century middle-class women in northern France, *Ladies of the Leisure Class*, gives a striking account of precisely the kind of convent education that Emma had. Smith points out how "convents prepared girls for the traditional world of the home" by emphasizing the overriding importance of "adherence" to an external social order: "In the process they learned that an order beyond themselves and their control, beyond their wants and inaccessible to reason, determined the order of their lives" (174). Through the regimentation of their lives in drab uniforms, a strictly organized routine of prayers, lessons, and walks, absolute obedience to their superiors, even a stylized handwriting, the girls were drilled in the priority of the group (such as a family) over the individual. This is a fundamental lesson that Emma rejects; at this early stage in her life she already asserts her willful spirits in her whims and personal choices:

> [Elle] s'irritait davantage contre la discipline, qui était quelque chose d'antipathique à sa constitution. Quand son père la retira de pension, on ne fut point fâché de la voir partir. La supérieure trouvait même qu'elle était devenue, dans les derniers temps, peu révérencieuse envers la communauté.   (99)

> [She] rebelled against discipline, as something alien to her constitution. When her father took her from school, no one was sorry to see her go. The [Mother] Superior even thought that she had of late been less than reverent toward the community.   (28)

So even in her adolescence Emma strays from the path designated for her.

In her marriage to Charles she does conform more to the customary pattern. Often marriages were arranged between families for economic reasons without much prior consultation of the prospective couple. Again, in *Ladies of the Leisure Class*, Smith gives vivid insight into the practices for negotiating marriages that would be considered advantageous for both parties (57–62). Emma's situation differs slightly from that outlined by Smith insofar as she had met Charles, and both were clearly attracted to each other. Seeing the young doctor's interest in his daughter, old Rouault makes a deliberate calculation to give her to him if he asks. Although Charles is not "un gendre comme il l'eût souhaité" 'not quite the son-in-law he would have liked' (83; 17), at least he will not demand much by way of a dowry. So old Rouault prompts Charles's tongue-tied stammerings to precipitate the desired proposal. Charles has to wait forty-nine minutes before the shutters are flung open, the agreed signal of Emma's acceptance. Readers are, at this point, positioned with Charles, so we don't know why it took Emma so long to make up her mind: was she merely being coy, or did she have genuine doubts? Flaubert has here introduced a tantalizing gap into the narration. One thing is certain, however: unlike her contemporaries, who envisaged marriage as a transaction of mutual convenience, not necessarily imbued with love or romance, Emma believes herself to be in love; "[Elle] cherchait à savoir ce que l'on entendait au juste dans la vie par les mots de *félicité*, de *passion* et d'*ivresse*, qui lui avait paru si beaux dans les livres" 'tried to find out what one meant exactly in life by the words *bliss, passion, ecstasy*, that had seemed to her so beautiful in books' (94; 24). This misguided conception of marriage will be the source of Emma's subsequent disappointment and problems.

She does not find in marriage, motherhood, and household management the fulfillment she expected to experience. The prevailing assumption was summarized by the British poet Coventry Patmore in an 1851 article entitled

"The Social Position of Women" as "the general feeling that women cannot be happy otherwise than as wives and mothers" (534). While positing "the social subordination of women" as "an irreversible natural law" (519) and conceding that "the position of woman is, at present, one of almost total *external* subjection" (530), Patmore writes, too, of a woman's "high place at the head of the small, but unspeakably important domestic realm" (521). Her "high calling" (522) was to be queen of the hearth or—to cite the title of Patmore's immensely popular poem, published in two parts in 1854 and 1856—"The Angel in the House." This idealization of woman's role in the home was a compensatory consolation for her lack of power outside the home. The distinction between the spheres of man and woman was tenaciously upheld throughout the nineteenth century. The woman's sphere comprised, in the widest sense, various household duties.

Household management was no simple task in the days before gas, electricity, refrigeration, washing machines, vacuum cleaners, and so on. Many of the chores that can nowadays be done without much effort, thanks to mechanical aids, had to be carried out manually. True, there were servants, but not as many as scholars once thought, as Patricia Branca has shown in her article "Image and Reality: The Myth of the Idle Victorian Woman." Emma, for instance, has just one general servant, Félicité, to help her. Yet the term *household management* subsumed a large spectrum of different kinds of tasks: the feeding of the family, including marketing and long-term provisioning for the winter; the cleaning and maintenance of the house, both daily and seasonal, which would comprise washing, ironing, mending of linens, sweeping of grates and chimneys, and replenishing the oil lamps. Often, clothing was made at home, and of course children, the old, and the sick had to be tended. All these diverse aspects of household management were the woman's responsibility. It was an onerous, demanding occupation that required energy, stamina, and devotion. And it was crucial because the family's health, comfort, and even survival depended in large measure on the housekeeper's competence.

Because of its importance, household management was simultaneously idealized and professionalized around the middle of the nineteenth century. Manuals were prepared as guides to set standards and to offer concrete advice on how to cope with the multiple obligations of housekeeping. The most famous of these manuals is *Mrs. Beeton's Book of Household Management* (1861), which provides instructions on topics ranging from plucking a chicken to selecting and supervising servants to handling hygiene in the sickroom. The book that Emma might have consulted is Cora-Elisabeth Millet-Robinet's *Maison rustique des dames* 'The Lady's Rustic Home,' a massive five-volume work that appeared in 1844–45 and had attained its eighth edition by 1872. Directed primarily at country women, it includes sections on the kitchen garden and farm, including the care of pigs, goats, bees, cows, and every variety of hen. But the first part, "Tenue de ménage" 'Household Management,' provides the duties of the mistress of the house and of the servants; dress codes; the maintenance of

furniture, drapes, linens, furs, heating, and lighting; the provisioning and con-
servation of wines, flour, meats, butter, vegetables, fruits, and so on. The second part, "Manuel de cuisine" 'Cooking Manual,' comprises everything from
elementary techniques to menus for each month. The third part, "Médecine
domestique" 'Home Medicine,' covers common medications, hygiene, emer-
gencies, children's diseases, bites, stings, poisonings, and death. Nothing gives
as complete a picture of the responsibilities of household management as does
perusal of a guide such as this one.

Besides its practical value, sound household management was regarded as
closely connected to moral virtue. Thrift, "careful expenditure and careful ac-
counting . . . also had its symbolic aspects of ordering existence," Erna Olafson
Hellerstein explains in "Women, Social Order, and the City: Rules for French
Ladies, 1830–1870." Emma's extravagance thus meets with her mother-in-law's
disapproval on both financial and moral grounds: she does not run her household as she should. Emma longs for fancy trappings such as fingerbowls, which
are not at all appropriate to her station on the social scale. Proper order in the
house was seen as the basis and emblem of good order in society, while, conversely, disorder in the family would mean disorder in society at large. This was
the central teaching of a seminal work by Paul Janet, *La famille: Leçons de
philosophie morale* 'The Family: Lessons in Moral Philosophy,' published in
1855, awarded a prize by the French Academy, and reprinted fourteen times
by 1890. Janet argues that household work is woman's duty and a moral necessity of her life and that she is naturally suited to household management because of the kind of mind she possesses. This view strikes us today as peculiar,
circuitous, and indeed offensive, yet it gained wide acceptance in nineteenth-
century France. Housework was recommended by physicians as a cure for that
mysterious female ailment, hysteria, which was thought to be fostered by the
reading of novels. That is why Charles's mother suggests that Emma needs "des
occupations forcées, des ouvrages manuels" '[to be] forced to occupy herself
with some manual work' (191; 90) instead of the idle reading of novels that
Emma prefers and that not only diverts her from her prescribed duties but has
a noxious effect by inflaming her imagination.

Only in the earliest days of her marriage does Emma attempt to be the angel
in the house:

> Elle s'occupa, les premiers jours, à méditer des changements dans sa
> maison. Elle retira les globes des flambeaux, fit coller des papiers neufs,
> repeindre l'escalier, et faire des bancs dans le jardin, tout autour du cad-
> ran solaire. . . .   (92)

> During the first days she kept busy thinking about changes in the house.
> She took the shades off the candlesticks, had new wall-paper put up, the
> staircase repainted, and seats made in the garden round the sundial. . .
>
>   (23)

So she acquires the reputation in Tostes of being a good housekeeper: "Emma
... savait conduire sa maison" 'Emma ... knew how to look after her house'
(101; 29). This is a high compliment. But before long, as her disillusionment
with her marriage sets in, she lets things slide:

> Elle laissait maintenant tout aller dans son ménage, et madame Bovary
> mère, lorsqu'elle vint passer à Tostes une partie du carême, s'étonna fort
> du changement. Elle, en effet, si soigneuse autrefois et délicate, elle
> restait à présent des journées entières sans s'habiller, portait des bas de
> coton gris, s'éclairait à la chandelle.   (126)

> She now let [everything] in her household go its own way, and the elder
> Madame Bovary, when she came to spend part of Lent at Tostes, was
> much surprised at the change. She who was formerly so careful, so
> dainty, now spent whole days without dressing, wore grey cotton stock-
> ings, and used tallow candles to light the house.   (47)

Later we hear from Charles that she prefers to stay in her room reading (147;
59).

Even before the move to Yonville, Emma is becoming "difficile, capricieuse"
'difficult, capricious' (127; 47), sometimes treating the maid harshly, at other
times overindulgently, asking for special dishes that she then did not touch. She
is certainly not the stable, self-effacing, self-sacrificing pillar of the household
that she is expected to be. After the move to Yonville, as she grows increasingly
engrossed in her amorous adventures and her daydreams, she becomes more
and more heedless of her daily duties in the house. Once, for a short while, she
tries to act out the role of attentive housewife: "On la vit prendre à cœur son
ménage, retourner à l'église régulièrement et tenir sa servante avec plus de
sévérité" 'She took interest in the housework, went to church regularly, and
looked after her maid with more severity' (171; 76). She warms Charles's slip-
pers by the fire, sees to it that his shirts have all their buttons, and contemplates
with pleasure all the nightcaps piled neatly in the closet. This brief interlude
serves to show that Emma knows well enough what she ought to be doing. She
does not, however, choose to do it for very long, finding it too boring and commonplace. Just occasionally, when her conscience bothers her, she makes
Charles his favorite dessert, pistachio cream (343; 195), but this favor is nothing more than a sporadic gesture, far from the constant daily attention a
woman is supposed to devote to the well-being of her family. She is merely
feigning an interest in domesticity when she asks her mother-in-law for her
recipe for pickling gherkins (262; 140) at a point when she is actively planning
to elope with Rodolphe.

Emma's unlovingness toward her daughter, Berthe, is considered contrary to
nature. She seems to have none of the nurturing, mothering instincts attributed
to women then and now. During her pregnancy she fantasizes about bearing a

son, who will enjoy all the freedoms denied to her as a female. But the moment she hears that the child is a girl, she turns her head away and faints. Her physical response has a figurative connotation as an expression of her disinterest in the child. That Berthe is put out to a wet nurse is in keeping with the practices of the time, when it was common for middle- and upper-class women to hire a surrogate breast. However, Emma's utter lack of tenderness toward the child is striking and dismaying. When she visits the baby at Mme Rollet's, Emma immediately puts her down in disgust when she throws up on Emma's lace collar (157; 66). Her attitude contrasts with that of Mme Rollet, who considers a little spitting normal. Later, when Berthe as a toddler lets some saliva drip onto her mother's silk apron, Emma pushes her away so roughly that the little girl falls and cuts her cheek on the brass knob of a chest of drawers. Guilt-laden, Emma insists on staying to watch at her bedside. But her reaction to her daughter is an alienating one: "C'est une chose étrange, pensait Emma, comme cette enfant est laide!" ' "It is very strange," thought Emma, "how ugly this child is!"' (181; 83). No wonder that Berthe is allowed to run about with holes in her stockings, to the horror of everyone in Yonville. The holes are the visible manifestation of Emma's neglect of her obligations.

The foil to Emma is Mme Homais, the pharmacist's wife: "c'était la meilleure épouse de Normandie, douce comme un mouton, chérissant ses enfants, son père, sa mère, ses cousins, pleurant aux maux d'autrui" 'she was the best wife in Normandy, gentle as a sheep, loving her children, her father, her mother, her cousins, weeping for others' woes' (161; 68). But this panegyric of her submissiveness and devotion to others is undercut by a potent current of irony as Léon contemplates her and realizes that she is

> si lente à mouvoir, si ennuyeuse à écouter, d'un aspect si commun et d'une conversation si restreinte, qu'il n'avait jamais songé, quoiqu'elle eût trente ans, qu'il en eût vingt, qu'ils couchassent porte à porte, et qu'il lui parlât chaque jour, qu'elle pût être une femme pour quelqu'un, ni qu'elle possédât de son sexe autre chose que la robe.   (161)

> so slow of movement, such a bore to listen to, so common in appearance, and of such restricted conversation, that although she was thirty and he only twenty, although they slept in rooms next each other and he spoke to her daily, he never thought that she might be a woman to anyone, or that she possessed anything else of her sex than the gown.   (68–69)

In this satiric, profoundly ironic novel, even the dominant ideal of the angel in the house is exposed to ridicule.

The effects of Emma's bad management are catastrophic for her entire household. Her extravagance is the direct cause of the family's bankruptcy. Like today's compulsive shopper who runs up an overwhelming debt on her credit card, Emma recklessly signs IOUs to Lheureux without realizing the extent of her expenditure. Obviously, she fails to keep precise household accounts, as prescribed for the angel in the house. Ultimately, it is her spending far beyond the family's means that causes her downfall when the bailiff arrives to seize most of the furniture and other possessions (369; 215). Even after Emma's suicide, Charles is faced with an onslaught of bills: from her piano teacher in Rouen, for a three-year subscription to a lending library, and from Mme Rollet, for mysterious services rendered (416; 249).

The corrupting effect of the angel gone astray impinges negatively on her husband, her daughter, and even her maid. Charles languishes and dies before long. Berthe, we are told on the last page, is sent to her grandmother's house, there being just enough money left to pay her fare there. When the old woman dies in the same year, a poor aunt takes charge of her, and the child is sent to earn her living in a cotton mill. The long hours, harsh conditions, and unhealthy environment prevalent in factories in the mid–nineteenth century bode ill for Berthe's future. As for Félicité, she takes to wearing Emma's dresses after her demise and then absconds with her young man, stealing all that is left of her mistress's wardrobe (416–17; 249).

It would be reductive to envisage *Madame Bovary* as a cautionary tale against the deleterious consequences of improvident household management, just as it would be to see it as no more than merely a satire against the harmful influence of romances on a young woman. This sociological dimension of the novel, however, must not be overlooked. Emma's grave shortfall, her failure to fulfill the role expected of a woman of her class at her time, scandalized nineteenth-century readers. As an "angel" gone astray, she spreads destruction to all around her. The seriousness with which her domestic default was taken must be understood as one factor in the censure that *Madame Bovary* met on its publication.

A Marxist Approach
to *Madame Bovary*

Edward J. Ahearn

In the popular (and political and journalistic and even academic) mind, a Marxist approach to anything seems illusory now that capitalism has "won." Yet recent world events have invalidated neither Marx's critique of capitalism nor even, perhaps, his premonitions about future world events. Although one encounters such skepticism regarding Marxist approaches to literature, there remains nevertheless a substantial body of persuasive Marxist literary theory and criticism. And, not coincidentally, a good deal of it concerns *Madame Bovary*.

Keeping in mind the theoretical dimensions of the literary use of Marx, I am concerned with showing how Marx's thought illuminates Flaubert's novel with regard to both aspects of that illegitimate dichotomy "content" and "form." Under the former fall Marx's arguments about history, industry, the city and countryside, class, the family, sex, desire, commodities, money, and capital, many of which are clearly structural elements in *Madame Bovary*. But for issues of form we will also need to consider Marx's thought about subjectivity, ideology, the aesthetic, what he (after Hegel) calls world historical consciousness, and the argument he develops in a crucial manuscript, "The Method of Political Economy." Often the materials from Marx take the form of summaries of extensive passages, for which I provide titles; when appropriate, I give page references to Robert Tucker's useful *Marx-Engels Reader*. Unless otherwise noted, references to Flaubert's letters are from the Norton Critical Edition of *Madame Bovary*, edited by Paul de Man; for the French text, see Geneviève Bollème's selection of the correspondence.

The simplest reason for studying Marx and Flaubert together is that they were contemporaries, major figures observing the same phenomena. Marx lived and studied in France from 1843 to 1845 and wrote about French political and socioeconomic events of that century in ways that correspond closely to *Madame Bovary* and *L'éducation sentimentale*. Although Flaubert's politics tended to be reactionary, he shared with Marx a vehement condemnation of both the bourgeoisie and French brands of socialism and communism. Despite his tendency toward aestheticism and formalism (his desire to write a book about "nothing"), his literary position stressed impersonality as a means of arriving at objectivity, and his favorite authors were those, like Homer and Rabelais, whose works constitute totalizing encyclopedias of their epochs (see his letters of 16 Jan. 1852, 6 Apr. 1853, and 7 Apr. 1854 [309–10, 314, 318]).

So what observations and arguments did Marx make that find echoes in Flaubert? As expressed at various stages of Marx's career—in the first part of *The German Ideology*, "The Method of Political Economy" (in *Foundations of the Critique of Political Economy*), and the first volume of *Capital*—modern Western history involved the final violent triumph of the bourgeois capitalist system over the feudal. France experienced this transition in the upheavals of 1789 and succeeding years and then, after Empire and Restoration, in the revolutions of 1830 (when what Marx calls the finance aristocracy came to power) and 1848 (when the commercial bourgeoisie joined the bankers and financiers), not to mention the Second Empire and the Commune of 1871, the last workers' revolution in France. Marx's analyses concerning France are presented in *The Class Struggles in France*, *The Eighteenth Brumaire of Louis Bonaparte*, and *The Civil War in France*. Despite Flaubert's subsequent hatred of the Commune, his similar historical acuity is evident in the example of Dambreuse in *L'éducation sentimentale*. As early as five years before the end of the Restoration, he finds it wise to shed all association with the aristocracy. Dropping the apostrophe from his name, he moves from the faubourg Saint-Germain to the nouveau-riche Right Bank, where he thrives first in banking and later in railroads and mining.

As for *Madame Bovary*, Dominick LaCapra considers the novel to be generally ahistorical yet views the slow chronological progress of its last parts as leading up to around 1848, so that in some sense Emma's suicide "replaces" the failed revolution of that year (173, 188, 201). I think that LaCapra is right and even that the book is more pertinently historical than he grants. We are given the date 1812 early on, when Charles's corrupt father is forced to leave the Imperial army (64; 3), and are told at the opening of part 2 that the Bovarys arrive in Yonville in 1835. We could have guessed that date when, earlier, we learned that d'Andervilliers, a minister under the Restoration, is preparing to run for office (106; 32); for this event to be possible, at least a few years must have passed since the revolution of 1830 and its dissolution in the illusorily democratic government under Louis Philippe. The ruins of the family château and the portraits of ancestors, together with the modern house the marquis now inhabits, also make him historically suggestive.

Such historical markers already indicate the importance of socioeconomic history, and *Madame Bovary* strikingly illustrates virtually every feature of the capitalist "mode of production" as Marx described it in mid-nineteenth-century France. In this vastly alienating system, money was (as it of course still is) used for the creation of money (Marx's definition of capital in volume 1, chapter 4, of *Capital*) as those with wealth exploited the labor power of others through the wage-labor mode. In such an arrangement money takes on an exaggerated importance at the expense of human values. Technology and industry increase both profits and alienation; the textile industry, originally a secondary activity of the peasantry, is the leading historical example.

Marx also showed that with the dissolution of feudal landed relations and the concentration of workers in the enormous cities of the eighteenth and nineteenth centuries, the country-city antagonism was vastly increased. Given recurrent cycles of expansion and depression, there came into being an "industrial reserve army," into which those on the margins of the middle class could fall. Since France was economically behind England in developing the capitalist mode, the provinces and the peasantry persisted in importance there far into the nineteenth century. In addition to concentration of money, population, and power in Paris, therefore, over the course of the century a class of secondary capitalist exploiters (moneylenders, lawyers, and bankers, assisted by heavy governmental taxation of the peasantry) effected an appropriation and transformation of landed provincial money into capital. But even in the countryside, the major mechanism of capitalism—the mass production of commodities and the creation of a demand for them—was progressing as the major source of profit making. As early as 1844, in his *Economic and Philosophic Manuscripts*, Marx railed at the enslavement he saw in such "object-bondage" (Marx and Engels 72), in the need to accumulate objects, and later, in the first chapter of volume 1 of *Capital*, he argued that commodities (mass-produced articles) are mysterious, fetishistic objects.

All these thoughts are important in Flaubert's novel. The country-city antagonism is a structural as well as thematic feature. Of rural background, Emma (like Charles) is educated in Rouen. All her life she yearns to get to Paris but never does. But the increasingly frenetic movement of the last part is expressed directly in her travels between Yonville and Rouen, the provincial capital. Characteristically, she responds to both cities in romantic, not economic, terms. It is apt therefore that what provokes her illness after Rodolphe's betrayal is the sight of him passing by her house, since that is the only route he can take to reach Rouen. The nonromantic and supremely economic Lheureux makes a more essential use of the country-city nexus: his wares are bought on weekly trips to Rouen, and by the end he has partially accomplished his goal of monopolizing transportation to that city.

Emma's most extended fantasy about Paris is provoked by the cigar case found on the way home from Vaubyessard. She imagines it as a unique object, sewn by the aristocratic lover of the viscount, almost literally embodying passion and aristocracy (117; 40–41). But, as Claude Duchet shows in his excellent study of objects in the book, she later buys an identical one for Rodolphe, so the case must be one in a series of mass-produced items. Emma's need to accumulate such objects submits her to Lheureux and becomes a compulsion in her relations with Léon. What more horrible fate for her therefore than to be deprived of all these possessions through the seizure that eventually leads her to suicide? And what more repulsive depiction of the inhuman profit motive than the character of Lheureux? In this character and his associates Marx's secondary capitalist exploiters acquire names—along with the moneylender, the notary Guillaumin, the banker Vinçart, not to mention Binet, the tax collector who also rebuffs Emma on her last day. By the end, paralleling Marx's arguments, they have entirely appropriated the Bovarys' wealth. Finally, the cigar case, that most compelling of fetishes, is not incidentally a product of the textile industry, which is in the background throughout and whose ravages are apparent on the last page as Berthe, without resources save for her labor power, joins the industrial pauper army as a worker in a cotton mill.

Furthermore, Marx's analysis of class, his depiction of the manipulation of desire within the commercial system, and his concept of ideology, which contributes to deluded consciousness, find parallels in *Madame Bovary*. Emma's background is rural and economically none too stable: Rouault's farm turns out to be less prosperous than it appeared, and Charles's first wife, the ironically named Héloïse, claims that Emma's grandfather was a shepherd. But Emma gets an education that "programs" her for romance and aristocratic aspirations. Without being able to analyze in detail the works to which she is exposed in chapter 6 of part 1, we may say that romance is linked to aristocracy and royalty, with which religion, romance, and sentimental nature poetry are associated through her readings of Chateaubriand and Lamartine. Her experience of the liturgy is described as sensual. She also reads romantic fiction, aristocratic keepsake books, and passages tinged with "orientalist" exoticism. She is indeed a passionate woman, but in keeping with Marx's arguments on ideology and class, this chapter shows her passion as having been formed literally by her reading—by her education and religious training.

How then can she be satisfied by the mediocre Charles, the rural petit bourgeois settings in which she lives? The one night at Vaubyessard corresponds to her aspirations, but Flaubert has her remember her rural upbringing as she glimpses the peasant faces outside the château. In her delusion about the cigar case, aristocratic status and passion are merged, though of course Emma gets only to dance with the viscount. The men with whom she actually has adulterous relationships, Rodolphe and Léon, constitute increasingly impoverished romantic and social replacements for him. There's the famous line about the debris of a poet in every notary (364; 211), and Rodolphe's name (Boulanger de la Huchette, roughly "baker-breadbox") sufficiently points to his unaristocratic status.

So desire has much to do with class in the novel, and in the end the relationships between Emma and the various men come down to money. As she makes her last attempt to get a loan, Lheureux thinks she is trying to seduce him, Guillaumin actually tries to seduce her, and Binet's horrified reaction may mean that she has made overtures to him. The narrator notes that Emma is unaware that she is prostituting herself in going to Rodolphe (382; 225), who reacts coldly when he learns that her motive is financial. In the culmination of a series of passages in which Emma confuses financial with romantic desires, the narrator notes, just before her suicide, that in her sufferings over her frustrated love she has forgotten the real reason for her despair: the question of money (387; 228). Here the libidinal has been entirely denatured by the economic.

Desire and objects, the inhuman profit motive, the obfuscating ideology of class and romance, and the tension between city and country are very much what *Madame Bovary* is about—but these elements are also structural features of Emma Bovary's story, of the novel as a whole. In the realm of literary study "proper," Marx has been thought reductive because of the base-superstructure-ideology metaphor that he once used (in the preface to *A Contribution to the Critique of Political Economy*) and that seems to relegate cultural productions to a nearly Platonic remove from economic reality. In response, we may first note Flaubert's own caricature of the purely aesthetic impulse, in Binet's productions (he has the egotism of a bourgeois and the jealousy of an artist, and the wooden objects he makes are presented as monotonously identical, useless, indescribable [139, 53; 379, 223]). For his part, Marx loved literature, frequently attributing to it the power to unmask oppressive societal conditions. In a passage on the Greeks and modern literature, he argued that literature cannot be reduced to the economic, explicitly stating his belief in the persistence of aesthetic value (Marx and Engels 245–46).

In the immediately preceding "Method of Political Economy" there is no "theory of levels," and the "artistic" is one of the ways in which the human mind "appropriates" reality, through a process of abstraction and observation arriving at the "concrete," which is described as "the concentration of many determinations . . . unity of the diverse" and as "a rich totality of many determinations and relations" (Marx and Engels 236–38). Flaubert, too, thought that he had arrived at the objectivity of science and that his protagonist was typical of unfortunate women crying in twenty French provincial towns. It is no accident that both he and Marx used another analogy, that of anatomy, to express such an encompassing and deeply structural perspective (see Flaubert's letters of 14 Aug. 1853 [315–16], 2 Jan. 1854 [317–18], and 22 July 1853 [Bollème, *Extraits* 140]).

Various formal features of *Madame Bovary* illustrate these propositions. In addition to the typicality of character just mentioned, description overwhelmingly functions to support the desire-class structure evoked earlier (pace some postmodernist critics; e.g., Culler, *Flaubert* 22–24, 75–76, 85–86, 91–92). Even Charles's hat, for Duchet, is an exaggerated version of all the tawdry commodities in the book. Moreover, as opposed to works of ideology that enforce the ideas of the dominant classes, Flaubert's novel exposes the viciousness and hypocrisy of bourgeois society, not only in the personages of Lheureux and his partners but particularly in the figure of the profoundly dishonest Homais, who spouts every possible cliché of the modern order and is crowned with success at the end. Richard Terdiman demonstrates how closely Flaubert's celebrated irony resembles that of Marx (198–226), LaCapra how the indeterminacy of the indirect narrative mode has a pervasively subversive effect (63, 125). And the book's depressing ending hardly provides the satisfying resolution sought, according to Fredric Jameson, by the "political unconscious"—quite the opposite.

The narrative form of the novel is also of striking interest. It opens with a biased individual narrator (though with marked class dimensions: provincial and urban) before "impossibly" continuing in the omniscient mode (67; 6)—with exceptions, notably the last encounter with Binet. This narrative structure may be seen as an approximation of Marx's effort to transcend subjectivity, class, and ideology and to reach a totalizing perspective. Moreover, some of the most directly "omniscient" passages concern economic matters, explaining the means by which Lheureux, Vinçart, and Guillaumin fleece the Bovarys (processes of which the Bovarys are ignorant). Far from perpetuating oppression and ideology, *Madame Bovary* is a striking example of a book that unmasks them. Put differently, had Emma been exposed to it rather than to Chateaubriand and romance novels, would her life have been different?

There are many pedagogical opportunities in the ideas expressed above, and I close by illustrating their pertinence in a major passage, the chapter that takes place at the agricultural fair. In a letter describing it (28–29 June 1853 [315]) Flaubert characterized it well as symphonic and comic, drawing together major and minor characters, expressing many central themes.

Characteristically, in this chapter description functions to stress the banality of the rural scene into which Rodolphe insinuates his seduction of Emma. His apparently aristocratic manner and dress, along with her memory of the viscount, perpetuate her driving desires. So does Rodolphe's use of the array of romantic clichés that correspond closely to her education. This seduction occurs literally on a different level from that of the political discourse below. Ideology is at work, and exposed, in both. Irony is at its most ferocious, not only in the reader's ability to judge Rodolphe's tactics but also in the famous counterpoint between Rodolphe and Emma and the prizes for hogs and manure (as well as the names of the winners!). Easily lost in all this commotion is the news that Lheureux has succeeded in bankrupting Tellier, through tactics that he will subsequently use on the Bovarys. The information comes from Guillaumin's servant—until the omniscient narrator's explanation on the last day of Emma's life, one of the rare suggestions that the notary might be involved. Did we catch this hint of the hidden economic plot (in both senses), or were we, with Emma and the others, distracted by the rest of the goings-on? Like the book as a whole, the fireworks at the end of the day fizzle, but Homais compensates by writing a propagandistic newspaper article comparing the event to *The Arabian Nights*. All these narrative levels and strands are encompassed by the totalizing perspective. In keeping with Flaubert's intention, the chapter synthesizes much that is important in *Madame Bovary* as a whole; as is apparent, it also abundantly reveals the rich convergences between the novel and the work of Karl Marx.

The Same or (M)Other:
A Feminist Reading of *Madame Bovary*

Susan L. Wolf

In a feminist reading of a canonical, male-authored text such as *Madame Bovary*, the search for the ideological underpinnings of patriarchy—the hierarchical system of stable meanings in which women are oppressed—should receive high priority. In this essay, I propose my own feminist readings of Flaubert's feminocentric novel, informed by both an awareness of the common devaluation of the feminine in androcentric culture and a sensitivity to the power of the signifier to encode that devaluation. To such ends, I enlist the aid of recent psycholinguistic theories as those most apt to ferret out embedded patriarchal meanings. At the same time, and inversely, the text whose structures of oppression are brought to light through the use of psycholinguistic theory may be revealed, I argue, to be a spectacular illustration of aspects of that theory. As a teacher, I have found my students' reception of critical theory to be closely allied with its power to generate compelling readings of specific texts which, until that time, had appeared as marginal or enigmatic at best. In what follows, I direct my attention to two such texts: the novel's initial focus on Charles Bovary's childhood and traumatic first day at school (which, despite its striking position at the outset, is often dismissed by students as an aberration, unconnected to Emma's story or to the novel as a whole) and Emma's relation to the blind man and his ditty at the novel's end, which still puzzles even as it elicits student interest.

I have twice begun class discussions of *Madame Bovary* with the observation that although, like most readers, I have long considered it a female-centered novel, its initial syntax, or ordering of episodes, would seem to contradict me and tell a different tale. I ask my students to consider what patriarchal myths or gestures Flaubert is reinscribing by beginning his novel—whose title indicates, ostensibly, that its subject is a woman—with the complete (if succinct) account of the psychosocial development of a man. If what begins, because it begins, is eminent, as Edward Said writes, what cultural work does the text accomplish by the surprising initial omission of the female protagonist so clearly promised by the title (32)? Emma owes her late entrance, it would seem, to the need to establish the prior account of a man's life into which her own existence might be inserted and thus acquire meaning, all of which serves to connote her secondary, dependent status. It is the novel's syntax, moreover, that permits a first interpretation of the title. Through its exclusion of a given name, repository of personal identity, and its insistence instead on marital status, the title informs us that the woman to whom it refers is important not as an individual but only to such extent that she assumes the function of her title. This omission of "Emma" from the title is underscored by what the reader notes as the virtual absence of all reference to Emma's childhood, an absence that finds an echo later in the enormous difficulty the reader experiences in gaining access to the childhood world of Emma's daughter, Berthe. Flaubert's silence on the subject of Emma up to age thirteen has the unfortunate effect of suggesting that members of the female sex present no real interest until the stirrings of puberty place them on the royal road to womanhood. "According to a certain dominant ideology," Luce Irigaray writes, "the little girl can thus have *no value* before puberty" (25).

To be sure, Flaubert does not linger over Charles's most formative years (to which he devotes, aside from the classroom scene of almost mythical proportions, all of one page). In a few deft strokes, however, he makes his reader understand how absolutely crucial such experience is to the construction—or thwarting—of an identity. If, as the syntax of Flaubert's novel would suggest, the boy's tale may be held out as the model (however nonexemplary) of childhood experience under which the little girl's story is subsumed and thus erased, it is because androcentric culture operates on a tacit "a priori assumption of the same" (Irigaray 27). Indeed, it would seem that Flaubert anticipates Freud by over half a century in his equation of the little girl with, and his subsequent dismissal of her as, "a little man" (Irigaray 25–27). Since children in this view are sexually undifferentiated, her story would prove a simple redundancy after his, a pointless repetition. The challenge for students, as I see it, lies in uncovering the connection between this radical suppression of feminine identity during the "mirror stage" of human development—Lacan's term for the decisive moment at which the child sees his or her own image in the mirror as whole, complete—and the subsequent restriction of woman to the role of the mirroring other (Emma's sexual desire, especially as it is ultimately reduced and parodied by the blind man's verse). How, in other words, does "the little man that the little girl is" become a woman (Irigaray 27)? Freud tells us that she does so by becoming progressively less of a man, by relinquishing important aspects of her masculinity only to spend the rest of her life, tragically, "envying" these lost aspects of herself in her male lovers (Irigaray 27).

I dwell on the irony of Charles Bovary's presentation as "eminent" only briefly to say that it is but the first of many ironies and gender indeterminacies in a novel in which both abound. Indeed, Charles is more often depicted as feminine than as masculine, and the sign under which the reader first encounters him—intense humiliation at the hands of his classmates—has the effect, one could argue, of feminizing him. This reversal might be understood as a parody of the patriarchal plot, which insists on the strict maintenance of all hierarchies (active versus passive, masculine versus feminine) as well as on the primacy of his story. It was because of this conflation of gender roles in fact— particularly the subsequent masculinization of Emma Bovary—that Flaubert seemed most subversive to contemporary critics such as Baudelaire. Yet Baudelaire's ecstatic characterization of Emma Bovary as "almost a man," which I would rephrase more negatively as "man but" (the French translation of which, my students tell me, is none other than *homme mais*—or Homais, Emma's textual double), completes the erasure of Emma's femininity begun in childhood, as it returns her to the predictably inferior variation of the paradigmatic, eminent male ("*Madame Bovary*" 401–02). Actually, Baudelaire's lavish but problematic praise of Mme Bovary's masculinity finds an astonishing echo in the ironic homage Homais pays (indirectly) to Emma: "C'est une femme de grands moyens et qui ne serait pas déplacée dans une sous-préfecture!" 'She's a highly capable woman who would not be out of place in a sous-préfecture!' (172; 76; trans. mine). This damning praise contrives in the space of one short sentence both to elevate and to denigrate Mme Bovary. After a beginning that confidently asserts what Emma is and places her on a footing of equality (as highly capable as a man), Homais's compliment rapidly degenerates into a more negative assessment of what she might not be (out of place) and sets up a rigid hierarchy. By the time the reader arrives at the word *sous-préfecture*, there can remain little doubt as to the true nature of Homais's homage. In its relation of inferiority to the term *préfecture*, the *sous-préfecture* clearly evokes the devalued status of woman vis-à-vis man. Some doubt is even cast on whether Emma, for all her *grands moyens* 'capabilities,' can actually aspire to the inferior term of this opposition. In a broader frame of reference, Flaubert's gender confusions seem to participate in a tendency in his work to collapse the concept of difference altogether, a trend that reaches its apogee, arguably, in *Bouvard et Pécuchet*, a work during the reading of which many students report difficulty in keeping the two protagonists distinct. This experience, once students discover it has relatively little to do with their basic competence as readers of French, can lead them to the discovery of a major Flaubertian preoccupation.

The underlying hysteria suggested by such lack of differentiation leads me back to the discussion of the title of Flaubert's novel, which refers ambiguously and simultaneously, as critics have noted, to Charles's mother and to his first wife, Héloïse, as well as to Emma. Of the title's three place holders, it is the half-concealed, half-revealed reference to Charles's *maman* (Mme Bovary, *mère*)—reiterated acoustically by the given name Emma—that particularly attracts my attention. This return of the mother in the signifier *Emma* plays like the return of the repressed, or, as Shoshana Felman might say in reference to Lacan's work, the repressed returns, but with a difference (*Lacan* 44). The question, What difference does *Emma* make? is a vital and interesting one that can involve students in the elucidation of the relation of a male author to the figure of the mother and the act of writing, and I return to examine that question shortly.

In his article "Female Sexuality" Freud finds the origins of later developments of hysteria in the phase of exclusive attachment to the mother, which he calls the pre-Oedipus phase. I ask students to look at the first scene of *Madame Bovary* as one that we might place on the edge of the (prehysterical) pre-Oedipus, with this difference: for Freud's division of early childhood experience into preoedipal (preobjectal or undifferentiated relation to the mother; there is as yet no division into subject and object) and oedipal (conflicted, divided relation to the father), I substitute Lacan's equivalent yet displaced concepts of the imaginary and the symbolic (without discarding Freud's categories, however). The imaginary and the symbolic recast Freud's developmental phases as linguistic stages. The imaginary would thus signify "preverbal" and the symbolic, language, "the sound system that depends on difference and the absence of the reference" to which Lacan also refers as the law/name of the father, metaphors that are often used interchangeably (Lacan 65–67; Homans 7). Shifting the frame of reference to the scene of language allows me to identify more accurately the specific dynamics of the first episode of *Madame Bovary*. Indeed, these first few pages, which recount the repeated and largely unsuccessful attempts made by a young schoolboy to articulate his name amid general classroom derision and pandemonium, provide an ideal context in which to evoke the recasting of the Freudian oedipal drama as the Lacanian primal scene of linguistics.

In both theories the locus of high drama involves the passage from the preverbal, preoedipal and paradisiacal relation to the mother to the oedipal stage, the symbolic or language stage, which occurs only under the threat of castration. The difficulty of this passage inheres in the separation itself, which, in addition to being accomplished under threat of bodily mutilation, is experienced as an act of violence against the mother. In the novel, it is the classroom and the stern law of its master that in the most obvious way fulfill the paternal role by enforcing the separation of the boy from his mother (prohibition of incest, induction into the social order), but as careful attention to the signifying material reveals, Flaubert situates the real struggle on the plane of language. The linguistic point of passage, the hurdle young Charles must clear to leave behind the mother and gain entry into the symbolic, would seem to reside in a single word: *Charbovari*. Students may thus read the first scene of *Madame Bovary* allegorically, as the fall into language.

A more spectacular or faithful performance of Lacanian theory—Charles is truly at center stage, surrounded by an audience of jeering boys—would be difficult to imagine. Here, the means of entry into the father's law, or language, resides precisely in the father's name, exactly as Lacan would have it. But that name can only be mumbled and maimed. It is this difficulty of articulating the name of the father, moreover, that points up the burdens it already represents for Charles (who has experienced nothing but rejection from his own father) and will represent in the future for the unwitting Emma in her accepting to bear the name of Bovary.

The nonseparation or running together of the first (Charles) and last (Bovary) names indicates that another separation has not yet occurred: namely, that of the child from his mother. Struggle though he may, Charles simply cannot seem to effect the crucial leap that would land him squarely in the symbolic. Still tied to the preoedipal mother, what emerges from his mouth is not-quite language, a kind of vocable-babble, an utterance that straddles the imaginary and the symbolic. The inability to articulate fully the proper name would also reveal an insufficiency of self. Possessing neither self nor (m)other, Charles Bovary becomes the target at which his classmates boisterously and hysterically aim their own unresolved castration and separation anxieties. Flaubert describes the scene as one of complete uproar: "Ce fut un vacarme . . . (on hurlait, on aboyait, on trépignait, on répétait: *Charbovari! Charbovari!*)" 'A hubbub broke out . . . (they yelled, barked, stamped, repeated "Charbovari! Charbovari!")' (63; 3). Charles's classmates' increasingly strident inflections of *Charbovari* utterly transform Charles's unassertive whisper into its exact opposite, suggesting nothing so much as the word *charivari*, although the text does not state it. The opposition of *Charbovari* and *charivari* suggests to students the limits of the intelligible and thus provides additional evidence that the scene they are witnessing is taking place in the confines of the imaginary, an impression that is further reinforced by the depiction of Charles's cap.

Indeed, Charles's infamous *casquette*, described in minute detail during this episode, may be understood in much the same terms as the classroom hubbub. Flaubert characterizes it as "mutely expressive"—"une de ces pauvres choses, enfin, dont la laideur muette a des profondeurs d'expression" 'one of those poor things, in fine, whose dumb ugliness has depths of expression' (62; 2)— and thus speaks of it as a sort of silence. Also evident in its completely heteroclite, incomprehensible form is that it represents something like babble, or a deafening din. A similar opposition to the one previously encountered thus emerges. This is a hysterical object, simultaneously mute and shouting, part of this hysterical text with its roots still firmly lodged in the preoedipal "breeding ground" for hysteria, as noted earlier. Moreover, such an object as Charles's cap does not so much signify (it is meaningless, a "stupid" object) as it signals the reassuring yet troubling presence of the preoedipal mother (Culler, *Flaubert* 174). The cap is, finally, like the initial scene itself, a monstrous entity excentric to language.

The mother banished from the novel's title thus returns like unfinished business. The creation of Emma, linguistic reenactment of *maman*, provides further proof of what I have called elsewhere the "impossible loss of the Mother." If in Emma, however, the mother returns, it is with an important difference, as noted earlier. Simply and briefly put, Flaubert brings back the mother to renegotiate the separation from her that was previously experienced as failed or incomplete, the attempt at separation that surfaced textually as Charles's traumatic encounter with language. Sartre has hypothesized a difficult and late insertion into language for Flaubert, referring to the author of *Madame Bovary*, in what seems a great paradox, as his "family's idiot." For an author who stumbled so badly when it came time to leave the imaginary for the symbolic, if we defer to Sartre's account, Emma's difference resides in the golden second opportunity she holds out to him to achieve the much desired separation (3). This time Flaubert will not stumble, nor will he mumble incoherently and suffer the humiliation of a Charles Bovary. The solution of Emma's death, Flaubert's "suiciding" of his female protagonist (Schor, "Triste Amérique"), accomplishes unequivocally, and in its most literal sense, this separation from the mother. A male author's successful work of individuation on the plane of fiction is achieved only at the price of the (textual) mother's life. By way of summary, I recall to students how this particularly drastic exchange of male for female was in fact suggested from the beginning by the novelist's focus on Charles's tale and his occulting of Emma's.

I turn next to examine the mother's (Emma's) death, for this scene dramatizes yet another nightmarish encounter with words: the ditty voiced by the blind man just seconds before Emma dies. Students of Flaubert have long found the blind man a puzzling and intriguing figure and often sense that his function is far more crucial than his number of appearances in the text might suggest. His loss of sight links him metonymically to Emma on the plane of castration. Why castration? Freud, in his article "The Uncanny," explains that a number of infirmities—chief among them, blindness and loss of limb (one thinks of Hippolyte here)—have an eerie way of evoking the dread associated with castration; indeed, they are its equivalents in the unconscious (397). Since Freud insists on defining woman as a castrated version of man, it is easy to see how woman, too, might be inscribed in the list of evocative objects. One might read the entire novel, in fact, from Charles's aborted speech act at one end to the final appearance of the blind man at Emma's death scene, as the construction of a chain of the incurable and the monstrous: loss of speech—loss of limb—loss of sight—woman. Emma, moreover, seems to sense an uncanny bond with the blind man on at least one occasion, throwing him her last five-franc piece as she rushes to her own destruction. It is perhaps not Freud, however, who has the last say here but again Lacan, whose theories may prove insightful to students as they try to come to grips with the blind man's words.

Just as Emma dimly recognizes herself in the blind man's mirror of monstrosity, his ditty speaks a tale whose images seem to present views of her that she herself encountered without seeing them fully. It is tempting to interpret the blind man's words as an illustration of Lacan's well-known aphorism "[T]he unconscious is the discourse of the Other" (Lacan 312; Felman, *Lacan* 124). Emma's unconscious, in other words, is the expression of the other, the discourse pronounced in a raucous voice by the blind man (the other of man, castrated man). At the same time, the blind man's ditty (which speaks Emma's unconscious) is revealed to be the discourse of patriarchy, denying women subjecthood as it condemns them to the position of objects in an economy of male desire. Emma's unconscious is decidedly not her own.

The ditty spoken by and through the blind man (for him, too, it is another's discourse) is the story of the appropriation of female desire. Nanette, the ditty's farmhand and feminocentric focus (a reminder to Emma of her own origins), is the male poet's possession, for he refers to her as "Ma Nanette" (401). Indeed, she is his creation, a mere figment of his desire. By endowing her with the appropriate lack or need (lack of penis, penis envy) he tailors her being to his own requirements. The heat of a sunny day is said to make Nanette, toiling in the fields, "dream of love" (400; 238), but this notion looks, rather, to be a comic projection of the poet's own lustful dreams. Endowing Nanette with penis envy in its most literal sense is the time-honored and unvarnished means by which the poet may ensure a place for, and the proper narcissistic reception of, his own sex and sexual appetites. Nanette's dreams of love, in other words, at once reflect and facilitate the poet's desire to "know" Nanette, a desire that the ditty further accommodates by the convenient summoning of a hot gust of wind around Nanette to undress her. For students of the text, however, Nanette remains virtually unknowable, a mere shadow with no real depth, definition, or body of her own. The ditty gives us to understand that the notion of woman itself may be little more than a symmetrical construct, a masculinist fiction born far more of the need to create a reassuring reciprocity or sameness of desire than of the need to acknowledge or explore the difference of the (self or) other. Nanette exists only to provide the poet a self-representation, a mirror in which he may rejoice in his masculinity; woman thus functions as man's complementary, nonthreatening other (see Gallop 70). This piece of popular verse, which may be said to serve as a parody and reductio ad absurdum of aspects of Flaubert's novel and Emma's life, also offers students material with which to effect a powerful critique of patriarchy, which, this text reveals, has use for woman only insofar as she constitutes a defense against the recognition of true otherness. In a gesture that is doubly ironic, Flaubert enlists the ("castrated") blind man as the instrument of dis-semination of this most crucial of in-sights.

Whereas for Oedipus knowledge leads to blindness, readers of *Madame Bovary* discover that for the female protagonist, in a curious and fascinating reversal of the male order, blindness leads to knowledge, to a bitter enlightenment. What the blind man's words reveal in a blinding—and illuminating—flash to the dying Emma and her readers, I suggest, is the impossibility of ever simply assuming in patriarchal culture that a woman's desires are authentically her own. While Emma had undoubtedly convinced herself that she possessed a degree of agency in her relations with her lovers and, when they failed her, in committing suicide, the discourse of the other makes it painfully clear that in her adulteries, as in her life and death in general, she was merely playing out her prescribed role, conforming blindly—if brilliantly—to patriarchy's script.

A Psychoanalytic Approach
to *Madame Bovary*
Lauren Pinzka

A psychoanalytic approach to *Madame Bovary* allows for an analysis of content and form, while adding a dimension to the novel's characterizations. The advantage of such an approach is that it allows the students a means by which to structure their observations of plot and characterization while teaching them to look beneath the surface and to perform close textual readings by focusing on word choice, syntax, and homophones. Psychoanalytic issues like gender, family dynamics, and sexuality engage students because they are central to our existence. The psychological aspects of the novel give it its universal appeal. I suggest several approaches from which to choose, depending on the students' level as well as on the purpose of the course.

On the simplest level, *Madame Bovary* may be read in the light of several of Freud's most significant premises. Given that some students will reject the universality of psychoanalysis, it is often useful to emphasize that Freud's analysis of the bourgeois family is especially pertinent to a study of the nineteenth-century novel, this one in particular. Both Freud and Flaubert were attempting portraits of disturbed women from their own phallocentric but not unsympathetic viewpoints. Despite his belief that human nature remains fundamentally unchanging, Freud acknowledged that the Oedipus complex had a social history (*Standard Edition* 4: 264; cited in Gay 48), which became more significant as the nuclear family emerged in the nineteenth century and was greatly influenced by the writings of Rousseau. Indeed, Rousseau's advocacy of motherhood continues to shape women's lives even today. The nineteenth century marked a turning point for women as the workplace changed from inside to outside the home and the woman's family role "became centered on child care and taking care of men" (Chodorow 4–5). The bourgeois mother was reduced to a moral role model for her children, far removed from the vulgarity of the workplace. Freud's analysis of the nuclear family of the nineteenth century provides a structural framework for the reading of the nineteenth-century novel. Freud was influenced not only by his patients but by fiction writers who he believed intuitively knew what he was trying to "prove" scientifically.

In a survey course, I avoid long theoretical exposés, which can build resistance; instead I assign guide questions and exposé topics to the students, including the following:

> Characterize the family relationships in the novel, or note the occurrence and significance of the repetition of key topoi ("timeless themes," motifs that appear widely and at various periods in literature) like the *tourbillon* 'whirlwind' or the mysterious songs and voices in the text.

Then, after the students have had the chance to enumerate their findings and to produce their own explanations (often quite creative), I guide them through a more psychoanalytic analysis, all the while insisting on the sociocultural context. When I introduce psychoanalysis slowly and in conjunction with other approaches, the students more readily accept its validity, particularly if they begin to see patterns from one book to the next. In my experience it is important to moderate one's direct use of Freud in the undergraduate classroom and to put it in a framework as feminist and literary as possible. Obviously, I am more inclined to provide an earlier and heavier theoretical component in a course specifically on psychoanalysis and literature.

I give examples of the kinds of thematic points that may be enriched by a psychoanalytic point of view but present my ideas in summary form to progress to a more rewarding and lesser-known use of the methodology. An obvious point of departure is a discussion of the above-mentioned relationships between the characters. The following section is designed to illustrate the sort of sociopsychological analysis that this approach permits. It is essential to emphasize continually to the students that we are not discussing real people (as clear as this point seems to us) and that any correlation between theory and fiction has different causes than would similar findings about human subjects who have indeed experienced childhood traumas.

In the following paragraph I provide an example of a Freudian and Lacanian analysis. Charles's relationship with his mother functions in part as one of Flaubert's many uses of the literary cliché. She is a disappointed wife who "reporta sur cette tête d'enfant toutes ses vanités éparses, brisées" 'transferred onto this child's head all her scattered, broken vanities' (66; 5).[1] In Freudian terms, Charles becomes her penis substitute, but Lacan provides a more nuanced analysis that insists on differentiating between the symbolic phallus and the organ that children confuse with it in their equation of power with masculinity. That confusion is inevitable as they assess the culture and family that make up the "symbolic order" in which they find their place. Since Charles's mother as a woman cannot "be the phallus," she tries "to have the phallus" through her husband, but because she perceives both his inadequacies and her own as a woman in a male-dominated society, she turns to her son.[2] Emma, who cannot "have the phallus" through Charles, either, attempts to replicate the compensatory strategy. To her chagrin, she has a daughter and is hence deprived of the phallus and must reach outside her family to obtain it. Rodolphe, always associated with violence, aggression, and stereotypically masculine objects like cigars and whips, clearly fulfills that function in her life and allows her to believe that she can obliterate her sense of emptiness by association with a powerful, "phallic" man. Louise Kaplan notes the prevalence of this female strategy and considers it a form of "female perversion" (222).

One way of encouraging a literary approach while discussing characterization is to encourage the students to become careful readers of the nuances of Flaubert's text. Flaubert's famed insistence on "le mot juste" 'the exact word' provides such a concrete approach. One might question the unconscious reasons (along with the conscious ones like phonic quality, also a feature of the unconscious) for which a particular word appeared to be the necessary one for the author. Charles's mother's happiness in regaining her dominion over her son is a case in point: "Elle fut ingénieuse et caressante, se réjouissant intérieurement à ressaisir une affection qui depuis tant d'années lui échappait" 'She was clever and caressing, inwardly delighting at recapturing an affection that had eluded her for so many years' (415; 248). The words *caressante* and *se réjouissant* (with the sexually charged *jouir*, referring to orgasm, inscribed within) reveal Flaubert's conscious or unconscious awareness of the reciprocal nature of the erotically charged love bond between mother and son. The verb *ressaisir* adds a domineering, almost violent, edge to her love. The violent nature of eroticism, a key component of Freudian theory, subtly pervades *Madame Bovary*, an issue that I address later in this essay. In analyzing the sentence quoted earlier, about how Charles's mother transfers her dreams onto her son, I invite discussion on the significance of the prefix of *reporta*. It is surely a conscious attempt to emphasize the repetitiveness of the elder Mme Bovary's life (Tanner 250) but perhaps also signals an unconscious perception of the compulsively repeated nature of the feminine response to a phallocentric society.

A relationship that lends itself well to thematic as well as formal analysis is the symbolically oedipal relationship between Emma and Léon. Students can provide details like the enclosed, womblike nature of their meeting places, including the red curtains surrounding the bed in their shuttered hotel room. Furthermore, Emma calls Léon "Enfant." The students can note the singsong quality of the syntax of "Elle l'appelait enfant:—Enfant, m'aimes-tu?" 'She called him child:—Child, do you love me?' (339; 192). The form adds immensely to the meaning of the passage.

Putting psychoanalysis in a sociocultural context, one may read the various symbols of castration as a literary representation of the decline of the father figure, perhaps related historically to the decline of the monarchy. The relationship between Charles and Emma is initiated only because her father has a broken leg. Both Charles's father and Charles are depicted as failures, although Homais and Rodolphe (the only one of Emma's lovers to represent the phallus) win out over Emma (following Flaubert's lead, Naomi Schor suggests that Homais symbolizes *homme* 'man' and also notes the phonetic similarity between *Emma* and *femme* 'woman' ["For a Restricted Thematics" 12]). Larivière, male authority par excellence, and possibly a stand-in for the author's father, fails to save Emma, suggesting a possible revenge fantasy on the part of Flaubert. In *L'idiot de la famille* Sartre argues at length that Flaubert disliked his father and took pleasure in parodying him in the form of Charles, a second-rate "officier de santé" who was not even a real doctor (H. Barnes 362). We cannot dismiss the role of the text as a stage for acting out the author's own fantasy life (Bellemin-Noël 43). We must, however, always take the text as focus because "the distance between text and author is extremely variable" (Frappier-Mazur

332). Furthermore, as I stated earlier, to avoid reductionism, it is important to link a psychoanalytic interpretation to others. Inherent in Emma's suicide is the struggle between Romanticism and science, both of which Flaubert nullifies. In "For a Restricted Thematics," Schor links gender, castration, and an opposition between speech and language in an analysis well worth assigning for discussion in an advanced class.

Ion Collas's Madame Bovary: *A Psychoanalytic Reading* provides the instructor with other discussion topics. He interprets Homais as an evil mother figure in the book, whose pharmacy-confectionery provides not only food but also poison (46). Lheureux clearly functions as a sort of evil mother-provider to Emma, bringing on her suicide when he abruptly cuts off financial sustenance.

A psychoanalytic interpretation may be layered onto a cultural reading of Emma's obsessive acquisition of commodities; the Marxian term *commodity fetishism* suggests such a union. Fetishism displaces desire from the body to objects in an unconscious attempt by the male subject to replace the phallus missing from the body of the woman (which therefore represents to him the vicarious threat of castration) and by the female subject to repossess the phallus of which she has been unjustly deprived. Emma repairs her "castration" by assuming masculine attributes. She thus becomes a phallic woman, a fetishized woman (see Kaplan 34–35, 63). Frappier-Mazur aptly evokes "fetishistic confusion between the sign and the thing" (343), a conspicuous delusion in *Madame Bovary*, which emphasizes the erotic power of the swishes of skirts, illustrated plates, and even doorknobs. I refer the reader to Tony Tanner's treatment of the subject. Kaplan notes Flaubert's use of characteristically fetishistic items like shoes, corsets, and whips (36) but, more interesting, notes that he also fetishizes "the false beliefs and deceptive ideologies of social progress" (203).

Two provocative elements of *Madame Bovary* for undergraduates are its breakdown of gender and the violent nature of its eroticism. The two elements are in fact intertwined, and their examination can be a fruitful exercise in careful textual reading. For instructors particularly interested in the topic from a psychoanalytic if not literary approach, I recommend Kaplan's *Female Perversions: The Temptations of Madame Bovary*. She provides a provocative analysis of Emma as a locus of various feminine forms of sexual perversion, including sexual bondage and self-mutilation, effectively linking gender stereotyping to sexual perversion. Kaplan also emphasizes Flaubert's transgressions as a response to an increasingly rigid enforcement of gender conformity socially necessary to solidify the nineteenth-century bourgeois family (5). The goal of sexual perversion is to abolish gender distinctions because one fears a secret inner desire to be of the opposite sex (64). Flaubert, with his well-known ambivalence about his own gender identity, consciously or unconsciously participated in that fantasy by creating a female protagonist. (For insight into Flaubert's character and sexual ambiguity, I recommend his letters and Sartre's *L'idiot de la famille*.) Furthermore, as Kaplan astutely remarks, "Bovary was supposed to have been Flaubert's curative immersion in banality, an attempt to expunge from his writings the theological mysticism that just barely disguised the sado-masochistic fantasies in *Temptations of Saint Anthony*" (202).

The literary text is in part a fantasy in which traces of the preconscious (the psychic apparatus somewhere between, and with access to both, the conscious and unconscious systems, the waking state a prominent example) are inserted within the framework of the unconscious, the actual creator of the work of art (Lyotard 383). Literature is not literally fantasy; rather, fantasy precedes and fuels literature. Behind fantasies are primordial fantasies: for example, the primal scene, seduction, and castration fantasies. Primordial fantasies reflect the conjunction of the real (biological facts) and the symbolic (the oedipal triad) (Laplanche and Pontalis, "Fantasme" 1854–55n45). Jean-François Lyotard maintains that these original, or primary, fantasies are repressed in the unconscious, leaving a configuration (which he terms the figure-matrix) that represents not the fantasies themselves but a repetition of the operations that made this figure possible (327). The figure-matrix imprints itself on other material, disguising itself with elements from reality (246), so it is not a recognizable form but a creator of signifiers, or word presentations, present in spite of syntactic rules (327). In reading the literary text, therefore, we never can locate the figure-matrix, only its effects. Our project is to look at those word presentations and thing presentations that exist despite rationalized discourse.

If perversion is a socially transgressive means of regulating aggression and a quest for ecstasy, as Kaplan maintains (125, 482), then perhaps writing represents the very same act for the author. And just as, in the writer's attempt to master traumatic childhood events, scenarios of sexual perversion "divert attention away from the underlying or latent motives, fantasies, wishes and desires" lurking behind them (Kaplan 10), we may assert that the scenarios of the text smooth over its own latent content.

To begin a discussion of the sadomasochist fantasies generating the text, I ask the students to be attentive to associations between pain and pleasure and to examples of dominance and submission. I then slowly lead them through the relevant theories of Freud and more modern thinkers to help students frame the play of violent eroticism and gender in the novel.

The opening scene of the novel is of particular importance because it sets the tone of the work and because the narrative point of view is different from that of the rest of the novel: "Nous étions à l'étude" 'We were in class' (61; 1) suggests that the narrator may be one of the children who will ridicule the hapless Charles. The implications of a sadistic narrator cruelly mocking his characters may be elaborated. I mention a few details to illustrate how one might analyze this passage. By designating Charles "le nouveau" 'the new boy,' the narrator suggests that he is about to be initiated into a strange rite. The students' and the teacher's physical and psychological violence are clear enough. The sexual element may be harder to identify. A careful reading uncovers a narrative crescendo and decrescendo mimicking orgasm, depicted with a definite suggestion of pain ("aigus," "trépignait" 'sharp,' 'stamped their feet' [63; 3]) and sexual release with its accompanying liquidity ("quelque boulette de papier lancée d'un bec de plume qui vînt s'éclabousser sur sa figure" 'some paper wad flipped from the tip of a pen that came splashing in his face' [64; 3]). The comparison of a few stifled laughs to a "pétard mal éteint" 'poorly extinguished firecracker' (63; 3) suggests an impotence often associated with the character of Charles Bovary. Although Flaubert clearly intended to portray Charles as a victim, the sexual dimension of the humiliation may very well be on the level of unconscious fantasy transposed to the text.

Charles's behavior can be examined according to Freud's theories of male masochism. A male masochist compulsively seeks to be punished by a "phallic woman" who in fact masks his father, thus satisfying his repressed homosexual desire for his father (Freud, "Child" 196). The male masochist is thus permitted "to identify with the degrading position assigned to women in the social order, but without losing face" (Kaplan 25). We note that Charles's early tormenter is a father figure, the teacher, but that he turns instead to phallic women like his first wife—"sa femme fut le maître" 'his wife was master' (70; 8)—and then Emma, who repeatedly exhibits masculine attributes. The phallic woman is usually a demeaned woman (Kaplan 24), as Emma clearly becomes in the course of the novel. In Freud's study of infantile beating fantasies, male masochists start by fantasizing that they are being beaten by father figures but repress that stage in favor of a continued fantasy of being beaten by a virilized woman ("Child" 200). That Flaubert's portrait of the male masochist so closely corresponds to Freud's studies is uncanny. Such coincidence can lead to an examination of the relation between unconscious fantasy and literary production.

One can then easily contrast Charles to Rodolphe, who corresponds to the male sadist, a caricature of masculinity based on prowess, aggression, and domination that stave off "a terrifying primitive violence" (Kaplan 12). At the basis of male perversion is a fear of women that translates into misogyny, plainly in view in the portrait of Rodolphe.

Students will be surprised by Freud's belief from clinical observation that the roles of sadist and masochist are interchangeable because masochism is at the root of both. The sadist's pleasure is in vicariously enjoying the masochist's pain ("Instincts" 127–28). Although Freud defines sadomasochism as taking sexual pleasure in causing or receiving pain (127), Kaplan explains that actual practitioners claim that the real dynamic is one of dominance and submission (448). Emma's plight can be analyzed as the female castration complex perpetuated by the clash of female desires and ambitions with the social roles traditionally assigned to women (Kaplan 105).

One can show that Flaubert, like Freud, considers the terms *masculine* and *feminine* culture-bound, convenient but inaccurate shorthand for biological differences ("Instincts" 134). The students will easily note, along with Baudelaire, that Emma wishes she were a man: she expresses envy for men's freedom; she yearns for the vicarious experience of such freedom through having a son; after her affair with Rodolphe is under way, she wears a lorgnon like a man and breaks the social taboo that forbids women to smoke. Concurrently, Flaubert acts out through Emma his own wish to be a woman—not without expressing much of his typical misogynistic ambivalence.

Another of Kaplan's assertions adapts itself well to Flaubert's text: women engage more often in sexual bondage than in sadomasochism (210). Emma provides a good example of a "love slave" motivated not so much by pain and pleasure as by desperate need, seeking castration, abandonment, and death through the medium of love and pleasure (Kaplan 218). Yet her status as the fictional creation of a male author changes the equation significantly. Like Flaubert, she exemplifies gender ambiguity. Subsequent examples confirm that Emma has indeed evolved from her masochistic phase to a sadistic one. The remark that Léon has become Emma's "mistress" (351; 201) calls attention to the ironic sexism of linguistic convention, which indicates that a female master is in fact a subordinate. Violence and power are so firmly associated with masculinity in our conscious and, as Freud insists, in our unconscious that we cannot create a feminine form for a dominant partner.

For a more advanced class, the instructor may want to introduce an equally interesting Lacanian reading. I do not have space to elaborate many examples but refer the reader to Tanner's excellent *Adultery in the Novel*. His attention to theory, theme, and textual detail is exemplary. To give a hint of the approach, I direct the reader to Tanner's analysis of various motifs in the novel, such as that of the open mouth, metaphor for gaping need and the satisfying of appetites (243). Language, emanating of course from the mouth, is an integral part of the equation. He details the process of Emma's "morselization," linking it to the Lacanian notion of the unstable self that realizes itself as a series of imaginary fixations and misconstructions (96). The empty self engenders an endless preoccupation with filling up space, both physical and verbal. Tanner relates this emptiness-fullness to the relations among language, demand, and desire. "The more Emma tries to express her feelings . . . the more she is doomed to encounter, not a metaphorical emptiness, but the emptiness of metaphors" (268). Lacan's belief that we are at the mercy of language is never truer than in the novelistic world of Flaubert.

NOTES

[1] All translations are mine, though I indicate the corresponding pages in the Norton edition for cross-referencing purposes.

[2] For an explanation of these terms, see Laplanche and Pontalis, *Language* 439–41, 312–14.

FORMAL APPROACHES

Will the Real Emma Bovary Please Stand Up?

Dean de la Motte

As the essays in this volume eloquently attest, *Madame Bovary* has inspired countless critical discussions, many known well beyond nineteenth-century French studies. What Albert Thibaudet called "le laboratoire de Flaubert" has become "le laboratoire de la critique," where generations of scholars, like Homais in his *capharnaüm*, have bustled about concocting interpretive "solutions" to the challenges posed by the author's text. Such an immensely fertile proving ground for theoretical concepts, however, is potential quicksand for undergraduate teachers and students alike. Just as the novel may be the ideal choice for a graduate seminar on narrative theory, so may it also entice a professor to lead students into a labyrinth of theoretical terminology, authors, and critical schools that is perhaps best avoided in an undergraduate survey course. The temptation to rely too heavily on theory is great, particularly to those of us recently issued from the rarified atmosphere of graduate school; indeed, even as I developed my argument, I had to remain ever vigilant to keep the pedagogical aims of this essay in mind.

I stress here, however, that in no way does the approach outlined in the following pages represent an attempt to bury the polemics of literary theory and pedagogy under the belletristic impressionism, rightly taken to task by Gerald Graff, that assumes literature would teach itself "if the encumbrances of scholarship, criticism, or theory could somehow be prevented from getting in the way" (10). Nor does such an approach seek, as Margaret Tillett does in *On Reading Flaubert*, "to imagine that one possessed the last edition [of *Madame Bovary*] corrected by him in his lifetime, without any notes or comments"

(13). On the contrary, my approach strives to foreground many of the significant theoretical problems discussed since the publication of *Madame Bovary*. Colleagues will no doubt agree that undergraduate resistance to theory is nearly universal and can perhaps be overcome only through subterfuge. The purpose of this essay is to suggest that one way substantive theoretical issues may be smuggled into the classroom is through the interpretation of Emma Bovary herself. By generating discussion about who, what, and how she "is" and about how she has been viewed, instructors may lead students from traditional humanistic, thematic readings toward more complex considerations. I sketch four different approaches to Emma Bovary, each tied to a traditional period or genre of literary history and each of which has, at one time or another, been used to describe her: tragic, romantic, realist, and modern. My essay is "thematic" only in that it erects a series of provisional thematizations of Flaubert's character that complement (or deconstruct) one another and enrich our reading of the novel.

Tragic Emma

Is Emma a tragic figure? With this question one opens Flaubert's text to many of the central issues of critical discussion. If the tragic hero is driven beyond the limits of convention, decentered by desire (Oedipus's desire to know, Phèdre's desire for Hippolyte), then Emma clearly qualifies. Her overweening desire for the forbidden or impossible, and the violent outcome of her inability to suppress or moderate it, makes her at least an epigone of Racine's famous heroine.

The parallels between Flaubert's novel and Racine's tragedies—*Phèdre* in particular—extend well beyond the hackneyed sense of tragic (as in Emma's "tragic demise") to the very structure, style, and thematics of the text itself. In one of his letters to Louise Colet, Flaubert confided:

> Ce qui me tourmente dans mon livre c'est l'élément *amusant*, qui y est médiocre. Moi, je soutiens que les *idées* sont des faits. . . . Je suis convaincu d'ailleurs que tout est affaire de style, ou plutôt de tournure, d'aspect.　　　　　　　　　　(*Correspondance*, ed. Bruneau, 2: 238)

> What worries me in my book is the element of *entertainment*. That side is weak; there is not enough action. I maintain, however, that *ideas* are action. . . . Besides, I am convinced that everything is a question of style, or rather of form, of presentation. (*Madame Bovary*, ed. de Man, 313–14)

Dearth of action, purity of style: here again the comparison with Racine is instructive, particularly as it bears on Flaubert's heroine. From a distance of three centuries, it is all too easy to see in Racine only the epitome of classical rigor and clarity (and even here the resemblance to Flaubert's cult of the mot juste is striking) and to forget that contemporaries accused him of the very sins later attributed to Flaubert's novel: "crude realism," love as a subversive rather than ennobling force, and "the interplay of common, if intense, passions in characters of no exceptional grandeur" (Harvey and Heseltine 90). But the most striking parallel is the central mechanism that links *Phèdre* and *Madame Bovary*: a woman's overweening desire for what cannot be possessed drives the plot toward its unfortunate dénouement.

A consideration of Emma as tragic serves to introduce students to a number of important concepts, some of which may be elaborated in later discussions: Flaubert's cult of style at the expense of plot (one of the main reasons he has been claimed as a modern); his supposedly mimetic portrayal of reality and its deflation of the ideal; the dynamics of unfulfilled and unfulfillable desire and its relation to the narrative structure of *Madame Bovary*.

Finally, students may be asked to agree or disagree with Thibaudet's statement that "Flaubert's novel is as Jansenist in spirit as Racine's *Phèdre*, and he has treated Emma's death as a damnation" (379–80). It is important to point out that Flaubert's novel created controversy precisely because of its lack of authorial judgment. Further, Emma's "tragedy of dreams" may be—unlike Phèdre's—what Victor Brombert calls the "tragedy of the very absence of tragedy" (*Novels* 90). Inscribed in Emma's story is the metamorphosis of desire, from the tragic heroine's lust for forbidden love to the romantic search for transcendence to the atrophied modernist quest for impossible closure. Desire, like art, becomes important in itself, while its ends are obscured: "Au bout d'une distance indéterminée, il se trouvait toujours une place confuse où expirait son rêve" 'At the end of an indefinite distance there appeared always a confused spot where her dream faded' (118; 41; trans. modified).

Romantic Emma

English-speaking students often confuse the French words *romantique* and *romanesque* and in doing so reenact the errors of Emma Bovary. In Flaubert's merciless skewering of Romanticism he chooses the most sentimental, and some of the least enduring, of texts; indeed, Emma's kind of reading is perhaps even at the origin of the confusion, for what our students would call romantic (and erroneously translate as "romantique") has precious little to do with the Romanticism of the Schlegels, Coleridge, Hugo, or Musset and includes little or no irony, Romantic or otherwise. Emma's "bastard Romanticism" (Tillett 14) is deadly serious and necessarily free of the narrator's ironic tone.

The textual evidence to support a reading of Emma as romantic is overwhelming; one need only refer to part 1, chapter 6, the famous flashback to her formative literary education and life at the convent. Students should be warned that hers is a distorted Romanticism, a distillation of the most sensational *romanesque* from the *romantique*. At this point one might mention Harry Levin's interpretation of her as a female Quixote. A brief digression on the tendency of Flaubertian criticism—until well into the twentieth century—to stress the tension in the novel (and in Flaubert's own psyche) between the romantic and the realist, is also appropriate.

Finally, a number of basic but theoretically charged questions may be raised here: What does Emma truly desire? Is her romantic weltschmerz—"ce ne sont pas les remèdes de la terre qu'il me faudrait" 'it is no earthly remedy I need' (177; 80)—due partly, primarily, or wholly to her reading? Will the suppression of novel-reading (proposed by Mme Bovary *mère*) "cure" her? Speculation about what would happen if things were otherwise in a work of fiction—often a singularly Bovarystic activity—is valuable if it prompts students to consider the status of fiction and of the subdiscourses at work in *Madame Bovary*. For Flaubert does not propose a viable alternative to romantic cliché; we are confronted with a most unattractive choice, between the stock phrases of Rodolphe's seduction and the bureaucratic "manure!" (215; 107) of the agricultural fair.

Romanticism is arguably the big loser in the battle of competing discourses or ideologies in *Madame Bovary*, but when Emma's diluted brand of Romanticism is swept away by a tide of irony, does anything identifiably Romantic remain? And, further, how does it inform the structure of the text? Her Bovarysm is utopian, a quintessentially Romantic urge, and no matter how easily we dismiss the forms it assumes (always derivative: novels, newspapers, fashion magazines), the core of dissatisfaction is constant and undeniable. At the heart of Flaubert's novel is the clash between the utopian urge and Emma's grim reality. This view of the novel, of course, dates back to Baudelaire, who saw in Emma "a truly sublime example of her kind" and "real greatness," for even in her narrow circumstances "she is . . . in pursuit of the ideal" (*"Madame Bovary"* 341, 342).

Realist Emma

For several decades the view that the skillfully rendered reality of Emma's mundane existence was the foil to her romantic excess held sway in criticism, until critics began to explore the destabilizing, problematic aspects of Flaubert's peculiar brand of realism. Paradoxically, to consider Emma Bovary as primarily a realist depiction of a suffocating bourgeoise circa 1850 is to introduce some of the most theoretically complex issues at stake in the study of *Madame Bovary*.

Apart from the novelist's comments—as when he claimed that his "pauvre *Bovary*, sans doute, souffre et pleure dans vingt villages de France à la fois, à cette heure même" (*Correspondance*, ed. Bruneau, 2: 392) 'poor Bovary, without a doubt, is suffering and weeping at this very instant in twenty villages of France' (*Madame Bovary*, ed. de Man, 316)—evidence of his realism appears to abound, especially in his descriptions of Emma's narrow universe. Students, particularly those who read the novel in French, have troble both deciphering and appreciating its descriptive passages. When they question the relevance of details, they stumble on an important issue in recent discussion of the novel. Critics have traditionally sought to recuperate descriptive detail for thematic or narrative purposes, to "let nothing escape, but integrate it in a larger scheme by giving it a meaning" (Culler, *Flaubert* 22). Roland Barthes challenges this tendency by suggesting that certain unrecuperable descriptive details "say, in the last analysis, only this: *we are the real*" ("Reality Effect" 16). I introduce students to Barthes's "reality effect" as well as to Mieke Bal's subsequent attempt to demonstrate how the description of Rouen anticipates the outcome of the novel (87–111). Remaining focused on realist Emma, we also explore the possibility that even, and perhaps especially, those details that cannot be made to contribute to the narrative can thematically reinforce the purposelessness, stasis, and ennui of Emma's environment.

Modernist Emma

The difficulties presented by fictional details demonstrating the paradoxical claims of realism attest to the richness (and indeterminacy) of Flaubert's text. It is indicative of the novel's polyvalence that it can serve as a dividing line between Romanticism and realism and as a forerunner of modern and even postmodern narrative. Indeed, the approach I take to *Madame Bovary* takes for granted the modernity of Flaubert's text. Since Jean Rousset's landmark discussion in 1962 of the novel as an "anti-novel" in "*Madame Bovary* ou le livre sur rien," criticism has largely privileged Flaubert the innovator at the expense of his acclaimed realism and the tragedy and Romanticism it seeks to deflate (see Brombert, "Flaubert and the Status of the Subject"). If we remain focused on Emma Bovary, however, can we read her as a forerunner of modernist characterization? Is she the fixed "center of it all," as Percy Lubbock maintains (qtd. in de Man 350), or is she a protomodernist figure who escapes critical recuperation?

Clearly Emma is unstable in more ways than one. Her invented sins at confession; her deception of Charles in her affairs both amorous and financial; her mercurial changes of mood, when she becomes "finicky" and "capricious" (127; 47); her dressing and behaving like a man; her preference for fiction over life; even the inconsistencies in the color of her eyes: all reveal in her the dissembler. Yet Emma is less fragmentary than displaced, and in this she anticipates the antiheroes of Kafka and, to an extent, of Beckett. The desire for a presence (completeness, closure) forever withheld is the motivating force behind her frequent and varied metamorphoses.

Emma's instability is paralleled by Flaubert's exploitation of the *discours indirect libre*, which may be introduced to students at this point. The almost imperceptible passage from the narrator's to Emma's consciousness announces both the ironic, polyphonic novel of modernism and modernist fascination with psychological processes (James, Proust, Joyce). Flaubert's innovation has, unfortunately, become nearly imperceptible to students and is perhaps best explained by contrast with earlier works like Balzac's *Père Goriot*, in which the reader has no doubt who is "speaking" or "thinking."

The uncertainties of Flaubert's text itself seem to authorize, if not demand, a reading of Emma Bovary from a shifting perspective in which students are asked to explore her various dimensions, as well as the questions each raises. Such a reading reveals that the polyvalence of *Madame Bovary* is nevertheless "contained" by and in the thematic constant of desire. The incompatibility of desire and reality lies, of course, at the heart of the novel. Nearly all our theoretical concerns—Flaubert's original use of voice, his dialogism and resulting all-pervasive irony, even the debate on the function and status of description—appear rooted in the inexorable conflict or *décalage* 'dislocation' between desire and possession (possession and "the real" are, in a sense, identical in Flaubert). In the same way, the development of modern fiction may be traced in and around *Madame Bovary* through the vehicle of desire in its many guises: narrative, sexual, spiritual.

I find this approach useful because, without requiring an immersion in theoretical materials often inappropriate for beginning students of literature, it immediately situates the novel in the context(s) of traditional literary movements, genres, and periods and yet points up the inadequacy of such tenuous, even arbitrary, divisions. Ideally, students will come to see that their successive readings of Emma Bovary are complementary rather than contradictory; that the "real" Emma Bovary is tragic, romantic, realist, and modern; and that her desire reconciles and transcends traditional classification. What Flaubert wrote of the sentences in a book also applies to our versions of his protagonist: "Il faut que les phrases s'agitent dans un livre comme les feuilles dans une forêt, toutes dissemblables en leur ressemblance" (*Correspondance*, ed. Bruneau, 2: 545) 'The sentences in a book must quiver like the leaves in a forest, all dissimilar in their similarity' (*Madame Bovary*, ed. de Man, 318).

Myth and Symbol in *Madame Bovary*

William Nelles

Undergraduates frequently find it difficult to identify and analyze literary symbolism, especially in a realist narrative, probably because their attention is focused on the "what" of their reading experience (what will happen next?) to the extent that they neglect the more subtle "how" of the literary structure (how is the author creating meaning and significance?). *Madame Bovary* provides an excellent model for teaching undergraduates how to read for symbolic structures. The three parts of the novel can, for pedagogical purposes, be characterized as clustering around three distinct symbolic centers: part 1 around cattle, part 2 around horses, and part 3 around water.

Cued in advance to look for this pattern in their initial reading assignment, students will probably remark the symbolism of Charles's name: Bovary is similar to the French *bovin*, "relating to cattle." We may also make the point that symbolism is usually overdetermined; like most writers, Flaubert takes out something of an artistic insurance policy on his symbolism, and readers who miss one instance will catch another. The symbolic point of the metaphor of Charles's "ruminant son bonheur" 're-chewing his happiness' (93; 24), for example, operates independently of the vocabulary of translation: Charles is compared to a ruminant animal. The use of cattle as a derogatory metaphor for passive and dull people is so securely established that *Merriam-Webster's Collegiate Dictionary*, tenth edition, gives as the second meaning of the word "human beings esp. en masse"; *Le petit Robert* gives a similar pejorative secondary connotation for *bétail*. The teacher who likes puns may even wish to quote Jonathan Culler's observation that *Madame Bovary* is "not a realist novel so much as a vealist novel" ("Uses" 78).

Having introduced the basic idea for the reading of part 1, we may digress for one meeting to give a historical overview of the symbolic significance of horses in art. Students often seem to believe that literary symbolism consists of a set of private signals mysteriously flashed between authors and teachers, a secret code inaccessible to the average reader. Indeed, many students probably think that much of the symbolism we discuss exists only in our heads, merely the product of our overheated imaginations. We can show (at least in this case) that we're not just making it up. Flaubert is in fact demonstrably drawing on a long tradition of the symbolic use of the horse, not inventing an idiosyncratic code but, rather, taking a common tool out of the writer's toolbox. To use Michael Riffaterre's terms, we want to demonstrate that many symbols are not only part of a given writer's personal "idiolect" but also part of the public "sociolect" that "belongs to both reader and writer" (2).

Because many students find visual images more striking and memorable than words, I begin by showing a slide of a fifteenth-century Bavarian engraving that depicts Prudence (conveniently labeled by the artist "ymago prudencie") holding

a horse by the reins, representing the proper control of the passions by the intellect. Next I show a slide of two panels carved in a fourteenth-century French
ivory casket illustrating the story of Aristotle, Alexander, and Phyllis. The first
panel shows the philosopher lecturing the youthful Alexander on the powers of
the intellect while Phyllis flirts with him behind his teacher's back. The second
panel shows Phyllis riding Aristotle like a horse (he even wears a bit and bridle) as Alexander looks on from his hiding place at this evidence of the powers
of the passions. (One might emphasize the use of the "comic strip" format here
to remind students of the many forms narrative takes.) Full understanding of
the joke presupposes knowledge of this traditional symbolism of the horse;
having been introduced to it, students will see the humor immediately and realize that it depends upon a reversal of the usual horse symbolism: passion is
the rider and reason the horse. The implicit gendering of this symbolism may
then be shown explicitly with a slide of Paolo Veronese's *La Virtù che frena il
Vizio* ("Virtue Restraining Vice"), which depicts a man (Virtue) brutally reining
in a bitted and bridled woman (Vice). Veronese's sixteenth-century Italian
painting rounds out the series of visual representations I use, and at this point
I remind the students that these three slides represent three different visual art
forms from three different centuries and three different regions, underscoring
the traditional and public, not original and private, nature of this symbolism.

Following the discussion of these analogues from the visual arts, I move to a
fourth genre, century, and nation, playing the students a tape of a popular 1989
song by the Canadian musician K. D. Lang, "Pullin' Back the Reins," which
utilizes precisely the same metaphor of the horse as passion and the rider as ra-
tional judgment: "pullin' back the reins / trying to remain tall in the saddle."
This modern song, immediately accessible to most students, helps demonstrate
that the use of this symbol is not merely an ancient historical practice and that
reading symbolism is not a form of archaeology. Teachers not familiar with
contemporary music will find that students are a good source of up-to-date
musical references. Students will probably have brought up other examples
themselves by now, including at least the cliché "unbridled passion," and will
have recognized that they are already familiar with this metaphor.

After this excursion into interdisciplinary studies, I hand out a page or two
of selected appearances of the horse-and-rider symbolism in written discourse.
Naturally, most teachers will want to substitute some of their own favorite examples, literary as well as artistic and musical (and other types altogether), for
the ones I have been suggesting; once students begin looking for horse symbolism, it appears everywhere. One plausible starting point is circa 406 BC
with the mythological allegory of the soul in Plato's *Phaedrus*: "Let the soul be
compared to a pair of winged horses and charioteer joined in natural union. . . .
One of his horses is noble, and of noble breed, and the other is ignoble and of
ignoble breed; so that the management of the human chariot cannot but be a
difficult and anxious task" (153). The ignoble horse, which seems to represent
the passions, becomes especially difficult to control in the presence of the

beloved: "Then the charioteer is worse off than ever; he falls back like a racer at the barrier, and with a still more violent wrench drags the bit out of the teeth of the wild steed and covers his abusive tongue and jaws with blood . . ." (161).

Typical and usefully explicit occurrences of the motif in its standard form, the "unmarked case," are found in Charlotte Brontë's *Jane Eyre*, which appeared only ten years before *Madame Bovary*: "Reason sits firm and holds the reins" (203); "His chest heaved once, as if his large heart, weary of despotic constriction, had expanded, despite the will, and made a vigorous bound for the attainment of liberty. But he curbed it, I think, as a resolute rider would curb a rearing steed" (369). Relevant citations presenting variations on the basic theme might range from dream explication in Sir Thomas Malory—"the brydyll signifieth abstinens" (562)—to psychological analysis in Sigmund Freud:

> Thus in its relation to the id [the ego] is like a man on horseback, who has to hold in check the superior strength of the horse. . . . Often a rider, if he is not to be parted from his horse, is obliged to guide it where it wants to go; so in the same way the ego is in the habit of transforming the id's will into action as if it were its own.   ("Ego" 25)

James Joyce's *Ulysses* provides a complex but interesting permutation that rounds out the survey by combining the reversal of roles seen in the Aristotle-Alexander-Phyllis example with the gendering of Veronese's painting: namely, the scene in which Leopold Bloom, the male representative of the "scientific" temperament (558) and reason, is transformed into a horse and ridden by Bella Cohen, "a massive whoremistress" (429) who evidently represents the flesh and the passions. When Bella mounts Bloom, she is transformed into a male, "Bello," and referred to by masculine pronouns: "[H]e throws a leg astride and, pressing with horseman's knees, calls in a hard voice" (436).

Having had this overview of the spectrum of possible forms that this basic symbolic structure can take, which should demand only one class period, students may then begin consideration of the many references to horses in part 2. Naturally, not every horse that appears in a work of art automatically symbolizes sexual passion; a horse may simply appear as a plot device—say, as a means of transportation—or as a realistic index of social class (only the well-to-do could afford to ride them) or even, given the proper context, as an allegorical representation of Karl Marx (Orwell's *Animal Farm*). A given symbolic system remains potential until it is actualized in a specific context through which an author calls this particular symbolism into effect. A good place to begin analysis of Flaubert's use of this symbolic technique (or of almost anything else in the book) is the scene that takes place at the agricultural fair. One useful assignment for the next class meeting, which will focus on the development of the horse symbolism in part 2, might be a short written explication of the following key passage:

... les vaches, un jarret replié, étalaient leur ventre sur le gazon, et, ruminant lentement, clignaient leurs paupières lourdes sous les
moucherons qui bourdonnaient autour d'elles. Des charretiers, les bras
nus, retenaient par le licou des étalons cabrés, qui hennissaient à pleins
naseaux du côté des juments.   (203)

... the cows, one leg folded under them stretched their bellies on the
grass, slowly chewing their cud, and blinking their heavy eyelids at the
gnats that buzzed around them. Ploughmen with bare arms were holding
by the halter prancing stallions that neighed with dilated nostrils looking
in the direction of the mares.   (98)

The contrast between the placid cattle and aroused horses could hardly be
more conspicuous, and students should find the symbolic connections to the
characters of the story fairly easy to make. The repetition of "ruminant" 'chewing their cud,' previously applied to Charles, will allow the students to attach
the cow symbol first to him and then perhaps to the villagers as a group, as they
recall the simile introducing Yonville "comme un gardeur des vaches qui fait la
sieste" 'like a cowherd taking a nap' (134; 50) or note that the mayor is emblematically named Tuvache. The description of the stallions and mares will recall for many students (at least in the Bible Belt) Jeremiah 5.8—"Each neighs
after another man's wife, like a well-fed and lusty stallion," an apt allegorical
précis of the story of Rodolphe and Emma (as stallion and mare) that will
ensue. They begin their liaison ostensibly because of their shared interest in
riding, of course, and Homais's warning before their first ride is ironically
prophetic: "Prenez garde! Vos chevaux peut-être sont fougueux!" 'Be careful!
Your horses may be skittish!' (224; 113). After the affair ends, Emma no longer
wants a horse: "Elle voulut que l'on vendît le cheval; ce qu'elle aimait autrefois,
à présent lui déplaisait" 'She wanted her horse to be sold; what she formerly
liked now displeased her' (281; 153). Her former interest in horses, a symbol
of the flesh, is replaced for the moment by an interest in religion, a symbol of
the spirit.

Even the seemingly unrelated subplot of Hippolyte's operation, the narrative
of which is intercalated with the several stages of the affair, contributes to the
horse imagery. The name Hippolyte means "unyoker of horses," emblematic of
the course the affair between the two lovers (as symbolic horses) will take, and
the operation, which aims to correct "cet équin, large en effet comme un pied
de cheval" 'the equine foot, wide indeed as a horse's hoof,' "fortement accusé
d'équin" 'with a strong tendency to equinus' (243; 126), is significantly unsuccessful, foreshadowing the point that Emma's own "tendency to equinus," her
passionate nature, cannot be excised, even by her brief religious fervor, and will
reappear when she meets Léon again. The stable boy's name has a second relevant connotation here; many teachers using *The Norton Anthology of World
Masterpieces* (Mack) will have previously assigned Racine's *Phèdre* and might

profitably remind students of the Hippolytus of that play. In act 1 he is a stranger to passion who could make "the wild steeds / Obedient to the bit" (191), but he gives way to his passion by act 5, when "tangled in the reins, he fell" and was "dragged by the horses" to his death (228). Given Racine's status as a cultural icon in France, we can reasonably assume that Flaubert expected his readers to make this intertextual connection between the names.

The first sexual encounter between Emma and Rodolphe is a particularly interesting scene to analyze from this point of view. The text tells us that Rodolphe "attacha les chevaux" 'fastened up the horses' (226; 114) before he and Emma consummate their affair and that he has to mend "une des deux brides cassée" 'the one of the two bridles that had broken' (228; trans. mine) after they have given way to their passion. Having pointed this out, one can ask students to locate the point at which the bridle breaks; they should have no answer, as the text makes no specific mention of it. After helping them search fruitlessly for a while, one can offer a (trick) solution to the problem: the only description of the bridle breaking is "elle renversa son cou blanc, qui se gonflait d'un soupir et, défaillante, tout en pleurs, avec un long frémissement et se cachant la figure, elle s'abandonna" 'She threw back her white neck which swelled in a sigh, and, faltering, weeping, and hiding her face in her hands, with one long shudder, she abandoned herself to him' (228; 116). In other words, while the mending of the bridle is literally depicted in the text, its breaking is depicted only figuratively, when the characters' passions escape from their control; the symbolic level momentarily subsumes or displaces the literal level. Indeed, it should be emphasized that only one bridle breaks; Rodolphe is by no means carried away to the extent that Emma is, as his later callous behavior establishes.

Teachers may adapt this same approach to the explication of other symbols in the book as well; for example, one could introduce the pervasive symbolism of water and the river, which reaches its full development in part 3, by showing slides and citing musical and literary parallels that develop water as the symbol of the unstable and evanescent. Indeed, most sustained narratives—especially those of classic realism, which rely on relatively stable and consistent symbolic patterns—would lend themselves to this approach.

Naturally, it is an oversimplification to view the symbolism of the novel as so compartmentalized, and one merit of this approach is that the students should see that limitation as well. They can see, for instance, that all three of the major symbolic clusters I have mentioned are represented in each of the three parts. The horse symbolism, to return to my chosen example, begins in part 1, at least as early as the first intimations of discord between Charles and Emma: "[I]l ne put, un jour, lui expliquer un terme d'équitation qu'elle avait rencontré dans un roman. Un homme, au contraire, ne devait-il pas tout connaître . . . vous initier aux énergies de la passion . . . à tous les mystères?" '[O]ne day he could not explain some term of horsemanship to her that she had come across in a novel. A man, on the contrary, should he not know everything . . . initiate you into the energies of passion . . . all mysteries?' (101; 29). Innocuous at first reading, the train of thought leading from "horsemanship" to "passion" to "all mysteries" seems loaded with meaning when reconsidered in the light of traditional equine symbolism. Some might trace the symbol's development from even earlier passages, finding it significant that Charles's horse takes fright and stumbles (73; 10) as he approaches Emma's home for the first time.

Dozens of other symbolic systems run throughout the book. Some, like those discussed above, are nearly universal; the equation of the horse and rider with passion and reason is relatively stable over a wide range of texts and clearly belongs to the broad sociolect of literary idiom. Others, like the several mentions of butterflies, the cigar case, or the dancing floor wax on Emma's shoes, to take three examples at random, belong to the author's personal idiolect, acquiring specific connotations within a context that may not be assumed to exist in other works. Flaubert writes of the satin dancing shoes that "[s]on coeur était comme eux: au frottement de la richesse, il s'était placé dessus quelque chose qui ne s'effacerait pas" 'Her heart resembled them: in its contact with wealth, something had rubbed off on it that could not be removed' (116–17; 40). Dancing shoes and wax probably do not carry this meaning in other texts, and comparing such a particularized symbol with a more generalized symbol like the horse should help students begin to move toward more sophisticated notions of the manifold forms that symbolism can take. By this time students should have learned not just a few things about the uses of myth and symbol in *Madame Bovary* but also a few things about reading any work for its symbolism. They can become active interpreters of symbolism rather than members of a passive—and perhaps skeptical—audience for the teacher's explanations.

Vision and Language: Teaching
Madame Bovary in a Course on the Novel

Michal Peled Ginsburg

One of the difficulties in teaching a course on the novel is engaging students in a discussion of formal features. Whereas students normally accept the importance of formal considerations for the reading of poetry, they still, by and large, hold to the "realistic fallacy" that the language and form of the novel are transparent vehicles for a content—a "message" or a representation of the world. When we try to show them the importance of formal features in "formalist" novelists such as Henry James (if we dare teach James to undergraduates) or Alain Robbe-Grillet, they tend to consider the question of form as that of mere technique and see the predominance of formal preoccupations as detrimental to the "important" things—what the novel tells us about the world. Flaubert's *Madame Bovary* is an excellent novel for dealing with problems of form in a way that engages students and shows them that formal considerations are not mere technique, that form and thematic content cannot be separated, even in a work that has been hailed as a masterpiece of realism.

The realistic fallacy that the meaning of novels is transparent or available immediately, independent of any formal mediation, is encouraged by the kind of omniscient narration practiced by Dickens and Balzac, in whose works the narrator is a disembodied eye or voice. This is why in teaching traditional novels (as opposed to modern or postmodern ones) it is important to insist that students scrutinize carefully the operation of narrative voice and point of view. Students should be shown not only that "who sees" or "who speaks" makes a difference with regard to what we, as readers, perceive or hear but also that point of view and narrative voice do not necessarily converge. *Madame Bovary* allows us to see this complex problem in a fairly clear way partly because it thematizes the issues of language (the theme of reading) and vision (the theme of dreaming). The students can then see not only how the formal apparatus functions but also how it is in fact inseparable from the thematic preoccupations of the text.

The issue of point of view or of "who sees" may be approached first since it is raised at the very beginning of the novel. Since the novel is called *Madame Bovary*, the first obvious question is, Why does the novel start with Charles rather than Emma? One can show that the beginning of the novel establishes a relay structure. It starts with a narrator who says "we" and who "sees" Charles. The characterization of Charles in these first pages as ridiculous depends on this collective, external point of view, which sees him as different. The description of Charles, his family and life, continues to be the focus of the narration until the moment in which Charles himself becomes the one who sees; we meet Emma when Charles sees her for the first time, and the first detailed description of Emma is through his eyes: "Charles fut surpris de la blancheur de ses ongles. Ils étaient brillants, fins du bout, plus nettoyés que les ivoires de Dieppe, et taillés en amande. Sa main pourtant n'était pas belle, point assez pâle. . . . Ce qu'elle avait de beau, c'étaient les yeux. . . ." 'Charles was surprised at the whiteness of her nails. They were shiny, delicate at the tips, more polished than the ivory of Dieppe, and almond-shaped. Yet her hand was not beautiful, perhaps not white enough. . . . Her real beauty was in her eyes . . . .' (74; 11).

But just as in a relay, the "we" narrator who remembers Charles fades out shortly after it has conjured up this character, having "lost its memory"—"Il serait maintenant impossible à aucun de nous de se rien rappeler de lui" 'It would now be impossible for any of us to remember anything about him' (67; 6)—and the narration is carried on by an unspecified third-person narrator (about whom more later on). This fade-out is repeated with Charles himself who, after seeing Emma, retreats to the margins: not only does he become a secondary character but he also loses those qualities that allowed him to be a point of view on the world (the abilities to see, feel, understand, remember).

Having demonstrated this relay structure, the teacher should ask students to reflect on its implications. First, one may say that this structure suggests that in Flaubert there is no categorical difference between narrator and character (which means, finally, that narration is always the view of a specific subject rather than the objective representation of reality by a godlike, disembodied omniscient voice). Every character is potentially a narrator to the extent that it sees something and that it allows what it sees to take its place of seer. But this structure also suggests that, in Flaubert, "spectacle"—what is seen—always takes the place of the eye-I that sees, replacing and thus eliminating the seer. This spectacle is finally the reality the novel represents, and students can now see that this reality is generated by a particular point of view but also can exist as reality only if that point of view is suppressed and eliminated. This observation might lead to a discussion of the ideological agenda of realist writing.

The relay structure suggests that Emma herself, like the "we" of the beginning of the novel and like Charles, should have a "vision" that would then replace her, only to be replaced by another vision, and so on, ad infinitum. But, in fact, the relay structure that has been launched is arrested with Emma. Having had this point introduced to them through the form of the narration, students can see that Emma's status as the central character of the novel is the result, or the complement, of her not being a narrator, a point of view on the world. Emma does not become a seer but remains an object seen by others (a character rather than a narrator). For instance, in the first encounter between Emma and the various men who shape her life, we are not given her point of view (Gothot-Mersch, "Le point de vue" 257; Rousset 114). Though we understand why this is the case in her encounter with Charles, we would think that by the time she meets Léon or Rodolphe she would be the seer, the one whose point of view produces or shapes what is seen. Yet this is clearly not what happens; when Emma enters the Lion d'Or for the first time, we don't see the people, and Léon, through her eyes but, rather, the reverse:

> Mme Bovary . . . s'approcha de la cheminée. Du bout de ses deux doigts elle prit sa robe à la hauteur du genou, et, l'ayant ainsi remontée jusqu'aux chevilles, elle tendit à la flamme, par-dessus le gigot qui tournait, son pied chaussé d'une bottine noire. Le feu l'éclairait en entier, pénétrant d'une lumière crue la trame de sa robe, les pores égaux de sa peau blanche et même les paupières de ses yeux qu'elle clignait de temps à autre. Une grande couleur rouge passait sur elle, selon le souffle du vent qui venait par la porte entr'ouverte.
>
> De l'autre côté de la cheminée, un jeune homme à chevelure blonde la regardait silencieusement.   (143–44)

> Madame Bovary . . . went up to the fireplace. With two fingertips she caught her dress at the knee, and having thus pulled it up to her ankle, held out her black-booted foot to the fire above the revolving leg of mutton. The flame lit up the whole of her, casting its harsh light over the pattern of her gown, the fine pores of her fair skin, and even her eyelids, when she blinked from time to time. A great red glow passed over her with the wind, blowing through the half-open door.
>
> On the other side of the fireplace, a fair-haired young man watched her in silence.   (56)

Similarly, in Emma's first meeting with Rodolphe we get his view of her rather than the reverse (195; 92).

All three descriptions of Emma as seen by men are highly eroticized; implicitly or explicitly, they already indicate that Emma is seen as an object of desire. We are not told, however, what Emma's feelings, impressions, or desires are when she first meets these men. Her feelings toward Léon are stated only when she realizes that he loves her: "Regardant de son lit le feu clair qui brûlait, elle voyait encore, comme là-bas, Léon debout. . . . Elle le trouvait charmant; elle ne pouvait s'en détacher. . . . N'aime-t-il pas? se demanda-t-elle. Qui donc?. . . mais c'est moi!" 'Looking from her bed at the bright fire that was burning, she still saw, as she had down there, Léon standing up. . . . She thought him charming; she could not tear herself away from him. . . . "Is he not in love?" she asked herself; "but with whom? . . . With me!" ' (167; 73). Similarly, we get a glimpse of her feelings toward Rodolphe only at the end of the agricultural fair when, as she hears Rodolphe's words, "une mollesse la saisit . . . elle sentait toujours la tête de Rodolphe à côté d'elle. La douceur de cette sensation pénétrait ainsi ses désirs d'autrefois" 'something gave way in her. . . . She was conscious of Rodolphe's head by her side. The sweetness of this sensation revived her past desires' (213–14; 105–06). These two scenes should illustrate to students the "content" of a formal or stylistic feature: in the novel Emma does not exist as a desiring subject before she is made such by the men who see her and choose her. Just as the novel makes clear that Emma's desires are not really "her" desires, since they are generated by or borrowed from the literature she reads, so her specific desires (of Léon, of Rodolphe) are generated only in response to the desires of men who see (create) her as an object of desire. It is certainly not immaterial that the literature which shapes Emma's desires is written by men: in the chapter dealing with her readings we do not find Mme de Staël or George Sand mentioned. The heroines of the novels Emma reads are the images of perfect femininity as conceived by men, in response to their desire. When Emma dreams of becoming like one of these heroines, she desires to become the ideal object of man's desire (Ginsburg, *Flaubert Writing* 84–85). The fact that the relay structure does not continue in the way we would have expected it can thus mean that, having been created or seen by a male point of view, Emma herself, a woman, is not allowed to become a point of view that sees and shapes reality, who sees or fashions man from her own point of view as a woman (according to her own desires). This observation can be a first stage in a feminist reading of the novel.

Yet though Emma does not see Charles, Léon, or Rodolphe but, rather, is seen by them, one cannot conclude that she does not become a seer at all. Emma's visions are her dreams:

> Mais, en écrivant, elle percevait un autre homme, un fantôme fait de ses plus ardents souvenirs, de ses lectures les plus belles, de ses convoitises les plus fortes; et il devenait à la fin si véritable, et accessible, qu'elle en palpitait émerveillée, sans pouvoir néanmoins le nettement imaginer, tant il se perdait, comme un dieu, sous l'abondance de ses attributs. Il habitait la contrée bleuâtre où les échelles de soie se balancent à des balcons, sous le souffle des fleurs, dans la clarté de la lune. Elle le sentait près d'elle, il allait venir et l'enlèverait tout entière dans un baiser.
>
> (364)

> But while writing to him [Léon], it was another man she saw, a phantom fashioned out of her most ardent memories, of her favorite books, her strongest desires, and at last he became so real, so tangible, that her heart beat wildly in awe and admiration, though unable to see him distinctly, for, like a god, he was hidden beneath the abundance of his attributes. He dwelt in that azure land where silken ladders swung from balconies in the moonlight, beneath a flower-scented breeze. She felt him near her; he was coming and would ravish her entire being in a kiss.   (211)

Students' response to such passages is that Emma's tragedy is that her dreams never come true: the perfect lover she dreams of never comes and takes her away. This response is perfectly valid if we understand it to mean that her "vision," instead of becoming a reality, remains a dream (and that it does so is conveyed by the vocabulary of the passage, which is both vague and romantic). If in Flaubert every character is indeed potentially a narrator, Emma remains a character who dreams instead of becoming a narrator who sees a reality. We have seen that this limitation may be read as a gender bias on the part of Flaubert, who cannot allow reality (and men) to be seen from the point of view of a woman. In the novel, it is explained as Emma's narcissism—her inability to see anything other than, or different from, herself. Depending on the sophistication of the students in the class, one may push this point farther by showing the complicity between the traditional characterization of woman as narcissistic (able to see only herself) and her removal from the arena of action or production (in this case, the production of literature).

Emma's narcissism is not always obvious to students since they rightly observe that Emma dreams of a romantic world, different from her own dreary reality. Both these aspects of Emma's dreams are manifest in the following passage, which may serve as an example:

> Avec Walter Scott, plus tard, elle s'éprit de choses historiques, rêva bahuts, salle des gardes et ménestrels. Elle aurait voulu vivre dans quelque vieux manoir, comme ces châtelaines au long corsage qui, sous le trèfle des ogives, passaient leurs jours, le coude sur la pierre et le menton dans la main, à regarder venir du fond de la campagne un cavalier à plume blanche qui galope sur un cheval noir.   (97)

> With Walter Scott, later on, she fell in love with historical events, dreamed of guardrooms, old oak chests and minstrels. She would have liked to live in some old manor-house, like those long-waisted chatelaines who, in the shade of pointed arches, spent their days leaning on the stone, chin in hand, watching a white-plumed knight galloping on his black horse from the distant fields.   (26)

The point to make apropos of this passage is that the "difference" is purely a matter of decor or setting and costume, which, however, leaves the "role" intact. Emma sees herself as a lady of the manor who sees a knight coming toward her. Though the lady lives in an old manor house and wears gowns with long-waisted bodices, she shares Emma's basic predicament and spends her day dreaming, looking, expecting someone to come to her, waiting for her dream lover to become real. But her dream, like Emma's, does not become a reality: just like the perfect lover Emma conjures up while writing to Léon, so the knight, in this dream within a dream, is seen coming toward the lady but never actually reaching her; he never comes true. Emma cannot dream about anything other than . . . dreaming; even when she is about to elope with Rodolphe—have her dream come true—all she can imagine is longing, dreaming, going elsewhere (264; 141–42). Whenever her dreams arrive at a point where an activity other than looking, dreaming, desiring, going elsewhere may manifest itself, they expire, since she literally cannot imagine a predicament other than her own (see, for example, the dream about Paris: 118–19; 41–42).

The only difference Emma can see is that of scenery or setting, so although she retains her sameness and creates nothing but her own mirror image, she can still create (for herself and also for the reader) the illusion of difference. Her preoccupation with the smallest details of clothes and scenery, furniture and accessories epitomizes her desire to create an illusion of difference where actually only sameness and repetition exist. What characterizes her both as a dreamer (a potential though abortive narrator) and as a character is her belief that a change in decor is sufficient to create a difference in experience (so that when she wants to become a saint she buys a cross, etc.). This belief and the attempt to create a semblance of difference explain her entanglement with Lheureux and why her drama of desire is also the story of financial ruin.

So far I have treated point of view as a question of vision, but point of view also involves speech and language; it is as much a question of "who speaks" as of "who sees," and the two do not necessarily coincide. Though in principle it is clear that the point of view of an utterance is manifested not only by syntactic features but also by semantic ones, in practice such a claim leads only to endless discussions of whether it is realistically possible that such and such a character would use such and such a word. This is why the issue of narrative voice—or of point of view on the phraseological level (Uspenskii's term)—may best be approached through a discussion of naming (see also Prince, "On Attributive Discourse"; Mathet). Students will find it easy to understand that what a person is called gives us some indication as to who the caller may be (if I am addressed as Professor, the caller may be a student but will probably not be my daughter). If in a certain passage Charles is called M. Bovary or "the country doctor," the point of view on the phraseological level is exterior and even distant (as opposed to passages in which he is called Charles). But the peculiarity of *Madame Bovary* is that such an external point of view may occur in passages where what we read is what Charles himself sees, thinks, or feels. Take the first meeting between Emma and Charles: as Charles enters the farm and Emma appears to him, we read, "Une jeune femme, en robe de mérinos bleu garnie de trois volants, vint sur le seuil de la maison pour recevoir M. Bovary" 'A young woman in a blue merino dress with three flounces came to the threshold of the door to receive Monsieur Bovary' (73; 10); and later, as he gazes at her neck and hair, we read, "[L]aissant voir à peine le bout de l'oreille, [ses cheveux] allaient se confondre par derrière en un chignon abondant, avec un mouvement ondé vers les tempes, que le médecin de campagne remarqua là pour la première fois de sa vie" '[J]ust showing the tip of the ear, [her hair] was joined behind in a thick chignon, with a wavy movement at the temples that the country doctor saw now for the first time in his life' (75; 11).

In addition to this discrepancy between vision and naming, the way characters are named may change from sentence to sentence, indicating such a shifting narrative voice that no single narrator could be the source of the passage as a whole. For example, in a short paragraph dealing with the insufficiency of Charles's education at the hand of the village priest, an intimate narrative voice that refers to Charles as "the child" 'le gamin' and that can be read even as the reported voice of one of the parents complaining that "Charles could not go on like this" clashes with a distant and formal voice that refers to Charles's parents as Madame and Monsieur: "Charles ne pouvait en rester là. Madame fut énergique. Honteux, ou fatigué plutôt, Monsieur céda sans résistance, et l'on attendit encore un an que le gamin eût fait sa première communion" 'Charles could not go on like this. Madame Bovary took strong steps. Ashamed or rather tired out, Monsieur Bovary gave in without a struggle, and they waited one year longer, so that the child could take his first communion' (67; 6).

Whereas the analysis of vision has shown a well-identified point of view, the analysis of naming shows a narrator who cannot be pinned down; whereas the narrator as a seer is clearly distinct from the character it sees (the character, as I have shown, has to be different in order to exist as a "real" character), the analysis of language shows a narrator who tends to get confused with its characters. This confusion becomes obvious with an analysis of free indirect discourse, a mode of narration that accounts for a large portion of the novel.

What is parallel to the relation between seer (narrator) and what is seen (vision, character) is the relation between the voice that quotes or reports (narrator) and the voice that is quoted. While in reported speech the two are distinct, they blur in free indirect discourse (where syntactic or semantic marks of reporting are missing or, if present, clash with marks of direct discourse). Free indirect discourse, hence, is an utterance whose speaker cannot be determined: the speaker may be the narrator, one of the characters, both, or neither (Ginsburg, "Free Indirect Discourse"; Perruchot). The chapter in which Emma's education is described, for example, starts with a straightforward narration: "Elle avait lu *Paul et Virginie* et elle avait rêvé la maisonnette de bambous" 'She had read "Paul and Virginia," and she had dreamed of the little bamboo-house' (94; 24). The narrator is distinct from the character he describes, Emma, and from her vision: the dream is clearly hers. But as the chapter progresses, this distinction starts to blur—for example, with the appearance of "vous" 'you' and the evocation of "Sultans à longues pipes" 'Sultans with long pipes' (98; 27). Toward the end of the chapter, in the description of Emma's reaction to her mother's death, we read, "Emma fut intérieurement satisfaite de se sentir arrivée du premier coup à ce rare idéal des existences pâles, où ne parviennent jamais les coeurs médiocres" 'Emma was secretly pleased that she had reached at a first attempt the rare ideal of delicate lives, never attained by mediocre hearts' (98–99; 27). We cannot tell now whether the narrator, in talking about "the rare ideal of delicate lives," is reporting only Emma's views or in fact shares her judgment (he does not say something like "She had reached what she considered to be the rare ideal"). The situation, however, is even more complex because if the narrator is both quoting Emma and speaking for himself, Emma, too, is "quoting" or reporting— the clichés of romantic literature. The utterance, then, cannot be attributed to a distinct speaker, since it has its origin in neither Emma nor the narrator but in the stock of language from which they both draw.

The difference between Emma and the narrator is not that they use different languages but that, whereas Emma is totally unaware of the cliché nature of language (the language of literature but also of Léon, Rodolphe, and Homais), the narrator is conscious of it (as his orchestration of political platitudes with Rodolphe's banalities at the agricultural fair amply demonstrates). But if the narrator is hence ironic when he speaks of the "rare ideal of delicate lives," his irony cannot be seen as merely directed toward Emma; it is also a self-irony. The combination of clichés and free indirect discourse in the novel makes all critique (of the characters) also a self-critique by and of a narrator, who has no language to speak of the characters other than their (cliché) language. For Flaubert there is no originality or individuality in language; language is, precisely, clichés or "common place" (Felman, "Modernité"). The loss of individuality in language may explain why as a voice or as language (as opposed to vision) the narrator is fragmented and undecidable. And since language is seen not as merely expressing thoughts or feelings (which are prior to and independent of it—the realistic fallacy again) but, rather, as generating desires and beliefs (the theme of the formation of desire and opinion by literature, exemplified by Homais as well as Emma), this lack of originality in language is not merely a question of form or style.

Flaubert's Moving Sidewalk

Beryl Schlossman

> Et il n'est pas possible à quiconque est un jour monté
> sur ce grand *Trottoir roulant* que sont les pages de
> Flaubert, au défilement continu, monotone, morne,
> indéfini, de méconnaître qu'elles sont sans précédent
> dans la littérature.
>
> And it is not possible that anyone who once stepped onto
> the great *moving sidewalk* of Flaubert's pages, with their
> continuous, monotonous, bleak, indefinite procession,
> could fail to recognize that these pages are without a
> precedent in literature.
>
> —Marcel Proust[1]

Many readers have been intrigued by Flaubert's use of the imperfect tense in his novels. The grammatical properties of the imperfect create the unfolding of a process through time without indication of either the beginning or the end of the process. In Flaubert's use of the imperfect, grammar and style intersect. The imperfect is employed as the grammatical support of a kind of subjective or interior time, the unfolding of a process or a progression within time that seems to reshape the sequence of the narrative to its own ends.

The use of the imperfect tense elaborates a lyrical frame of continuity, of dreams and daydreams, and of rhythmic eloquence. This frame of the imperfect tense contrasts with the moments of irony and realism that cut off its flights of wishful thinking and desire. Flaubert's transformation of the imperfect into a new style caught Proust's attention and led to his formulation of the "imparfait éternel" 'eternal imperfect' as the essential characteristic of Flaubert's writing.

Teaching Style: Continuity

Flaubert claimed that *Madame Bovary* presents an aesthetics of the impersonal. One of the specific stylistic effects of this new aesthetics is a spectacular continuity that does not allow for authorial interruptions of opinion, judgment, or commentary; the author's personality has been masked in the text. The author as a narrator of interruptions, the authorial speaker who enters traditional fiction with the power of coloring the text and commenting on it, has vanished. Instead of the author's personal voice, the novel offers stylistic means of communication that occur without interrupting the artful rhythms of the text; instead of an alternation of moral messages and events in the plot, *Madame Bovary* sustains a focus on rhythm, continuity, impressions, and language. Flaubert privileges evocations of images, trances, moments of vision, and "tableaux" that are integrated into an ostensibly uniform, impersonal viewpoint.

Proust's account of Flaubert's prose as a "moving sidewalk" captures the continuity that provides the fundamental principle of Flaubert's style in *Madame Bovary*. As Proust implies, the essential elements of Flaubert's style cannot be found in the category of a single trope or figure; the moving sidewalk of sentence constructions points to syntax itself as the place of style.

Flaubert's *trottoir roulant* is connected with several other categories that emerge in Proust's essay. Flaubert's prose valorizes impressions rather than actions and introduces a new use of parts of speech, especially the use of verb forms that culminates in the eternal imperfect.[2] Proust's reading indicates that the poetics of rhythm dominates Flaubert's new version of the novel (and its customary emphasis on a chain of events); within the new, smooth surface of an impersonal text—a text without explicit authorial intrusion—the eternal imperfect that characterizes the sidewalk of style gives rise to a new art of time. Proust's categories of the moving sidewalk, the representation of impressions rather than actions, and the new eternal imperfect anchor a reading of Flaubert's poetics of style in the shape of the sentence.

Teaching Style: Madame Bovary *on the Trans-Romantic*

In the background of the moving sidewalk, the larger frame of Romanticism and modernism brings both writers (and others, especially Baudelaire) into a relation to style that shapes their writings. The writer's relation to style is an investment and a vocation that transform the act of writing into the impersonal account that Flaubert demanded of his art. In every sentence, the oeuvre bears the imprint of the writer's investment in style. I have described this relation as trans-Romantic.

The poetics of *Madame Bovary* may be understood as an attempt on Flaubert's part to bring Romanticism beyond its own limits, rather than to shape an anti-Romantic discourse that Zola enthusiastically acclaimed as naturalism. The distinction is crucial for a reading of style because the influence of Flaubert's poetics on the writings of naturalism has obscured the importance of Romanticism for the writer of *Madame Bovary*. In this context, Flaubert's use of irony should be interpreted not as a rejection of Romanticism but, rather, as a working through of it.

Flaubert's ideal led him to a revision of Romanticism through the elaboration of a new style. After the lyrical *La tentation de saint Antoine*, harshly criticized by his friends Louis Bouilhet and Maxime du Camp, *Madame Bovary* was Flaubert's first work; it was also the first of his canonical texts of modernism. Innovative style became the central question of Flaubert's fiction: Flaubert envisioned form as inseparable from content. His famous epithet of the "book about nothing" gives an indirect account of *Madame Bovary* as a novel that privileges style rather than plot. My aim here is to demonstrate (for students who may or may not be familiar with Flaubert, literary criticism, and stylistics) that an understanding of Flaubert's new style is essential for a literary and historical appreciation of *Madame Bovary* and that the elements of this style are illustrated on every page of the novel.

The teacher who would like to include questions of style in presentations and discussions of *Madame Bovary* may find it useful to consider the following categories within the larger framework of the moving sidewalk or as representations of a new stylistic articulation of rhythmic continuity, subject to the dominant principle of the impersonal. These proposed categories of style form a constellation that may be presented to a class with the examples that I provide as illustrations or with examples drawn from other scenes in the novel. If a teacher is pressed for time, however, most of the categories can stand alone as an indication of what is at stake in Flaubert's new style in *Madame Bovary*.

Pronouns

At the beginning of the novel, Flaubert's surprising use of personal pronouns sets the stage for the "nouveau" (new boy), the strangely drawn character of Charles Bovary. Through his appearance, the novel presents a new style that absorbs silences and gestures within a discursive continuity. Flaubert's new style articulates moments of silence, gesture, fragment, and colloquialism without the use of a traditional narrator. The novel focuses on the character of Bovary as an introduction (and a conclusion) to the portrayal of his wife. The shifts in pronouns from "nous" in the first chapter to "il" and "elle" in the rest of the novel indicate that the "nouveau," the schoolboy Charles Bovary with his cap, has entered a new and unfamiliar fictional world that will undermine the stable categories associated with him. Charles seems to figure Flaubert's transition from the "old" style to the "new" style. Charles enters the scene; the traditional narrator vanishes.

The "casquette" (visored cap) is the first unplaceable and inconceivable object that Flaubert creates; its "ordre composite" (composite order) marks the transition from the grandiose and the heroic, the world of Walter Scott's novels, to the strange silences that occupy an important place in Flaubert's account of the prosaic world of daily realities. The *casquette* appears as "one of those poor things" (2) that dwell in Flaubert's new realm of impersonality.

After the first chapter of part 1, "nous" will have faded into the impersonal realm of "on" ("one") or the "vous" (impersonal "you") that appears to replace "on" in the novel's reveries before it imperceptibly melts into the use of the third person that dominates Flaubert's accounts of subjectivity. This "vous" appears briefly in Emma's reverie when she anticipates her flight with Rodolphe: "On marchait au pas à cause des grandes dalles, et il y avait par terre des bouquets de fleurs, que vous offraient des femmes habillées en corset rouge" 'The horses slowed to a walk because of the wide pavement, and on the ground there were bouquets of flowers, offered by women dressed in red' (264; 141).[3]

"On" blends the dreaming Emma and her lover into the projected ideal scene of the reverie; the sentence allows the couple to enter a scene inhabited by ideal and imaginary beings. The reverie focuses intensely on the scene and uses the people in it—both the potential travelers (including Emma and Rodolphe) and the anonymous decorative women who offer them bouquets— as rhythmic or aesthetic figures that fulfill desires for flight, freedom, and beauty. The bouquets offered to an impersonal "vous" recall Emma's wedding bouquet, dried out and burned; the red bodices that figure the carnal sensuality and ripeness of beauty contrast with the white color of the wedding dress and the "candide" (pure, white) quality of Emma: Flaubert shapes these stylized images of color into an opposition between the purity of the virginal bride and the bloom of adultery. Emma's bridal purity is given back to Charles (until his decisive discovery of her correspondence) when she is dead and laid out in her wedding dress and covered from head to toe with the long stiff veil.

Continuity: Three-Part Sentences

Emma's reverie of flight with Rodolphe (264; 141–42) provides the teacher with a sequence of "phrases ternaires" 'three-part sentences' that indicate some of Flaubert's most important stylistic goals and achievements in *Madame Bovary*. Flaubert posits part 2, chapter 12, as the chapter that follows the critical midpoint of the novel, Bovary's disastrous operation on Hippolyte. Following Emma's temporary break with Rodolphe, which marked her final attempt at resisting the corruptions of adultery, this chapter begins with the reconciliation of the lovers and ends with Rodolphe's decision to break with Emma following her plans to run away with him. The reverie of flight is presented as the antithesis (or counterreverie) to Charles's musings about their daughter; the sequence of sentences pivots on the oppositions between sleeping and waking, between "forever" and "never."

"Jamais" and "toujours": Emma imagines that she is leaving forever and that Rodolphe will take her away for all time. Flaubert's text provides ample retrospective irony to the teacher of *Madame Bovary*, since Emma will leave only at the moment of her death. The illusions that fill Bovary's reveries of Berthe's eternal happiness—"cela durerait toujours" 'this would last forever'—and Emma's reveries of departure for "l'immensité de cet avenir" 'the immensity of this future' will be destroyed later in the novel. The dreams of these two ill-matched characters have only one thing in common: the "fatality" that condemns them.

Charles falls asleep, prosaically dreaming of his daughter's future and the happy home life that she will provide for him before he and Emma find a "brave garçon" 'some good young fellow' who will give her unending happiness. Flaubert constructs the antithesis of prosaic and poetic dreams with Emma's waking into reverie: "Emma ne dormait pas, elle faisait semblant d'être endormie; et, tandis qu'il s'assoupissait à ses côtés, elle se réveillait en d'autres rêves" 'Emma was not asleep; she pretended to be; and, while he dozed off by her side, she awakened to other dreams.' The paragraph of Charles's reverie is separated from Emma's dream paragraph by the one-sentence paragraph of antithesis ("Emma ne dormait pas . . ."). The last word of Charles's dreaming ("toujours") is undercut by the abrupt break that begins Emma's reverie: "Au galop de qua-tre chevaux, elle était emportée depuis huit jours vers un pays nouveau, d'où ils ne reviendraient plus" 'To the gallop of four horses she was carried away for a week towards a new land, from where they would never return.' Emma's po-etic reverie includes vivid phrases that evoke the idealized qualities of the scenery and the exquisite pleasures that welcome the lovers. The highly con-trolled rhythmic power of Flaubert's sentences is thematized in Emma's reverie when the urgent temporal rhythm of her flight ("Au galop") slows to the even, repetitive constancy of "Ils allaient, ils allaient, les bras enlacés, sans par-ler" 'They went on and on, their arms entwined, without speaking a word.' The rhythm gradually slows down to a measured walking pace with the sentence that begins, "On marchait au pas" 'The horses slowed to a walk.' This sentence may be analyzed in class to point out the stylistic effects of Flaubert's three-part sentences.

The rhythmic division of the sentence may be illustrated as follows: (1) "On marchait au pas à cause des grandes dalles, (2) et il y avait par terre des bou-quets de fleurs, (3) que vous offraient des femmes habillées en corset rouge." Each of the three clauses contains a rhythmic emphasis or stress on the im-perfect verb that follows the pronoun or conjunction that introduces it. The sentence is rhythmically slowed down ("au pas," like the pace of its dreamer) by the described objects that elaborate the end of each of the three alexan-drine-length clauses. Each clause adds a vivid image to the reverie, and the verselike rhythm formally connects the content of the clauses; the bouquets in the central clause provide a spatial (and metonymic) link between the "dalles" of the first clause and the women who offer the bouquets in the third clause.

Verbs: Eternal Imperfect

Flaubert's use of verbs draws them out of the purely grammatical category and into the realm of style. In *Madame Bovary* the grammatical qualities of the imperfect tense enter a new framework of impression, description, and day-dreaming. The evocative quality of these verbs brings out a vision of subjectiv-ity: Flaubert's imperfect absorbs characters' momentary perceptions into a time frame of rhythmic continuity. An example that occurs early in the novel, when Charles Bovary returns repeatedly to Bertaux, is marked by the repetition of "Il aimait" 'He loved' (76; 12), followed by the mention of Bovary's arrival at the farm, the barn, the stables, Emma's father, and her clogs tapping on the tiles. The repeated imperfect "Il aimait" sets up a context of habit and sentiment, rendered in the modest frame of Bovary's subjective possibilities and of the shyness (tinged with the malaise of Bovary's adulterous desire?) that prevents him from naming the demoiselle Emma as the object of his love. The visit with the father is elided from the text that accounts for Bovary's impressions; the paragraph ends with the details of her "sabots" 'wooden shoes' walking ahead of him, and the following paragraph begins, "Elle le reconduisait toujours" 'She always accompanied him out' (76; 12; trans. modified by eds.). The sequence of "Il aimait" and Bovary's focus on Emma set the scene for a moment of perfection in the eternal imperfect, in a passage that is thoroughly imprinted with Flaubert's exquisite precision of observation, impression, and continuity. Flaubert's setting, the less subtle sequence of "Il aimait" leading into the details of Emma's "sabots," imperceptibly shapes the context for the passage about the "ombrelle" 'parasol,' in which Bovary's mediocrity and limited powers of observation lead into a lingering and melting moment of vision that Flaubert renders impersonally.

This impersonality is highly accomplished: the vision is offered in writing by Flaubert, but the perception belongs to Bovary. Although the lines could not have been written by a character like Charles, Flaubert's principle of impersonality enables him to posit this passage as Bovary's impression: "L'ombrelle, de soie gorge-de-pigeon, que traversait le soleil, éclairait de reflets mobiles la peau blanche de sa figure. Elle souriait là-dessous à la chaleur tiède; et on entendait les gouttes d'eau, une à une, tomber sur la moire tendue" 'The parasol, made of an iridescent silk that let the sunlight sift through, colored the white skin of her face with shifting reflections. Beneath it, she smiled at the gentle warmth; drops of water fell one by one on the taut silk' (77; 13).

The effect of continuity is produced by a range of meanings that include the ordinary use of the imperfect tense to indicate habitual past occurrences, but this ordinary usage is rendered more literary by its association in Flaubert with the event that lingers in the sentence that contains it. Flaubert's imperfect tense of reverie includes a hypothetical time frame that takes the daydreamer in any desired direction, beyond the limits and imperfections of daily life. In Flaubert's style, the imperfect tense articulates a number of moments of melting that combine past and present, the real world and the creations of desire, the impression and its disappearance into the fictions and fantasies of the observer.

Indirect Discourse

Although *Madame Bovary* indicates occasional hesitations in the author's use of indirect discourse, especially when the text combines direct and indirect discourse in a single conversation, "style indirect libre" 'free indirect style' is skillfully presented from the beginning of the novel. Flaubert captures voice, tone, and idiosyncrasies of expression (including colloquial speech and the clichés that cover a wide emotional range, from pathos to jokes).

In a narrative account of Bovary's first marriage, Flaubert shifts to this style. Bovary's wife feels neglected: "Le soir, quand Charles rentrait, elle . . . se mettait à lui parler de ses chagrins: il l'oubliait, il en aimait une autre!" 'When Charles returned in the evening, she . . . began to talk to him of her troubles: he was neglecting her, he loved another' (71; 8). The stylistic shift, the rhythm, the final exclamation, and the syntactical figure of disjunction vividly convey a tone of impassioned accusation. The following sentence continues the free indirect style—"On lui avait bien dit qu'elle serait malheureuse" 'She had been warned she would be unhappy'—before the final clause concludes the chapter with the narration of "et elle finissait . . ." 'and she ended. . . .'

When Charles meets Emma, Flaubert represents their first meal with several moments of dialogue, including a sentence in free indirect style introduced by a sentence of narration: "Mademoiselle Rouault ne s'amusait guère à la campagne" 'Miss Rouault did not at all like the country' (75; 11). "Mademoiselle Rouault" conveys Bovary's respect for the speaker of the sentence, and the expression of "ne s'amusait guère" evokes Emma's refined speech and her proper behavior, in contrast to the familiarity and uneducated expressions that appear in the free-indirect-style remarks of her father. The ailing Rouault awaits Bovary with a carafe of brandy "pour se donner du coeur au ventre" 'to keep up his spirits' (73; 10), and he invites Bovary "à prendre un morceau" 'to have a bite' (75; 11) before he leaves; when "le bonhomme Rouault" speaks to Charles in direct discourse in the following chapter, Flaubert continues the colloquial style that characterizes these examples of his free indirect style.

Irony and Idées Reçues

Much of Flaubert's irony is elaborated through the effects of clichés, or *idées reçues*, attributed to characters in the novel. These clichés often counterpoint the stylistic effects of Flaubert's narrative passages; the impersonal (or invisible) narrator uses the clash between the two levels of discourse to produce effects of irony. Dialogue (and free indirect style) introduces clichés into the text, without allowing them access to the impersonal narrative. In his vigilant rewriting, Flaubert attempted to prevent the infiltration of his narrative by the clichés that he passionately despised. Although the banal *idées reçues* that will occupy *Bouvard and Pécuchet* originate in ordinary language, Flaubert's deliberate use of them differs from ordinary language at the moment that it enters his novel. Teachers may find it useful to illustrate irony in *Madame Bovary* with examples of the stylistic figures of the cliché and the "lieu commun" 'commonplace.'

Two days before their intended flight, Emma and Rodolphe exchange a series of romantic clichés of love in a conversation in direct discourse. She tells him that he is everything for her, he replies that she is charming, she asks him to swear that he loves her, and so on. Flaubert's narrative interrupts this dialogue with a description of the night sky, the moon, and its reflections in the river; when he shifts to its effect on Emma and Rodolphe, Flaubert echoes the rhythmic sentences of Emma's nocturnal reverie, several paragraphs prior to the conversation. Time stops and memory takes over, until the images of the night scene gradually enter their consciousness. Flaubert interrupts the narration with Rodolphe's brief utterance of a romantic cliché: "Ah! la belle nuit! dit Rodolphe" ' "Ah! what a lovely night!" said Rodolphe' (267; 143). The evening (and the chapter) ends with Rodolphe's awakening from the reverie; he decides to leave Emma instead of running away with her. The irony of love in *Madame Bovary* is based on a disproportion of language. "Ah! la belle nuit!" is Rodolphe's answer to Flaubert's lyric description of the night. "N'importe! c'était une jolie maîtresse!" 'All the same, she was the prettiest mistress!' (268; 144) is Rodolphe's judgment of Emma and his answer to her idealized portrait of the lover who is "everything" to her. The dialogue between the characters trades one cliché for another, but Flaubert's narrative articulation of ironic contrast reveals the differences between Rodolphe's "awakening" and the end of Emma's reveries.

Within the impersonal continuity of Flaubert's style, the ironic resonances of the cliché and the *idée reçue* transform the Romantic forms of lyricism that shaped the sensibility of Flaubert's generation into the dissolving rhythms of reverie, "emportement," and the eternal imperfect. The "nouveau" of *Madame Bovary* is the trans-Romantic: the new aesthetic of the moving sidewalk.

NOTES

[1]All translations of Proust are mine.

[2]"Ce qui jusqu'à Flaubert était action devient impression. . . . Le subjectivisme de Flaubert s'exprime par un emploi nouveau des temps des verbes, des prépositions, des adverbes, les deux derniers n'ayant . . . qu'une valeur rythmique" (Proust 588–89) 'That which until Flaubert was action becomes impression. . . . Flaubert's subjectivism is expressed through a new use of verb tense, prepositions, adverbs, and the value of the latter two is . . . solely rhythmic.'

"Cet éternel imparfait, composé en partie de paroles des personnages que Flaubert rapporte habituellement en style indirect pour qu'elles se confondent avec le reste . . . donc, cet imparfait, si nouveau dans la littérature, change entièrement l'aspect des choses et des êtres" (Proust 590) 'This eternal imperfect, partly composed of characters' spoken words that Flaubert habitually reports in indirect style so that they melt into the rest . . . this imperfect, so new in literature, completely changes the look of things and beings.'

[3]Translations of *Madame Bovary* are mine. I have modified some of them according to the Norton edition. Page numbers for the translations refer to that edition.

Unwrapping the Comic

Michael Issacharoff

Madame Bovary is not usually thought of as a primarily comic novel. Its numerous tragic or pathetic scenes linger in the memory, apparently precluding the impression of humor, albeit camouflaged. "Very often," writes Erich Auerbach, "the reader is moved by [Emma's] fate in a way that appears very like tragic pity" (490). Emma's suicide and painful death, Charles's desperate though futile attempt to save her, Emma's dreams, and Charles's frustrated love and death prevent many readers from perceiving the explicitly comic and ironic elements, many of which are linked to the more subversive, ambivalent undercurrents of the novel. But Flaubert's purpose, as Claudine Gothot-Mersch reminds us (Introduction lxiii) in citing his comment (in a letter to Louise Colet of 8–9 May 1852), was to combine lyricism and grotesque humor ("le comique qui ne fait pas rire, le lyrisme dans la blague") (*Correspondance*, ed. Bruneau, 2: 85). In this respect, the tone of *Madame Bovary* prefigures, in many ways, Eugène Ionesco's notion of tragic farce. Especially similar is the way in which Ionesco elevates language to comic protagonist status, in plays such as *La cantatrice chauve* and *Jacques ou la soumission*, powerfully enough to dominate his dramatis personae, and the way Flaubert explores the comic and other possibilities of unattributable discourse. The protean quality of Flaubert's narrative discourse, taken together with the sophistication required for unwrapping his novel's ironies, makes reading *Madame Bovary* an intricate matter indeed. The comic element is designed to counterbalance pathos, thereby underscoring the ambivalence of the book. It represents, too, the reader response inscribed in the novel by its author.

Students—particularly women—frequently identify with Emma. Indeed, one of the problems in teaching a novel like *Madame Bovary* to undergraduates is the necessity to show how it *requires* in the reader not empathy but distance. The ironic and comic modes presuppose readerly sophistication, entailing detachment rather than empathy. In fact, therein lies a further pitfall for the inexperienced reader: the lack of an "admirable" character with whom to identify.

When approaching *Madame Bovary* for the first time, however, most students soon realize that the main characters are impossible candidates for role models. Emma is hopelessly romantic; Charles absurdly mediocre; Léon, Rodolphe, Lheureux despicable; and Homais a pathetic (though ultimately triumphant) buffoon. Though there are, of course, minor characters presented in a positive light—Catherine Leroux and Dr. Larivière instantly spring to mind—their presence is too short-lived for them to act as empathic foils. Therein lies a strategy for initiating undergraduates into the mysteries of narrative and readerly detachment: the lack of an admirable major character to elicit an empathic response.

Starting with the issue of character portrayal and the writer's use of indirect presentation—Charles as presented by the ephemeral, introductory "nous," Emma as perceived by Charles (see Rousset 112–17), and so forth—it is possible to illustrate the novel's predominant mode of ironic detachment. Alan Raitt has shown that, contrary to the view of commentators who have alleged authorial inexperience or clumsiness, Flaubert's opening "nous" should be seen in conjunction with other distancing devices used elsewhere in the novel.

An obvious source of the comic in fiction is the use of grotesque or emblematic names, a tradition going back to the Renaissance. *Madame Bovary* is no exception and perpetuates this well-established comic heritage with, among the minor characters, such obvious candidates as Tuvache, Lieuvain, Mme Dubuc, Lestiboudois, Boudet, M. Lehérissé and M. Cullembourg, Maître Hareng, Léocadie Leboeuf. As has been pointed out often before, there is clearly a bovine connection between Tuvache, Leboeuf, and Bovary. This onomastic device was put to good use in the theater by Flaubert's contemporary Eugène Labiche, whose plays are rich in the invention of such grotesque names as Rochepot, Claquepont, Machavoine, Dardenboeuf, and Bigaro. Names like these are designed to undercut the utterances or actions of their bearers and thus entail significant referential consequences.

Irony, on the other hand, requires clear demonstration and illustration for American and Canadian undergraduates, most of whom are otherwise inclined to misread such works as *Candide* and *Madame Bovary*, taking them at face value. The best plan is to include required reading of standard works on irony, such as those by Douglas Muecke and Wayne Booth. Students will then be equipped at least to identify the more obvious instances of irony and then to distinguish effortlessly between verbal irony and situational irony. Assignments could include identifying examples of each type of irony, thereafter assessing their relative significance within the broad context of *Madame Bovary*. It will then be an easy matter to illustrate Flaubert's characteristic technique of ironic juxtaposition, particularly in the clearest example in the novel: the agricultural fair (2.8).

In that scene, ironic and comic effect is achieved, for example, through the incongruous juxtaposition of spaces and the discourse belonging to each: the balcony with Rodolphe's banal seductive patter; the raised platform from which Lieuvain and Derozerays deliver their stereotyped speeches and the ground level with the mumbling of the peasants and the lowing of the cattle. This device is akin to the use of the split set in farce. Like Georges Feydeau's practice in *L'hôtel du libre échange*, Derozerays's remarks—ostensibly addressed to the country folk listening to him but skillfully intermingled with snatches of the Rodolphe-Emma dialogue—can be taken to refer derogatively to Emma and Rodolphe.

Juxtaposition can amount to (grotesque) analogy, thereby enhancing comic effect. In the *Comices* scene (the agricultural fair), for example, the narrator, by juxtaposing Lieuvain's droning and the lowing of the cattle, implicitly equates them:

[L]a voix de M. Lieuvain se perdait dans l'air. Elle vous arrivait par lambeaux de phrases qu'interrompait çà et là le bruit des chaises dans la foule; puis on entendait, tout à coup, partir derrière soi un long mugissement de boeuf, ou bien les bêlements d'agneaux qui se répondaient au coin des rues. En effet les vachers et les bergers avaient poussé leurs bêtes jusque là, et elles beuglaient de temps à autre. . . .   (213)

Monsieur Lieuvain's voice was lost in the air. It reached you in fragments of phrases, interrupted here and there by the creaking of chairs in the crowd; then, the long bellowing of an ox would suddenly burst forth from behind, or else the bleating of the lambs, who answered one another from street to street. Even the cowherds and shepherds had driven their beasts this far, and one could hear their lowing from time to time.

(105)

But irony in *Madame Bovary* is not confined to the considerable roster of verbal and situational instances. Perhaps the most significant use lies in the writer's systematic attempt to undermine discursive attribution. At almost every turn, it is difficult to determine with any certainty the identity of the narrator and the source of utterances. He is neither stable nor the same throughout the novel. Many critics have focused their attention on this problem, ranging from those, such as Michal Peled Ginsburg, who link narrative indeterminacy to the issue of point of view and free indirect discourse (see *Flaubert* 97–107) to those, such as Jean-Paul Sartre, Claude Duchet ("Discours"), and Ruth Amossy and Elisheva Rosen, whose emphasis is more linguistic, with observations on the use of the cliché and its impact on the rest of the novel. Sartre insists that Flaubert's use of cliché, even if apparently disclaimed ironically by such riders as "comme dirait M. Prudhomme" 'as M. Prudhomme would put it,' stems from the fact that Flaubert was a bourgeois: "il parle *en* bourgeois *parce qu'il est bourgeois*" 'he speaks *like* a bourgeois *because he is a bourgeois*' (Sartre 2: 624; trans. mine). Duchet underscores the link between clichés, italicized discourse, and what he calls "le discours social," while Amossy and Rosen point out suggestively (as others have) that the use of clichés and stereotyped similes, unattributable to a specific character or voice, undermines, if not thereby deconstructing, the very notion of fictional character and voice (78–82).

Comic effect is also achieved, in the agricultural fair scene and elsewhere, through the use of narrative summary ironically condensing, for example, the verbosity of seduction ("Rodolphe, avec Madame Bovary, causait rêves, pressentiments, magnétisme" 'Rodolphe was talking dreams, forebodings, magnetism with Madame Bovary') or the pretentiousness of official rhetoric ("et tandis que M. le président citait Cincinnatus à sa charrue, Dioclétien plantant ses choux . . . le jeune homme expliquait à la jeune femme que ces attractions irrésistibles tiraient leur cause de quelque existence antérieure" 'and while the president was citing Cincinnatus and his plough, Diocletian planting his cabbages . . . the young man was explaining to the young woman that these irresistible attractions find their cause in some previous state of existence' (215; 106).

Rouault is the target of similar comic condensation in the narrator's summary: "Il fuma dans la chambre, cracha sur les chenets, causa cultures, veaux, vaches, volailles et conseil municipal" 'He smoked in the room, spat on the andirons, talked farming, calves, cows, poultry, and municipal council' (127; 48). Particularly significant is the writer's characteristic device of juxtaposition, underscored by the implication that the *veaux* and the *vaches* are no different from the *conseil municipal*.

The most unsophisticated students in early literature courses have problems apprehending the very notion of "aboutness." The widespread tendency is to read for the plot, with the mistaken assumption that plot and meaning are coextensive. (At a much more sophisticated level, this is the pitfall of some formalist, narratological approaches to fiction.) Thus, when asked the most elementary question about a fictional work (What is the novel *about?*), students often respond with poorly disguised attempts at plot summary. In such cases, it has proven especially effective to use as (critical) starting point either students' own suggestions of principal theme or those offered by critics (e.g., "The Tragedy of Dreams" [Brombert, *Novels*]; "The Inadequacy of Dreams" [Brombert, *Flaubert par lui-même*]; "The Frustration of Dreams," "The Failure of Emma's Attempt to Find a World Ordered to Her Expectations" [Culler, *Flaubert*]; "The Book about Nothing" [Rousset 109]).

Having grasped the requisite two-step procedure implicit in the reading of any narrative, students are suitably prepared for the next problem: the tone of the work. The problem peculiar to a novel like *Madame Bovary*, of course, is its primarily negative universe. Naturally, a negative universe goes hand in hand with the ironic and comic mode.

After a survey of the manner in which characters are presented, it becomes clear that, whereas all major characters are portrayed negatively by the narrators, it is the portrayal of the *male* characters that is a significant source of comic and satirical effect. This is particularly true of Charles (as a child), Homais, and Rodolphe (during the agricultural fair). While Emma is of course criticized for her gullibility and in particular for confusing life and literature (given her exposure to and naive reading of Romantic fiction), the attack is not especially comic, despite disparaging references to Romantic stereotypes and Emma's interest in them.

What is sometimes overlooked is the importance of the comic impact of the opening chapter of the novel, the description of Charles's famous cap and the absurd initial impression he creates on his classmates—who make fun of him by repeating his name over and over again: Charbovari—and hence on the reader. Many critics have pointed out the wordplay between the name thus pronounced and *charivari*. Thus the tone is set right from the first chapter and the comic effect underscored by virtue of its being the reader's initial vision of the character and of the book. The motif of repetition is thereby explicitly linked to derision at the outset. In fact, the whole novel is inscribed between the two signposts of the comic and the ironic: the comic of the opening scene and the heavy irony of the closing sentence: "[Homais] vient de recevoir la croix d'honneur" '[Homais] has just been given the cross of the Legion of Honor' (425; 255).

The motif of repetition signals both the comic and the ironic modes of *Madame Bovary*. Repetition is one of the fundamental keys to Flaubert's novel, to its deliberately ambivalent tragicomic flavor, and ranges from the use of the imperfect tense—emphasizing habitual or iterative action—to the citation, of clichés in particular, that Duchet has dubbed *discours social*. Clichés are highlighted derisively in the novel through the use of italics, reiterated, yet disclaimed by the novelist. Clichés also feature prominently in those passages in which characters such as Homais reveal their incapacity to communicate other than in borrowed, predigested thought. Using the epitaph chosen for Emma by Homais (*Madame Bovary* 420; 292), Ross Chambers has shown how stereotyped discourse is designed to function at several ironic levels—not simply to reflect the *bêtise* of their users but also to elicit other, more sophisticated levels of reader response. Jean Ricardou has pointed to a comic phonic network generated in the first scene of the novel by a series of words beginning with the *C* and *B* of Charles Bovary's name together with another series stemming from the comic proliferation of the lexeme or syllable *veau* (nou*veau*, *Vau*frylard, *veau* à l'oseille, etc.) ("Belligérance" 101–02). Jonathan Culler, taking up the cue, extends this observation to outline a strategy for reading the novel antirepresentationally, showing that the purpose of this phonetic reiteration is to undermine extratextual reference ("Uses" 7–8).

Repetition itself is an ambivalent motif and device. Though Camus suggests that we should imagine Sisyphus happy, the iterative mode that underscores Sisyphean destiny acquires a comic, tragic, or at least negative value in Flaubert's novel. (At times, to enhance the novel's ambivalence, Flaubert gives repetition a positive value, so it is not necessarily an index of boredom or monotony. As Diana Knight has rightly pointed out, at times it coincides with moments of pleasure, as in the case of Emma's Thursdays in Rouen [66–67].) But most action itself is undermined through the privileging of the imperfect tense and becomes meaningless (because repetitive) or guaranteed to end in failure. Iteration—be it that of Emma's abortive love affairs, when considered in retrospect, or of Homais's or Rodolphe's discourse—is either absurd or grotesque. It is hard to consider the presence of the repetition motif in *Madame Bovary* without thinking of its ambivalent status in *Trois contes*, as a mark of *bêtise* and anticlericalism in "Un coeur simple" (the parrot's discourse), of prophetic discourse in "La légende de saint Julien l'Hospitalier" and "Hérodias." Just as ironic juxtaposition underscores the spirit of the three tales if they are taken as a triptych, in *Madame Bovary* it is essential to consider in tandem all the iterative devices and motifs, ranging from the imperfect tense used to represent repeated action, clichés and other stereotyped speech, and lexical repetition to narrative events and so forth. From this feature of the text alone one can observe the deliberately ambivalent mode of the novel. *Madame Bovary* can be read as Emma's failure to impose on her existence a repetition of her dreams and memories of Romantic fiction. Ultimately, it is when repetition eludes the control of Flaubert's protagonist and other principal characters that it is set on a collision course with the comic. Conversely, it is when Emma succeeds—in stage-managing her death—that the novel acquires its pathos.

It is important to dispel once and for all the myth, based in part on remarks in Flaubert's *Correspondance*, of impersonal, detached narration. In fact, narrative intrusion is far from exceptional in *Madame Bovary* and is often a signal of the comic. Occasionally, such intrusions include the narrator's comments or privileged information. The window motif, for example, recurs frequently, in one instance with this observation: "Emma était accoudée à sa fenêtre (elle s'y mettait souvent: la fenêtre, en province, remplace les théâtres et la promenade)" 'Emma was standing in the open window (she often did so: in the provinces the window takes the place of the theatre and the promenade [193; 91]). Elsewhere, Rouault is taken to task for his illiteracy and banality, when Emma reads a letter from her father:

> Elle resta quelques minutes à tenir entre ses doigts ce gros papier. Les fautes d'orthographe s'y enlaçaient les unes aux autres, et Emma poursuivait la pensée douce qui caquetait tout au travers comme une poule à demi cachée dans une haie d'épines.   (239)

> She held the coarse paper in her fingers for some minutes. A continuous stream of spelling mistakes ran through the letter, and Emma followed the kindly thought that cackled right through it like a hen half hidden in a hedge of thorns.   (124)

Intrusion is also particularly apparent in the narrator's comments on the Homais household.

Homais himself is consistently the most fertile source of the comic in *Madame Bovary*. In the narrator's summaries, in direct and indirect discourse, Homais frequently attains the stature of a Molièresque farcical character. Two brief examples—the first from the clubfoot scene, the second when he reprimands Justin for his clandestine reading of *L'amour conjugal*—will suffice to illustrate the device of comic summary:

> M. Canivet, ayant retroussé ses manches, passa dans la salle de billard, tandis que l'apothicaire restait avec Artémise et l'aubergiste, plus pâles toutes les deux que leur tablier, et l'oreille tendue contre la porte.   (251–52)

Monsieur Canivet having turned up his sleeves, passed into the billiard-room, while the druggist stayed with Artémise and the landlady, both whiter than their aprons, and with ears strained towards the door. (132)

Il marcha d'abord de long en large, à grands pas, gardant le volume ouvert entre ses doigts, roulant les yeux, suffoqué, tuméfié, apoplectique. (322)

First he walked up and down, with the open book in his hand, rolling his eyes, choking, fuming, apoplectic. (180)

Both examples are explicitly theatrical—the first serving as comic relief, the second emphasizing the gestural. In the case of indirect speech, Homais's demeanor is equally Molièresque: "Il citait du latin, tant il était exaspéré. Il eût cité du chinois et du groenlandais, s'il eût connu ces deux langues; car il se trouvait dans une de ces crises où l'âme entière montre indistinctement ce qu'elle enferme" 'He was so exasperated he quoted Latin. He would have used Chinese or Greenlandic had he known them, for he was rocked by one of these crises in which the soul reveals all it contains' (321; 180).

Finally, in Homais's direct speech, the effect intended is almost always comic or ironic, as in the scene in which he rants farcically to his family:

—Non laissez-moi! reprenait l'apothicaire, laissez-moi! fichtre! Autant s'établir épicier, ma parole d'honneur! Allons, va! ne respecte rien! casse! brise! lâche les sangsues! brûle la guimauve! marine des cornichons dans les bocaux! lacère les bandages! (320)

"No, leave me alone!" the pharmacist cried, "leave me alone! I tell you, I might as well be running a grocery store. Just keep at it, don't mind me and break everything to pieces! Smash the test-tubes, let the leeches loose, burn the marshmallows, put pickles in the medical jars, tear up the bandages!" (179)

A ubiquitous feature of Flaubert's novel, the comic surfaces in all the key scenes, starting with the opening chapter, a constant reminder of the readerly detachment intended. Like all other ambivalent elements in *Madame Bovary*, the comic offers an excellent introduction to Flaubert's aesthetics.

The comic serves to enhance the tension in the novel—between pathos and irony, between the realist and antirepresentational forces, between empathy and detachment, the desire to move and to distance. The comic devices used by the novelist—repetition, juxtaposition, grotesque analogy, naming, condensation, intrusion, clichés—are all double-edged. They underscore the ambivalence of the novel. They also teach us how to read it.

A Narratological Approach to *Madame Bovary*
Gerald Prince

Narratological criticism examines the narrative features of texts with the tools developed or refined by narratology. More specifically, it attempts to show how these features reveal, foreground, construct, and affect some of the forms and meanings generated by a text, some of the responses it can provoke, and some of the values to which it aspires. Narrative features are numerous (they include, for instance, the order in which situations and events are arranged, the point of view according to which they are depicted, the speed and frequency with which they are recounted, the kind of narrative voice that recounts them, as well as the modes of characterization and description favored by the text or the type of architecture it constitutes), and the analysis of any feature's textual functioning can provide a point of departure for a narratological account. Because of spatial and other constraints, I do not, in what follows, systematically explore all the narrative features of *Madame Bovary*. Rather, I address certain features that have attracted significant attention and discuss certain aspects of their operation.

The opening scene of the novel is presented by a homodiegetic narrator (one present as a character in the main narrative) who was among the boys witnessing Charles's first day in school (61–64; 1–3). After that initial scene, however, first-person gives way to third-person narration. Indeed, the possibility of an account of Charles's story based on memories of him is rejected. Henceforth, the heterodiegetic narration (one that does not issue from a character personified in the main narrative) proves difficult to attribute to a specific and well-defined storyteller, a stable and coherent subject position (Culler, *Flaubert* 109–22; Ginsburg, *Flaubert Writing* 82–107). At times the narrative voice sounds omniscient (e.g., 93, 103–04, 118–19; 24, 30–31, 40) and at times it does not (99–100, 189, 213, 342; 27, 90, 105, 195). In some passages it seems to emanate from a mere unidentified observer (115, 212; 39, 104–05); in others, it resembles that of a historian (e.g., 106; 32–33); in others still, it approximates that of a (social) philosopher given to generalizations (95–96, 259, 306–07; 25–26, 138, 169); and it shuttles quickly among these and additional forms (111–12, 259; 36, 138).

Compounding this variability is the irony at work in Flaubert's text (Culler, *Flaubert* 142–47, 185–207; Gengembre 108–09; Lafay 27–75). It can be so elusive that it (seemingly) appears, disappears, and reappears within the space of one or two sentences: "Il [Charles] ajouta même un grand mot, le seul qu'il ait jamais dit: 'C'est la faute de la fatalité' " "He even made a phrase, the only one he'd ever made: "Fate is to blame" ' (424; 255; trans. modified by eds.). Irony has so many disparate—sometimes antithetical—targets (Emma and the men in her life, her romantic extravagance but also the mediocrity of Tostes or Yonville, the silly books she reads as well as the people who—like Charles's mother—find these books dangerous) that the source or perspective governing it is hard to situate once and for all. Irony proves so pervasive that it threatens to contaminate the entire novel. Even Dr. Larivière, the one great artist in the world presented, the physician who loves his work and does it with exaltation and wisdom, may not quite escape its sting: "Et il allait ainsi, plein de cette majesté débonnaire que donnent la conscience d'un grand talent, de la fortune, et quarante ans d'une existence laborieuse et irréprochable" 'He went through life with the benign dignity that goes with the assurance of talent and wealth, with forty years of a hard-working, blameless life' (395; 234).

Perhaps an even more basic factor of narratorial indeterminacy is Flaubert's extensive use of free indirect discourse, which contains (mixed within it at least) two discourse events, two styles, two languages, two cognitive and axiological systems (see, e.g., 65, 101, 309, 371; 4, 29, 170–71, 216). Again and again, the narrative voice and the voice of one character or another coalesce to present situations and events, speeches or thoughts, emotions or perceptions (Gengembre, 73–74; Ginsburg, *Flaubert Writing* 101–02; Lloyd 81–85). In fact, there is hardly a character who does not contribute: Emma, Rodolphe, Léon, and Charles, of course, but also Emma's father, Charles's parents and his first wife, M. Guillaumin, Mme Caron, Mme Tuvache. Thanks to various markers (contextual or lexical, semantic or typographic), often it is simple enough to identify free indirect discourse and the voices it combines. In particular, such features as italics and exclamation marks can facilitate the enterprise: "Mme Bovary mère semblait prévenue contre sa bru. Elle lui trouvait *un genre trop relevé pour leur position de fortune*; le bois, le sucre et la chandelle *filaient comme dans une grande maison*, et la quantité de braise qui se brûlait à la cuisine aurait suffi pour vingt-cinq plats!" 'The elder Madame Bovary seemed prejudiced against her daughter-in-law. She thought she was living above her means; the wood, sugar and candles vanished as in a large establishment, and the amount of stovewood used in the kitchen would have been enough for twenty-five courses!' (102; 30). Just as often, however, the task turns out to be more problematic. Signs of another voice, marks of another language joining a narratorial voice and language, add up to no more than a word or two, a tinge, a trace (181, 373, 397; 82, 218, 234). Flaubert's transitions from one mode of discourse to another—from, say, indirect to free indirect speech—are so smooth as to be almost imperceptible ("Le clerc se récria que les natures idéales étaient difficiles à comprendre. Lui, du premier coup d'oeil, il l'avait aimée" 'The clerk retorted that idealistic natures rarely found understanding. But he had loved her from the very first moment' (308–09; 170). Because free indirect discourse is not always grammatically different from narratized discourse or narrative statement (something like "She was exhausted" might be a simple narratorial observation or the narratorial rendering of a character saying or thinking "I am exhausted"), we may interpret many passages in *Madame Bovary* as originating with a character or as involving no voice other than a narrator's. Who, for example, is the source of the explanation in "Deux jours après la noce, les époux s'en allèrent. Charles, à cause de ses malades, ne pouvait s'absenter plus longtemps" 'Two days after the wedding, the married pair left. Charles, on account of his patients, could not be away longer' (90; 22)? Even italics (e.g., 107, 156; 33 ["dog-cart" not italicized], 65 ["huts" not italicized]) do not necessarily help (Gengembre 72–73; Lafay 47–52), and the question "Who speaks?" frequently has no definitive answer.

If voice in *Madame Bovary* is changeable and elusive, so is the point of view that Flaubert uses to present situations and events (Culler, *Flaubert* 109–22; Ginsburg, *Flaubert Writing* 84–107; Sherrington 79–152). Some of the latter are rendered by a narrator whose place is unlocatable, who does not seem subject to perceptual or conceptual restrictions, and who presumably depicts "what is" or "what was" ("Il était debout, son mouchoir sur les lèvres, râlant, pleurant, suffoqué par des sanglots qui le secouaient jusqu'aux talons; Félicité courait çà et là dans la chambre; Homais, immobile, poussait de gros soupirs, et M. Canivet, gardant toujours son aplomb, commençait néanmoins à se sentir troublé" 'He was standing, his handkerchief to his lips, with a rattle in his throat, weeping, choked by sobs that shook his whole body; Félicité ran here and there in the room; Homais, motionless, uttered heavy sighs, and M. Canivet, still keeping his self-command, began nevertheless to feel uneasy' [394; 233]). But most of these situations and events are viewed through (the subjectivity of) major characters (112, 118–89, 201–02; 37, 88, 97) or minor ones (379–80, 388, 393, 415, 424; 223, 229, 232–33, 248, 255); and many are seen from the perspective of (uncharacterized) observers ("what one perceived"—e.g., 85, 89, 206, 412; 18, 21, 100, 246) or from a vantage point which is not quite that of a character but, rather, that of a proximate reading instrument ("what X or Y could or would have perceived"—e.g., 276, 311, 336; 150, 172, 190). Flaubert adopts so many different positions (including such unusual ones as in the cab scene or in the passage where Mmes Caron and Tuvache watch Emma pleading with Binet), moves so rapidly and evenly from place to place, and chooses so frequently to color one point of view with another that "Who sees?" can be as problematic a question as "Who speaks?" (e.g., 110–11; 36) and that no single perspective (not even Emma's) comes to dominate and orient the text.

The elusiveness of the narrator, the variability of voice, and the multiplication of viewpoints underlie the novel's brand of impersonality (and objectivity). As indicated above, it is not that, beyond the first few pages, *Madame Bovary* bears no distinctive narratorial mark. One can find many signs of a narrating "I" in the text, from the uses of "we" that pepper the narrative (96, 355, 413; 25, 205, 247) to the uses of present tense and deictics relating to the time of the narrating ("mais, aujourd'hui encore, il continue la culture de ses tubercules" 'but, to this day, he carries on the cultivation of his little tubers' [137; 51]) and the passages designating texts or worlds familiar to both the narrator and the narratee ("C'était un de ces sentiments purs qui n'embarrassent pas l'exercice de la vie" 'It was one of those pure feelings that do not interfere with life' [172; 76]). Rather, the novel is impersonal in that what is told does not pertain to a narrator as a person; does not illuminate a narrator's self; does not reveal, express, or situate that self. The narrative is objective because undetermined by a subjectivity (Culler, *Flaubert* 109–22).

The very switch from homodiegetic to heterodiegetic narration signals the rejection of narratives issuing from personal experience, animated by personal desire, shaped by and limited to one specific voice, aimed at profit and self-satisfaction. The very notion of a sovereign subject is put into question by the mingling of utterances, the invasion of one language (one's language) by another. Caught in the discourse of the other, the discourse of the self repeats it: what Emma considers most private or singular turns out to be most banal. And the insufficiency of single visions is foregrounded not only by their capriciousness (when Emma feels well disposed toward Charles, for example, she notices with some surprise that he has nice teeth [245; 127]) but also by their mere juxtaposition and incompatibility.

In effect, Flaubert's text counters narrationally what it denounces thematically through its criticism of the characters' narrative conceptions, longings, and practices. Thus Emma, who wants to replace existence with narrative, to reinvent herself and her life through narrative, recounts in order to possess, tells in order to receive, consumes and fabricates narratives in order to gratify herself. Her egoism makes her incapable of seeing in terms of a perspective other than her own (103; 31). Her stories are tied to commerce ("Il fallait qu'elle pût retirer des choses une sorte de profit personnel" 'She had to gain some personal profit out of things' [96; 26]) and to eroticism ("ses élans d'amour vague la fatiguaient plus que de grandes débauches" 'for these vague ecstasies of imaginary love would exhaust her more than the wildest orgies' [364; 212]). They prove trivial and incomplete when not deceitful (118–19; 41–42), biased, or—worse—unjust ("par quelle déplorable manie avoir ainsi abîmé son existence en sacrifices continuels? . . . C'était pour lui, cependant, pour cet être, pour cet homme qui ne comprenait rien, qui ne sentait rien!" 'what madness had driven her to ruin her life by continual sacrifices? . . . It was for him, for this creature, for this man who understood nothing, who felt nothing' [252–53; 133]), deluded, blind, deadly. What Emma is the victim of—and what the text repudiates—might be called an oral type of narrative, one that, like speech, develops in terms of particular circumstances, follows particular itineraries, fulfills particular goals. But speech (as opposed to language; *parole*, not *langue*) is deficient, especially in the realm of self-expression and self-realization. Flaubert's statements are well-known: "personne, jamais, ne peut donner l'exacte mesure de ses besoins, ni de ses conceptions, ni de ses douleurs. . . . la parole humaine est comme un chaudron fêlé où nous battons des mélodies à faire danser les ours, quand on voudrait attendrir les étoiles" 'no one ever has been able to give the exact measure of his needs, his concepts, or his sorrows. . . . The human tongue is like a cracked cauldron on which we beat out tunes to set a bear dancing when we would make the stars weep with our melodies' (259; 138); "la parole est un laminoir qui allonge toujours les sentiments" 'speech is a rolling-mill that always stretches feelings' (307; 169; trans. mine). Contrary to its protagonist, *Madame*

Bovary shuns the self, and to the oral it prefers the written—that is, what puts in doubt the pertinence of "Who speaks?"

Instead, the relevant question bears on "how it was." Partly because any given perspective, rather than being allowed to dominate for long, is made to blend with or yield to other perspectives that often undercut it; because any given voice is frequently muffled by other voices; and because free indirect discourse involves the use of the imperfect (the tense of what is static or repeated) and not the simple perfect (the tense of singular events), the characters lose autonomy and force. Conversely, the world surrounding them and interfering with them acquires density. It refers neither back to an unequivocal source nor forward to an ultimate significance. It resists and eludes the meanings attributed to it, the shapes conferred on it. It is there, as (mis)perceived and (mis)interpreted by a multitude of focalizers, composed only to be recomposed; but it is also there beyond any focalization.[1] Along with such other factors as the banality of the plot, the mediocrity of the characters, the links between their environment and their destiny, and the abundance of details referring to everyday life, the opacity of this world forms the foundation of the novel's realism.

Several other narrative features combine to increase the weight of the world while subverting the characters' centrality. For example, Flaubert avoids giving full and objective views of his creatures, preferring to show them in bits and pieces through the perceptions of others (think of the changing color of Emma's eyes: 74, 93, 110, 307, 385; 11, 23, 35–36, 169, 226) as if to subvert and dissolve their substantiality. He also tends to grant equal importance to objects and characters, humanizing the former (as in the celebrated cab scene) while reducing the latter's power to affect or control events (Gengembre 77–79). Structurally, Emma's story is framed by Charles's just as Emma herself is trapped by her marriage to him. The action follows an iterant pattern of hope, seeming fulfillment, disappointment, and failure, thus placing the heroine's life under the sign of repetition and sterility. And the novel frequently favors the mingling or the juxtaposing of distinct series of events, which not only gives rise to powerful ironies (as in the exemplary scene of the agricultural fair) but also puts into question the singularity of the characters' experience, the significance of their individual projects (Gengembre 50–61; Lloyd 54–65; Wing 41–77). Besides, the chronology of events lacks precision and is at times implausible. Only two (plot-external) dates are mentioned explicitly: 1812, the year Charles's parents probably married (64; 3), and 1835, the year a new road made Yonville easier to reach (134; 49). The time elapsed between Charles's first day at school in Rouen and his first encounter with Emma remains vague; it is not clear whether he dies the same year as the heroine or the year after; and though the novel suggests that Emma becomes pregnant around March (129; 49), she apparently gives birth before June (155; 65).

Moreover, flash-forward passages are neither frequent (fewer than ten) nor textually extensive. If flashbacks are more numerous (about forty), their most important function is to present the characters' antecedents (e.g., 61–71,

94–100; 1–8, 24–28). Chronology and chronological links matter less than du-
ration. *Madame Bovary* offers not so much a chronicle of French provincial
lives in the first half of the nineteenth century as an account of provincial life
(its subtitle is *Moeurs de province* ["Provincial Mores"]), and it favors atmos-
pheric rather than temporal realism, the truth of fiction over the correctness of
history. Molded by an immutable past, lacking in willpower, and cut off from
the future, the protagonists are imprisoned in a monotonous present ("Depuis
les événements que l'on va raconter, rien, en effet, n'a changé à Yonville" 'Since
the events about to be recounted, nothing, in fact, has changed in Yonville'
[137; 51]) where time as change and difference becomes time as repetition and
fate (Gothot-Mersch, "Aspects"; Vargas Llosa, *L'orgie* 194–211).

So the text prefers a viscous blending of events to a clear-cut temporal suc-
cession; similarly, in terms of narrative frequency it shows a penchant for iterative as opposed to singulative narration (e.g., 152, 161–62, 231–32; 62, 69,
118). Characters are caught in the glue of routine. Actions as well as experiences lose their freshness and vigor. Movement is nearly reduced to immobil-
ity, and this penchant for iterative narration decisively affects narrative speed
(Gans 42). Like most canonical narratives, *Madame Bovary* relies on an alternation of scene and summary (*récit*). But many of the scenes it presents are
typical—recounted iteratively—rather than unique (247–48, 258–59, 341–42;
129, 137–38, 194). What should be singular and eventful proves habitual and
ordinary. Showing and telling blend; background and foreground merge; scene
becomes summary. And just as the novel saps intranarrational distinctions, it
also blurs the boundaries between "narration proper" and description (Bal
87–112; Bollème, *La leçon* 141–95). The former inclines to stasis. The latter,
which is usually focalized and informed with the characters' thoughts or feelings, does not merely provide a (sociophysical) background for their actions or
a (sociophysical) explanation of their movements: in Flaubert's practice, it
takes on a (psycho)narrative role, signaling the birth of a project, the death of
a feeling, the change in a state of mind (see, e.g., Charles's visits to the Bertaux,
the Vaubyessard ball, or the opera scene in Rouen).

It is partly the way in which the narrative techniques undermine differences
(between description and narration, scene and summary, beings and objects,
various voices or points of view) that gives *Madame Bovary* its justly famous
compactness, its massive consistency, and makes it not only a "written" text and
a realistic fiction but also—and perhaps even more so—a thing of art.

NOTE

[1]*Editors' note*: "Focalizers" are words in a text that show who is perceiving the outside world and through what kinds of sensory impressions. They do not appear in omniscient narration and in other "objective" descriptions of a character whose thoughts
and feelings are not known. See Genette, *Figures III* 206.

DECONSTRUCTIONIST APPROACHES

Teaching *Madame Bovary* through the Lens of Poststructuralism

Dorothy Kelly

Flaubert's *Madame Bovary* is a paradoxical text: both a canonical, realist novel and a more modern antirepresentational novel. As such, it provides students of literature with a neat juxtaposition of modes that facilitates their understanding of the problems of narrative representation in modernity. In my courses on the French novel, I use *Madame Bovary* to highlight the conflict between standard notions about representation and the newer, postmodern critiques of representation. Indeed, poststructuralism is intimately linked to texts of the nineteenth century; Jacques Derrida's work on "différance" relates to Mallarmé's poems, and Jonathan Culler's work on postmodernism and uncertainty relates to Flaubert's novels. In my undergraduate novel courses, naturally, I do not give my students Derrida's *La dissémination* to read, but I do introduce them to the basic ideas that drive poststructuralism. The concepts of deconstruction and poststructuralism may be taught without the jargon and the philosophical background when one is doing close readings of texts.

My goals in teaching *Madame Bovary* in this way are to enable the students to take pleasure in the paradoxes of the text, to help them appreciate the beauty and complexity of the writing, and to make them question our assumptions about the way language relates to reality.

One does encounter problems in aiming for such goals; I have found, however, that the most difficult problems are those involved not in the concepts of deconstruction but, rather, in the nature of teaching *Madame Bovary* itself to undergraduates in a course that requires them to read several novels in French and to speak French in class. I first describe how I tackle these two basic problems, then turn to a summary of how I teach deconstruction to undergraduates through a reading of *Madame Bovary*.

The first problems for students are the sheer length of the novel and the complexity of its vocabulary. I assign fifty pages for each class meeting (three meetings per week) for three weeks. I emphasize, and reemphasize, to the students that they must keep up with the schedule to be able to participate in class discussions, which constitute a significant percentage of their grade. Each topic of discussion for a particular class deals only with material that the students have already read. I therefore work slowly through the text while highlighting important episodes as they come up, more or less in order. Although I find three weeks a long time to devote to one novel in a course on several novels, the students have expressed appreciation in their comments for such in-depth reading and would actually like to have more time to spend on the novel.

Another problem is that the students so lack confidence in speaking French that there is virtually no class discussion unless I use special methods. According to one particularly successful method, I begin the class with fifteen minutes or so of lecture and question-answer sessions, then divide the class into several groups and give each one a particular passage to discuss (using my prepared questions). I give them another fifteen minutes to work on this project, and then each group presents the results to the class as a whole. Often the discussions will spill over into the next class period and sometimes take it up completely. In this way, students have an opportunity to speak French in their small groups with minimal intimidation (an opportunity they value highly), and they also have a chance to discuss ideas and collect their thoughts before they have to speak to the class as a whole. I often write out questions on paper and hand them out to students; this is, after all, what they should be teaching themselves to do: to ask questions of a literary text.

For this exercise to work well, the passages and questions must be selected with care. At times, the whole class will work on a single passage; at other times, the work of each group will provide one piece in a larger puzzle, and when all the groups have finished their discussions, the completed picture may be seen. Below, I review five of the most important passages I discuss, the problems I give each group to tackle, and how these passages contribute to the students' understanding of *Madame Bovary*.

To begin, students in each group take turns reading sentences from the description of Charles Bovary's hat at the beginning of the novel. As each group translates these sentences into everyday French, one student who is identified as having a bit of artistic talent draws a picture of the hat as directed by the other students in the group. The vocabulary here is complicated, and I usually provide a sheet of translated words, but I do not explain the English vocabulary (such as "shako") because the French itself is obscure. I ask the group, "Is this description of Charles Bovary's hat realistic? If a realist text gives the illusion of describing reality objectively, is this a realist text?" As they begin the drawing, students usually feel it is realistic because of the sheer quantity of the description. Then, as they work through it carefully, they change their minds. After we pass around the drawings (each group having made one), see how different they are, and have a good laugh, we address the more serious question of realism and representation. What is Flaubert saying about language here?

On the one hand, language does represent reality: a hat is described, and we all know what hats are, so the description poses no problem. But on the other hand, the excesses of Flaubert's language put that representation into question: the hats the students draw do not resemble anything that exists in the real world, nor do they resemble one another. This problem introduces us to the first major questions posed by deconstruction: What is the relation of language to reality? Does language map onto reality in a one-to-one correspondence of words into things? Does language thus come after reality (the word *hat* names a real object—a hat)? Or does language create reality for us (the new and bizarre hat)? Is the real a concept formed and contaminated by language? A final point convinces the students that this question is pertinent: the observation that the letters *c* and *b* are obsessively repeated in the description of the hat. If "clothes make the man," then the letters make the clothes (the French proverb "L'habit ne fait pas le moine" 'The habit doesn't make the monk,' ironically, works well here). Thus is language, in the initials of the name Charles Bovary, the origin of the realist description of the protagonist's hat; language precedes the reality of the hat (see Ricardou, *Nouveaux problèmes* 37–39). Other topics that may be discussed with this idea in mind are Emma's eyes (Julian Barnes's chapter on this subject in *Flaubert's Parrot* is excellent; 74–81) and Emma's wedding cake.

The next set of questions involves a slightly different approach to this topic. How do our fictions relate to reality? Do fictions (language) generate the thing (reality) as the *c*'s and *b*'s in the hat description do? Or does reality generate our fictions (language); do the hats of the world give rise to the word *hat*? Here I juxtapose two different sets of discussion questions: first, the problem of Emma's desire; second, the problem of Homais's fictions. These group discussions show how both of these hypotheses work in *Madame Bovary* and how both of them are undermined.

After we begin with a discussion of the nature of Emma's desire, such as her image of the ideal wedding and the ideas of "félicité" she gets from books, we conclude that she would like to turn the literary fiction of Romantic novels into her reality. (In classes on the French novel, it is often effective to assign a Romantic narrative, such as Chateaubriand's *René*, just before *Madame Bovary*, so that the rhetoric of Romanticism is fresh in the students' minds.) In her desire to have fiction (language) turn into reality, Emma would thus appear to adhere to the first of the options described above: fictions generate reality.

At this point I break the students into groups and have them investigate the relation of Emma's dream fictions to her reality. I give each group two small passages to study together: the first is a description of an ideal from fiction, the second its transposition to Emma's reality in the ball at Vaubyessard. The first group looks at the description of her ideals from her readings: "Elle aurait voulu vivre dans quelque vieux manoir, comme ces châtelaines au long corsage, qui, sous le trèfle des ogives, passaient leurs jours, le coude sur la pierre et le menton dans la main, à regarder venir du fond de la campagne un cavalier à plume blanche qui galope sur un cheval noir" 'She would have liked to live in some old manor-house, like those long-waisted chatelaines who, in the shade of pointed arches, spent their days leaning on the stone, chin in hand, watching a white-plumed knight galloping on his black horse from the distant fields' (97; 26). This group then observes that these dreams come true at Vaubyessard. She stays in a "château" rather than a "manoir" and becomes the "châtelaine" dreaming at her window: "Emma mit un châle sur ses épaules, ouvrit la fenêtre et s'accouda" 'Emma threw a shawl over her shoulders, opened the window, and leant out' (114; 38). The second group observes how the elements of the keepsakes become her reality: "le lévrier" (greyhound) there becomes her "levrette," (little Italian greyhound); the exotic "djiaours" (Giaours) turn into her dog's name, "Djali" (98, 104–05; 27, 31–32). The third group sees how the authors of the keepsakes, the "comtes ou vicomtes," turn into the vicomte of the ball (97, 113; 27, 37–38), and the "cygnes" become real (98, 114; 27, 39). As the students work on these individual passages in the groups, they are not particularly convinced, but when the groups get together and share their observations, the repetition of the realization of her dreams becomes convincing.

We wrap up the discussion of the realization of Emma's dreams with an evaluation. When her dreams become reality, is Emma satisfied? Why not? The students are usually quick to note that "swans" do not normally bring one happiness, and we discuss how the ideals of happiness in the books read by Emma are literary and cultural clichés that do not necessarily guarantee satisfaction when transported to reality. The transportation involves a degradation. I then point out to them that there are three ball scenes in the text: the scene at Vaubyessard, the visit by the man with the miniature dancers in the music box, and the ball scene at the end of the text, where Emma is in the presence of women of the lowest order. We discuss how each ball scene is a degradation of the one that precedes it. The conclusion to be drawn is that though Emma's fictional dreams do come true, they turn out not to be what she wanted. We also discuss the danger of her attempt to turn language into reality in the episode of the surgical operation: she makes Charles read scientific articles on clubfeet, she makes him try to turn the language that he reads into reality, and the consequences are disastrous for all. We also discuss the black liquid of putrefaction in the description of Hippolyte's foot that reappears in other images of bodily degradation and decay (those relating to the blind man and Emma) and that figures the decline of the ideal.

Next, we turn to Homais as the representative of the second relation of fiction to reality introduced above and the one that is the more traditional: reality generates language and fiction; reality precedes the language that merely re-presents reality. I give out only two passages for discussion and ask several groups to discuss the same passage: the first is a description of the pitiful fireworks display that takes place after the agricultural fair. The second is the piece written by Homais for the newspaper in which he extols the fireworks as follows: "Le soir, un brillant feu d'artifice a tout à coup illuminé les airs. On eût dit un véritable kaléidoscope, un vrai décor d'Opéra, et un moment notre petite localité a pu se croire transportée au milieu d'un rêve des *Mille et une nuits*" 'At night some brilliant fireworks suddenly lit up the sky. It was a real kaleidoscope, an operatic scene; and for a moment our little locality might have thought itself transported into the midst of a dream from the "Thousand and One Nights" ' (221; 111). This passage generates much humor in the class, and we turn to a discussion of the implications of this lie. For Emma, a fictional ideal becomes a degraded reality; for Homais, a degraded reality is rewritten into a lying fictional ideal. When I ask the class which point of view Flaubert takes, they invariably answer, "Neither one." I then ask, "What is the relation between fiction and reality in this text?" They usually begin to see at this point that the very problematization of that relation is in some sense the point of the book itself, and they arrive at a more complex understanding of the issues at stake in language and representation.

The fourth topic of discussion stems from the origin of Emma's desires in literary clichés and Homais's predilection for the clichéd bourgeois way of life. I ask the students to define just what a cliché is. In their answers, the concept of repetition appears, and from there I ask them whether all language is clichéd in a certain way. Then, as we turn to our group discussions, I choose the well-known juxtaposition of discourses in the scene at the agricultural fair. The first group discusses Lieuvain's name (*lieu commun?*) and the clichés of his discourse, the second discusses Rodolphe's clichéd seduction scene, and the third discusses the various animal sounds described throughout. After the groups have presented their material, the students are anxious to point out the humor involved in the juxtaposition of these clichés, and then the entire class looks together at the section in which the pace of the juxtaposition of these discourses accelerates and at the comical choice of vocabulary (215; 107).

We then discuss the effects of this juxtaposition: the nearness of one set of clichés to another shows the ridiculousness of each. Each discourse serves to undermine the others, and their mutual interaction shows the clichéd nature of all discourse. For understanding to occur, language must be a repeated code, but the very repetition renders the expression of a unique experience impossible. To add one final twist to the discussion, we do a close reading of three more passages. The first appears in the heart of the seduction scene, and it is a passage of great beauty and sonority. As Emma dreams of the past, the tender nature of her reveries are expressed by soft sounds: *ch, s, ge, l, j, f.* Her fall back to reality at the end of each clause is expressed by the harder sounds, *p, d, t, b, c.*

> Mais, dans *ce* geste qu'*elle* fit en *se* cambrant *sur sa chaise, elle* aperçut au loin, tout au fond de l'horizon, la vieille diligence *L'Hirondelle,* qui

descendait *l*entement la côte des *L*eux, en traînant après soi un long panache de poussière. *C*'était dans *c*ette *v*oiture *j*aune que *L*éon, *s*i, souvent, était re*v*enu *v*ers e*ll*e; et par *c*ette route là-bas qu'il était parti pour toujours! E*ll*e crut le *v*oir en *f*ace, à *s*a *f*enêtre; puis tout se *c*onfon*d*it, *d*es nuages passèrent; *il l*ui *s*embla qu'e*ll*e tournait en*c*ore dans la *v*a*l*se, *s*ous le *f*eu *d*es *l*ustres, au bras du *v*icomte, et que *L*éon n'était pas *l*oin, qu'i*l* a*ll*ait venir . . . et ce*p*en*d*ant elle sentait toujours la tête *d*e Rodolphe à côté *d*'elle.   (213–14)

But in making this movement, as she leant back in her chair, she saw in the distance, right on the line of the horizon, the old diligence the "Hirondelle," that was slowly descending the hill of Leux, dragging after it a long trail of dust. It was in this yellow carriage that Léon had so often come back to her, and by this route down there that he had gone for ever. She fancied she saw him opposite at his window; then all grew confused; clouds gathered; it seemed to her that she was again turning in the waltz under the light of the lustres on the arm of the Viscount, and that Léon was not far away, that he was coming . . . and yet all the time she was conscious of Rodolphe's head by her side.   (105–06)

We discuss the implications of this beauty in its context of a scene of literal and figural "bêtise": what do we make of the beauty of banal language? Another juxtaposition to make is that of "beauty" with the "beast" (*bêtise*) in the following "animal" images: "les grands bonnets des paysannes se soulevèrent, comme des ailes de papillons blancs qui s'agitent" 'the large bonnets rose up like the fluttering wings of white butterflies' (216; 107) as compared with the ridiculous, literal "bête-ise," of the words "chevalines, bovines, ovines et porcines" 'equine, bovine, ovine, or porcine' (214; 106) in Lieuvain's speech. Once again, we conclude that both the ridiculousness and beauty of language are at work here and that Flaubert does not let us settle into any one, comfortable place.

We end our discussion of the clichéd nature of language with a discussion of another famous animal quotation, the one in which Flaubert compares human language to a cracked cauldron on which we can beat out melodies fit only to set bears to dancing (259; 138). We then read the chapter "The Flaubert Bestiary" in *Flaubert's Parrot* and discuss the word play of his name. (I have a prop that I bring to class at the end of this lesson: a stuffed teddy bear called a Zoominary, made by Recycled Paper Products, which has a tag that reads, "My Name is Gustave [Flaubear]." Another moment of hilarity ensues.) We end the discussion of cliché by talking about Culler's "The Uses of *Madame Bovary*" and "vealism," which the students like enormously.

The fifth and final area of discussion is the end of the novel, and each group takes the same passage: the description of Emma's death. The questions I ask of them are "What is the realization that Emma reaches at the end? What does it mean that she gains this understanding, this 'insight,' from the words of a blind man? What does it mean that this understanding comes at the moment of her death? What do the words of the song have to do with her life?" The students, in answering these questions, come to an appreciation of the irony of her blindness and insight, of the ambiguous stature of knowledge gained from a blind man at the moment of death. Again, the slippery ground of Flaubert's work becomes the focus of discussion: we can be satisfied neither that she has gained a full understanding of her plight nor that she remains in the fullness of her "bêtise"; Flaubert's text situates her somewhere in between, just where the reader must remain. We also discuss Charles and the irony of his fate. Students are quick to laugh at him throughout the novel, but when they come to the final scene of his life in which he dies of love, they retreat from their condemnatory position and concede that he, in fact, is the incarnation of Emma's Romantic dream: she actually did have a lover who would die for her. They understand that this does not erase his bêtise but, rather, complicates it.

Our concluding remarks on the novel bring together the various questions asked about language, representation, understanding, and the way in which this novel makes any definitive answer impossible. We see how Madame Bovary asks fundamental questions about meaning and how it suspends the possibility of giving an answer. Does language repeat reality or construct it? Is there any certainty of meaning? Is language a ridiculous, repetitious cliché or a beautiful musical expression? Can it be both at once? Students come away from a reading of this classic with a love for the beauty of its expression, an affection for its humor, and a respect for the deeper understanding of the complexities involved in the way language functions in the world. If their initial naive reading usually entails a simplistic identification with the character of Emma, their reading at the end of the course entails a more sophisticated identification with a character and an author who represent the desire for, and the impossibility of, plenitude.

It is the notion of the suspension between two opposite interpretations that makes up what I term here the deconstructive, or poststructuralist, approach to Madame Bovary. What is especially important for the students to learn, I believe, is that language, cliché, and convention enter our relation with reality in a much more pervasive way than we tend to realize. In my course on Madame Bovary—indeed, in most of my courses—I am fond of telling my students a riddle that illustrates to them how language distorts the way in which we digest information to such an extent that it makes us "blind," like Emma, to obvious "truths" as well as to the extent of its own intervention. The riddle goes as follows: "A man and his son were driving across the border between California and Arizona and were involved in a terrible accident. The father was killed, and the son was rushed to the nearest hospital. When he arrived there, the surgeon cried, 'My son, my son!' Who is the surgeon?" If the students have not heard this riddle before, they are unable to see the most obvious truth: the surgeon is the mother. We discuss how the cultural and thus "clichéd" connotations of the word *surgeon* are so strong that they prevent us from arriving at a simple, self-evident solution, and they do so "invisibly." The students can thus see at work the way in which language structures our reality and makes us blind to a real and obvious answer. From the sexist implications of this riddle and the more general implications of *Madame Bovary*, students reevaluate their simplistic understanding of words as simple labels affixed to things and revise it to question the sometimes dangerous consequences this simplistic understanding of language can have.

NOTE

The interpretation set forth in this essay draws in part from Dorothy Kelly, *Fictional Genders* (Lincoln: U of Nebraska P, 1989).

Reading (in) *Madame Bovary*

James Winchell

> Il me semble que *René*, c'était moi. . . . J'avais, comme
> *René*, le coeur mort avant d'avoir vécu.
> —George Sand, *Histoire de ma vie*

> It seems that *René* was I and that I was *René*. . . . Like
> his, my heart was dead before I could live.

This essay proposes an exercise in "applied pedagogy" for the teacher confronting the challenge posed by *Madame Bovary* in the current dynamism of reading and reception among students first encountering this work. The multiplicity and diversity of approaches to teaching the novel—to which the range of essays in this volume testifies—should not blind the professoriat to the affective experience of reading the novel for the first time. Consequently, our critical dexterity and theoretical versatility should not anesthetize us to the concerns initially expressed by contemporary students when confronted with the "injustice" of Emma's fate.

With increasing energy and volubility, students motivated by feminist and ethical concerns feel strongly about the constitution of Emma's personality as a "manipulation" by a male author; her suffering and her self-destruction emerge from their reading as yet another "romantic" pseudotragedy in a lamentable history of "authoritarian" invasion and domination. The author, according to this line of reasoning, might be compared (on the grounds of his narrative "penetrations" or "invasiveness" of the heroine's consciousness) with the other men in the novel itself. Indeed, moved by the pathos and inevitability of Emma's downfall, contemporary students often feel compelled to criticize Flaubert instead of Homais, Rodolphe, Léon, or Lheureux.

This critical approach would have been dismissed out of hand in earlier academic environments as a wrongheaded confusion of two different ontological levels, the author's and the characters'. If teachers pronounce such a peremptory dismissal today, however, they in turn run the risk of wrongheadedness by insisting on too static a sense of ontological hierarchy in the face of a work that clearly pursues the problem of subjectivity and social (or intersubjective) formation as its central preoccupation.

Responsible pedagogy for the new millennium, therefore, assumes instead that the concerns and objections raised by today's students are valid responses based not on issues external to the text but, rather, on the most compelling, problematic locus of meaning thematically and formally treated by the novel itself: the processes of subjectivity implicit in the relations among reading, knowledge, language, and desire. Far from betraying yet another failure of

American education, therefore, the student's suspicion that Flaubert has violated Emma Bovary reveals a sophisticated distrust of authorial manipulation as a general precondition of reading romantic novels: if the author is ultimately responsible for the world in which Emma commits suicide, critical readers must distance themselves from the creator of such a world, even if it be related purely in symbols.

This attitude, far from violating literature's inherent autonomy, its freedom from contingency, insists on its relevance to the individual's experience of the real via the "sensuous complexion of works" (Adorno 133). For if we dream of robbers and awake in terror, Freud reasons, it is not the imaginary robber but, rather, the dreamer's fear that is palpably, psychically, and affectively "real" (*Interpretation* 497). Approaches to the artwork that are sensitive to issues of the reader's response, therefore, proceed from hypotheses based on the strange and complex authenticity of the common ground shared by readers, authors, and characters alike: the experience of reading itself.

Indeed, the act of reading (in) *Madame Bovary* poses a problem uncannily shared by both the fictional personage and today's reader: How does Emma herself know what she desires, and how does the reader know that Emma knows what she wants?

The answer to these questions comes in two stages (let us call them, for the time being, subjective and intersubjective) and informs the narrator's early exposition of the very formation of Emma's desire. In the last lines of part 1, chapter 5, the reader learns of Emma's marriage as the threshold event marking her passage from private individual to public personage. Emma's emotional energy—the private, even intimate, expectation upon which she had undertaken to marry Charles Bovary—has been preformed by her reading of books: her feelings regarding love and marriage have been predetermined or mediated by a secondhand language of "beautiful" emotions and sentiment. This vocabulary (*bliss, passion, ecstasy*) is inherently ideational, representing exorbitant states of body and soul as concepts at one remove from Emma-the-reader's subjective experience. While these concepts serve as linguistic ideals or models for the young woman's marital and extramarital future, however, they also leave her strangely in the dark regarding her own knowledge concerning her desire. This cognitive breakdown—between her readerly expectations and the emotions that fail to materialize for her in marriage—emerges, dramatically enough, only in her experience of postmarital blues. Her intersubjective, public experience of passion fails to resemble the concept of passion she had held within her subjective, premarital, or private desire.

The idea that there somehow exists a possible "autonomous" subjectivity unsullied by the world is itself a romantic idea, which modern criticism has worked energetically to unmask. The term *Bovarysme*, coined by Jules de Gaultier in 1902, designates the phenomenon of mimetic self-fashioning in characters who attempt to take as their own the desires of other people (or

characters in books) as models they deem worthy of imitation. Gaultier sees a
pattern of this behavior in many of Flaubert's characters, a continuous preoccupation with the psychology of "external mediation" that reveals the pro-
foundest preoccupations within the author's own psychology.

More recently, René Girard has pursued these phenomena in the novel as a
genre, deciphering a history of the confusion that results when characters pattern their own actions upon the desires of others, a novelistic procedure he
traces from *Don Quixote* to Stendhal to Flaubert to Dostoevsky to Proust and
beyond:

> The novelist allows his characters to act and to speak and then, in the
> wink of an eye, he reveals their mediators to us. He thereby underhand-
> edly reestablishes the veritable hierarchy of desire, all the while seeming
> to add his own testimony to the deluded self-explanations claimed by the
> characters themselves.   (*Mensonge* 29; trans. mine)

This revelation of the process by which readers of chivalric, religious, or ro-
manticist texts absorb and replicate the desire of the other is seen by Girard as
the genre-determining project of the "novelistic truth" '*vérité romanesque*'
against the "romantic lie" '*mensonge romantique*': "As soon as the influence of
the mediator makes itself felt, the sense of the real is lost and the character's
judgment is paralyzed"; "Emma Bovary desires *through* the romantic heroines
with which she has filled her imagination, [who have] destroyed in her all spon-
taneity" (17, 18; trans. mine). Flaubert's mise-en-scène of Emma's reading,
then, presents a crucial sequence of interpretive moments that merits a detailed discussion in the classroom to prepare for reading the work as a whole.

The chapter following the passage on marital expectation and disappointment is a key chapter in the novel (1.6). In this flashback, every single incident
or detail serves to unlock some aspect of Emma's reading as the formative experience of her youth. The reader learns that her education at the convent consisted of a jumbled mixture of religion and romanticism, of her own sexual
awakening transmuted through a weird mix of metaphysical desires and furtive
readings of prohibited books.

If one looks closely at the sequence of "texts" cited in this chapter, however,
it becomes clear that the issue is not books per se but, rather, the act of reading as the formative prelude to her experience of marriage. Reading is cited
here by the narrator as a forensic axiom, an explanatory precondition for the
experiential moment of Emma's acquisition of the public life-world surrounding her new position as Mme Bovary. The type of texts she has read, however,
fixes her expectations and magnifies her very sense of desire as if through a sort
of narcissistic microscope.

The narrator's tone is absolutely unambiguous regarding his critical target:
in his ironic rhetoric of praise and blame, it is not Emma's "fault" that she finds
herself in a world imbued with such texts:

Elle avait lu *Paul et Virginie* et elle avait rêvé la maisonnette de bambous, le nègre Domingo, le chien Fidèle, mais surtout l'amitié douce de quelque bon petit frère, qui va chercher pour vous des fruits rouges dans des grands arbres plus hauts que des clochers, ou qui court pieds nus sur le sable, vous apportant un nid d'oiseau.   (94)

She had read "Paul and Virginia," and she had dreamed of the little bamboo-house, the negro Domingo, the dog Fidèle, but above all of the sweet friendship of some dear little brother, who seeks red fruit for you on trees taller than steeples, or who runs barefoot over the sand, bringing you a bird's nest.   (24–25)

Everything points to an authorial criticism not of Emma but, rather, of the language of romanticism itself: the abuse of diminutives and scale ("little bamboo-house," "dear little brother," "trees taller than steeples"), exoticism and local color ("the negro Domingo," "barefoot over the sand"), and cloying nature ("the dog Fidèle," "a bird's nest") all attest to the narrator's distaste for these shopworn, deluded, and hollowly sentimental motifs.

By using the second person in the passage ("red fruit for you," "bringing you a bird's nest"), the author also economically conjoins the reader of *Madame Bovary* with Emma herself: the "you" in question uncannily, if only momentarily, collapses into one and the same reader, the one who is the subject of and subjected to the same dynamic mediations before the texts in question. While Emma has no access to the narrator's irony, however, the reader of the narrative does: by means of this tone, Flaubert alternately brings the reader toward and distances the reader from Emma's point of view. The technique of free indirect discourse, pioneered by Flaubert, permits a systematic exploitation of the movement of consciousness parallel to the movement of language in writing and reading.

The paragraphs following the "Paul and Virginia" passage, furthermore, constitute a tour through "readings" of every sort: indeed, the rest of the chapter presents a catalog of texts that informed Emma's premarital sensibility. By means of an associative description—in which Emma's visual perspective ("coupées çà et là" ["chipped here and there"]) suddenly overlaps the reader's—we learn of the romantic legends painted on the very plates used by Emma and her father during their trip to the convent when Emma was thirteen: "Les explications légendaires, coupées çà et là par l'égratignure des couteaux, glorifiaient toutes la religion, les délicatesses de coeur et les pompes de la Cour" 'The explanatory legends, chipped here and there by the scratching of knives, all glorified religion, the tendernesses of the heart, and the pomps of court' (95; 25).

Once installed in the convent, Emma's reading consisted of a book of "vignettes pieuses bordées d'azur, et elle aimait la brebis malade, le sacré coeur percé de flèches aiguës, ou le pauvre Jésus qui tombe en marchant [sous] sa croix" 'pious vignettes with their azure borders in her book, and she loved the

sick lamb, the sacred heart pierced with sharp arrows, or the poor Jesus sinking beneath the cross he carried' (95; 25); at confession and at sermon she represented herself in scenes of mystico-erotic passion, while the religious reading
in the evenings—an indistinct alternation of writings by the Abbé Frayssinous
and Chateaubriand—provoked in her a rapt attention to "la lamentation sonore
des mélancolies romantiques se répétant à tous les échos de la terre et de l'é-
ternité!" 'the sonorous lamentations of romantic melancholy re-echoing
through the world and eternity!' (95; 25)

Lest the reader lose track of Emma among so many forms of textual mediation, the narrator stops to remind the reader how completely Emma's subjectivity was formed by these mimetic or imitated feelings, so quiet and uneventful
was her subjective, unmediated experience. He goes so far as to create a condi-
tional clause that poses an alternative childhood for his character:

> Si son enfance se fût écoulée dans l'arrière-boutique d'un quartier mar-
> chand, elle se serait peut-être ouverte alors aux envahissements lyriques
> de la nature, qui, d'ordinaire, ne nous arrivent que par la traduction des
> écrivains.   (95–96)

> If her childhood had been spent in the shops of a busy city section, she
> might perhaps have opened her heart to those lyrical invasions of Nature,
> which usually come to us only through translations in books.   (25)

I have quoted this sequence of "textual experiences," which because of their
retelling in flashback actually constitute so many pre-texts for Emma's marital
dilemma, to show how often and how consistently the narrator poses the issue
of mediation as a primary concern not only for Emma but also for the reader.
Each example exploits, alternately, style and technique—irony, shifts in point of
view, free indirect discourse—to inform the reader of the artwork's polyvalent
allegory of reading in relation to meaning: instead of enabling Emma to accede
to her subjective relations with those around her, these romantic fantasies work
twice: to blind her by means of her reading of them and to reveal this process
of blinding to the reader of Emma, reading.

Instead of violating Emma, Flaubert thereby exposes for the reader an initially
sensitive subjectivity undergoing a progressively more dangerous objectification.
In so doing, and by insisting so thoroughly on reading as the formative moment
of this process, the author reveals the romantic lie as a force of brutality and deception closely allied with the world of masculinity (in its insensitive or ineffective
forms, as incarnated by Rodolphe and Charles, Lheureux and Léon, Homais and
Bournisien) that fatally constitutes the arena of Emma's action. To demonstrate
this point sufficiently, the author pursues the problem of reading exhaustively.

Flaubert's focus makes the catalog of texts in this relatively short chapter
especially striking in its range: the novel titled *Paul and Virginia*, the painted

plates, the pious vignettes, the sermons, the romantic tales smuggled into the convent by the *vieille fille*, the works of Walter Scott, songs and ballads, keepsakes and their illustrations where, "se détachent en écorchures blanches, sur un fond d'acier gris, de loin en loin, des cygnes qui nagent" 'sharply edged on a steel-grey background, white swans are swimming here and there' (98; 27). The ultimate development at the end of this list, however, is not a textual or romantic episode but, rather, an immediately affective experience with profound consequences for Emma: her mother's death.

The transition from the catalog of readings to the narrative of Emma's successive reactions to the loss of her mother is effected in a strange little paragraph that may surprise or bewilder the student but that serves as a reminder of the last, vanishing trace of Emma's self-presence:

> Et l'abat-jour du quinquet, accroché dans la muraille au-dessus de la tête d'Emma, éclairait tous ces tableaux du monde, qui passaient devant elle les uns après les autres, dans le silence du dortoir et au bruit lointain de quelque fiacre attardé qui roulait encore sur les boulevards.   (98)

> And the shade of the oil lamp fastened to the wall above Emma's head lighted up all these pictures of the world, that passed before her one by one in the silence of the dormitory, and to the distant noise of some belated carriage still rolling down the boulevards.   (27)

The texts on which this chapter is based fade into the background as this passage moves the reader toward an evocation of Emma's sensory focus or access to the nonimagistic data around her. The images of romantic clichés—the targets of so much authorial irony before this key paragraph—are now framed in the light of the oil lamp, but their content is no longer the focus; rather, because they "passed before her one by one in the silence of the dormitory," they serve to draw the reader toward Emma's position as a subject within that same silence. Finally, once collated with Emma's position, we, too, are placed within the auditory framework previously alluded to by an absence of sound ("the silence of the dormitory"), which is now expressed in terms of a presence: "the distant noise of some belated carriage still rolling down the boulevards." The narrative has moved from the lamp to its light to the image to the dormitory setting and its silence, finally arriving at Emma's unmediated perception of a far-off presence, itself becoming absent.

The sound of a disappearing carriage "heard" by the reader and Emma from practically the same physical position thus prefigures the disappearance of both Emma's mother and Emma's own subjective experience. The grief she feels is her last fragment of unmediated subjectivity disappearing into "the haze of fantasies she surrounds herself with" (Kovel 43); indeed, we learn that she cried a great deal and had an image fabricated from her dead mother's hair, but this mourning process reveals itself to be an imitation of mourning by means of which she can manage her feelings precisely through their "romanticized" reading and mise-en-scène: "The excessive volume of feeling worked to cancel out her diminished sincerity; meanwhile, she gained an audience: father, nuns (she was at the convent at the time), *but mainly herself, now identified with the lost mother watching and admiring her grieving daughter*" (Kovel 42; emphasis added). This interpretation is not based on extratextual material but is, rather, explicitly stated in the final "movement" of this crucial chapter. During Emma's mourning, the reader learns, "[elle] fut intérieurement satisfaite de se sentir arrivée du premier coup à ce rare idéal des existences pâles, où ne parviennent jamais les coeurs médiocres" 'Emma was secretly pleased that she had reached at a first attempt the rare ideal of delicate lives, never attained by mediocre hearts' (98–99; 27).

Her passage from romanticized reader to anesthetized mourner "n'ayant plus rien à apprendre, ne devant plus rien sentir" 'with nothing more to learn, and nothing more to feel' (99; 28) places her squarely in line with other products of romanticism, in terms comparable to George Sand's epigraph at the beginning of this essay. The flashback reverts to the narrative present in the last paragraph of this chapter as Charles Bovary arrives at the Rouault farm, but even this scene remains consonant with the drama of reading and Emma's vanishing subjectivity, her disappearing "self-presence." For it is not Charles's personality but merely "la présence de cet homme" ("the presence of that man") that finally drives her to act—by accepting his proposal—on what she believes is a "passion merveilleuse" 'wondrous passion' (99; 28). The premarital disappointment with which Flaubert's exposition of the effect of Emma's reading began thus comes together in Emma's post-honeymoon realization that the presence of Charles effectively hides the absence of a romantic hero, an absence whose deluded presence she had absorbed through reading and mechanically projected onto her husband-to-be.

Once students have been led through the exercise in "double reading" proposed here, the epistemological bases of Emma's violation or victimization may be organized in terms of the relation between reading and the other throughout the rest of the novel. In Léon's praise of reading (2.2), he describes to Emma the process of identification between reader and literary character as a sensuous process, playful and shapely:

> [E]t votre pensée, s'enlaçant à la fiction, se joue dans les détails ou poursuit le contour des aventures. Elle se mêle aux personnages; il semble que c'est vous qui palpitez sous leurs costumes.   (147)

> [A]nd your thought, blending with the fiction, toys with the details, follows the outline of the adventures. It mingles with the characters, and it seems you are living their lives, that your own heart beats in their breast.   (59)

Emma enthusiastically responds that this is true, signaling her acquiescence not only to the romance of reading but also to the romance of amorous engagement with her new interlocutor. The progressive objectification of Emma's personality—resulting ultimately in her poisoned corpse—is consistently effected in a frame featuring at least two readers: Emma and the reader reading her. Even Charles's mother, that sublime critical intelligence, realizes that Emma's bad taste in literature is killing her: "N'aurait-on pas le droit d'avertir la police, si le libraire persistait quand même dans son métier d'empoisonneur?" 'Would they not have a right to call in the police if the bookseller persisted all the same in his poisonous trade?' (192; 90) she asks in part 2, chapter 7.

This type of "scenography"—or the self-referential scene making of modern writing, reading, and the "writing of reading"—constitutes an important, even epochal, contribution in nineteenth-century fiction to an understanding of "reception" *avant la lettre* (Dällenbach 422). Flaubert's technical manipulation of reading implicates his reader in Emma's "frantic, unfaithful search" for her ruined subjectivity, yet *Madame Bovary* moves its audience "not simply by presenting the failure of object love in an isolated spirit, but by uniting us with the concrete, sensuous, socially embedded woman in whom that spirit dwells" (Kovel 46).

In a letter to Louise Colet dating from 14 August 1853—a date that falls during the composition of *Madame Bovary*—the author makes an important claim for this novel in relation to social oppression, the status of women, and the culture of France in the period. He states, "La poésie est une chose aussi précise que la géométrie. . . . Ma pauvre Bovary, sans doute, souffre et pleure dans vingt villages de France à la fois, à cette heure même" (*Correspondance*, ed. Bruneau, 2: 391) 'Poetry is as precise as geometry. . . . My poor Bovary, without a doubt, is suffering and weeping at this very instant in twenty villages of France' (*Madame Bovary*, ed. de Man, 316).

His writing of a subjective reading of the heritage of romanticism reveals, therefore, the geometric proliferation of masculine brutality, scientific incomprehension, and wasted lives in nascent modernity. Far from victimizing Emma Bovary, then, he initiates the reader into the very cultural and historical conditions under which women like her were objectified as a group. It is true that male authors are responsible for the texts that "poison" Emma's sense of desire and her very subjectivity; not every male author, however, is Gustave Flaubert.

Desire, Difference, and Deconstruction in *Madame Bovary*

Andrew McKenna

"Madame Bovary, c'est moi" 'I am Madame Bovary' (see Descharmes 103). This statement is revealing, not especially for what it tells us about the author of *Madame Bovary* but for what it can suggest to us as readers of the novel. For *Madame Bovary* satirizes not only Flaubert's own romantic illusions but romance in general and tells us something fundamental about desire and its representation that transcends the historical circumstances composing any individual life. Romance alleges the originality of desire, arguing that it springs spontaneously from the subject or that it is fatally attracted to the object (the destiny of Tristram and Isolde is sealed when they drink a love potion intended for King Mark). Flaubert's novel argues, Emma's sentimental education to witness (1.6), that desire requires a model or mediator to designate its objects, that it originates in the imitation of other desires, the desires of others. Where romance posits magic, mystery, or magnetism, the novelist uncovers mediation, mimesis.

This insight serves as the keystone of the fundamental anthropology elaborated by René Girard in *Things Hidden since the Foundation of the World*. In *Deceit, Desire, and the Novel* he acknowledges our greatest novelists, Flaubert principal among them, as a privileged source of theory about human affairs. The theory of mimetic desire is as simple and clear in its formulation as it is rich in its consequences, and its exploration takes us to the core of Flaubert's originality as a writer—as a stylist—and as a reader of modern culture. It also helps us to appreciate the relevance of a poststructuralist critique of representation, origin, and difference for a reading of Flaubert's novel.

The structure of desire is triangular in its operations: between the subject and the object of desire stands a mediator, living or dead, near or far, imaginary or real, who designates the object as desirable, who confers value on an object that is in itself devoid of intrinsic or natural merit. Desire is directed obliquely by verbal or visual representations: it is not attracted by objects immediately present to it. Emma's indifference to her natural surroundings is thus attributed to their very proximity (95–96; 25).

This compact of *imago* and *imitari* (which have the same etymon) is located at the origin of Emma's ultimately catastrophic dissatisfaction:

> Avant qu'elle se mariât, elle avait cru avoir de l'amour; mais le bonheur qui aurait dû résulter de cet amour n'étant pas venu, il fallait qu'elle se fût trompée, songeait-elle. Et Emma cherchait à savoir ce que l'on entendait au juste dans la vie par les mots de *félicité*, de *passion* et d'*ivresse*, qui avait paru si beaux dans les livres. (94)

> Before marriage she thought herself in love; but since the happiness that
> should have followed failed to come, she must, she thought, have been
> mistaken. And Emma tried to find out what one meant exactly in life by
> the words *bliss, passion, ecstasy*, that had seemed to her so beautiful in
> books.   (24)

Flaubert's use of the partitive article ("de l'amour") and then of the demon-
strative pronoun ("cet amour") is not easily translatable, though it more slyly
designates love as an objective entity, a commodity or a condition one might
acquire, like a new car or a new look.

This mention of thwarted desire is the reader's very first glimpse of Emma's
own consciousness, of her view of the world from within her own psyche, the two
previous paragraphs having described Charles's relaxation into the contempla-
tion of his own marital bliss—though here, too, only via some negative comparisons with the superiority formerly enjoyed by his schoolmates, "plus riches ou
plus forts que lui dans leurs classes" 'richer than he or cleverer at their school-
work' (93; 24). But it is misleading to speak of Emma's "own" consciousness. The
next chapter, justly famous for its derision of a vulgarized, retreaded romanticism, begins by listing her readings and the stock of derived enthusiasms that
hold sway over her imagination and that will literally poison her existence:

> Ce n'étaient qu'amours, amants, amantes, dames persécutées s'évanouis-
> sant dans des pavillons solitaires, postillons qu'on tue à tous les relais,
> chevaux qu'on crève à toutes les pages, forêts sombres, troubles du
> coeur, serments, sanglots, larmes et baisers, nacelles au clair de lune,
> rossignols dans les bosquets, *messieurs* braves comme des lions, doux
> comme des agneaux, vertueux comme on ne l'est pas, toujours bien mis,
> et qui pleurent comme des urnes.   (96–97)

> They were all about love, lovers, sweethearts, persecuted ladies fainting
> in lonely pavilions, postilions killed at every relay, horses ridden to death
> on every page, somber forests, heart-aches, vows, sobs, tears and kisses,
> little boatrides by moonlight, nightingales in shady groves, gentlemen
> brave as lions, gentle as lambs, virtuous as no one ever was, always well
> dressed, and weeping like fountains.   (26)

Like all great satirists, Flaubert is a master of the mixed catalog, evidenced
here by his switching back and forth abruptly, and so as if indifferently, between referent ("relay") and text ("page") and between characters, decors,
and moods. By his use of plural nouns, of the present participle ("fainting"
freezes the portrayed emotion, petrifying it), and of absolute qualifiers ("all,"
"every," "always"), Flaubert's enumerative sentence translates the presumed
uniqueness of heroic otherness as repetitious artifice; it renders extraordinary
affect as routinized affectation—as just the opposite, in a word, of what such

expe riences are supposed to be, of what Emma takes them to be: a superior form of existence.

Everything in this chapter concerns the way in which singularity is serialized, stereotyped, and broadcast in a fashion that heralds the mendacities of what we call our media age, a term designating the ascendancy of images over individuals. Even Emma's suicide is undertaken out of a "transport d'héroïsme" 'an ecstasy of heroism' (388; 229), and her grotesque death agony is accompanied by symbolic reminders of its literary origin in the "affreux goût d'encre" 'frightful taste of ink' (390; 230) caused by the arsenic that will finally pour from her mouth, after her death, as a "flot de liquides noirs . . . comme un vomissement" 'rush of black liquid . . . as if she were vomiting' (406; 342). Flaubert thus exacts a kind of symbolic revenge against all the writings that inform and deform an adolescent imagination. And the novel's critique of mediation, or subjective imitation, thus proceeds apace with a radical interrogation of media, of representation or of language as such.

Our students never fail to appreciate the continuity between Emma's imaginary apprenticeship in her convent school and their own massive exposure to films, television programs, best-selling novels, and magazine advertisements that regale them with variously gorgeous depictions of aesthetic attraction and emotional gratification. As Eric Gans argues cogently in his monograph on *Madame Bovary*, Emma is the prototype of the modern consumer, the purchaser who, by deferred payment for a host of discretionary commodities, is promised a better life and exceptional standing among one's peers (47–51). Her being a provincial foreshadows our thoroughly suburbanized culture, whose capital cities serve chiefly to furnish a roster of desirable effigies.

Even our cult of the automobile in a supremely mobile society is presaged by Emma's multifarious peregrinations, her constant sojourns to and from Rouen in the *Hirondelle* for shopping and trysting. Her alcove escapism—and ours—is caricatured in her seduction by Léon in a cab, where her vacillation is overcome by the prestige of a Parisian model:

—Ah! Léon! . . . Vraiment . . . je ne sais . . . si je dois . . .
Elle minaudait. Puis d'un air sérieux:
—C'est très inconvenant, savez-vous?
—En quoi? répliqua le clerc. Cela se fait à Paris!
Et cette parole, comme un irrésistible argument, la détermina.   (316)

"Oh Léon! Truly . . . I don't know . . . if I should . . ."
She simpered. Then, in a serious tone:
"It's very improper, you know, it isn't done."
"Everybody does it in Paris!" replied the clerk.
This, like a decisive argument, entirely convinced her.   (176)

The same phrasing characterizes Emma's surrender to Rodolphe's earlier siege, as her resistance to going riding with him is vanquished by the prospect of a suitable outfit: "L'amazone la décida" 'The riding outfit decided her' (224; 113). In both cases Flaubert's ironically concise syntax portrays Emma not as an active subject of desire, not as an autonomous agent of decision, but as the object of a decision that is mediated by an image, a costume, a preestablished role.

Flaubert's psychology, though he shares it with other great novelists, is properly revolutionary for the way it overturns traditional conceptions of subjectivity. For we normally conceive the subject as the source of reflections and choices made about objects and persons external to it, and we judge it accordingly. The canonical structure of subject and object is what Flaubert's novel literally deconstructs by its ubiquitous detection of the role of mediation, modeling, mimesis.

And middling, as in middle class. For Flaubert's psychology is of a piece with his sociology and his semiology, his study of sign systems, as he equates the triumphal expansion of the bourgeoisie with the proliferation of media, of which the pharmacist Homais is the paragon. Homais is the little man (as signaled by the diminutive *-ais*), the irrepressibly up-and-coming man as liberated by the nonsensical formula "les immortels principes de '89" (142; 55) (if immortal, how do we date them?). He is the eminently public man (by contrast with Emma's deluded cult of private, personal emotions) who would make a name for himself (he has no first name in the novel, and even his children are named for official values [154; 63]) by his dedication to publicity, self-advertising, and journalism. As a pharmacist, he is neither scientist nor physician but a middling, meddling blend of the two, whom we may neologize as the amalgam for all that his success owes to the *bêtise* with which Flaubert identifies modern culture and for all that *bêtise* betokens of an incongruous fusion of elements.

Bêtise as a heterogeneous mix is elsewhere emblematized by the "composite order" of Charles's hat (62; 2); by Emma's wedding cake, a Disneyesque concoction of three tiers representing classical, medieval, and romantic-pastoral styles (88; 20); and of course by Emma's romantic schooling. Flaubert provides an objective correlative of *bêtise* in Yonville-l'Abbaye itself, a double-named (non)district—"a mongrel land"—situated at the confines of other regions; its sandy, rocky soil requires excessive manure (134; 49), a persistent motif in the novel. From Homais's runaway chemical analysis of his region's atmosphere in the next chapter, we learn that its "faisceau" 'bundle' of natural elements and animal exhalations engenders "miasmes insalubres" 'poisonous fumes' (145; 57).

The pervasiveness of *bêtise* is such that we cannot define it, for there is almost nothing with which to contrast it. We cannot translate it simply as stupidity, as Flaubert's translators are nonetheless condemned to do, for it is precisely as a nonsimple quality, as lacking in essence or discrete properties, that it obsesses Flaubert's conception of modern culture. Françoise Gaillard (215) and Claude Perruchot (255) alike describe it as the other's share of the self. Its emblem is written language, which is why Homais's garrulous appearance in the novel is heralded by a description of his house as one that, "du haut en bas, est placardé d'inscriptions écrites en anglaise, en ronde, en moulée" 'is plastered from top to bottom with inscriptions written in longhand, in round, in lower case' (136; 51). A series of twelve items importantly designates products to the pharmacist: "Eaux de Vichy, de Seltz et de Barèges, robs dépuratifs, médecine Raspail, racahout des Arabes, pastilles Darcet, pâte Regnault, bandages, bains, chocolats de santé, etc." ("Vichy, Seltzer and Barrège waters, depurative gum drops, Raspail patent medicine, Arabian racahout, Darcet lozenges, Regnault ointment, trusses, baths, laxative chocolate, etc."). To the reader they designate words. They symbolize representation, the prestige of naming rather than material realities. (Laxatives come last for reasons I discuss below.) The paragraph concludes with a twofold repetition of the proper name, "Homais, in gold letters," together with labels—"Pharmacist," "Laboratory"—that testify to the glory of classification.

Homais is the true man of letters in his new historicized form, incarnate in the letter itself as it symbolizes for Flaubert what it meant to Plato, Rousseau, and Saussure: mindless repetition, thoughtless duplication, mechanical reproduction (which is the original sense of cliché as photographic replica) (Derrida, *Of Grammatology* 46–65). In its mute opacity and elemental insignificance, the letter, the material sign, is the archetype of routinized formulation, of conventional, unreflective, unoriginal, and therefore strictly irresponsible conception—of received ideas, in a word, whose *Dictionnaire* Flaubert compiled during his whole adult life. The printed sign insistently reiterating the proper name served Flaubert as the mark and the model of arbitrary and therefore imperious determination, delimitation, and definition by which what we call experience or reality suffered progressive impoverishment (see Gaillard, esp. 208–10). The author of *Madame Bovary*, and still more of *L'éducation sentimentale* and *Bouvard et Pécuchet*, saw this process of semiosis as a destitution or degradation proceeding apace with what the bourgeois hailed as progress: cultural artifice devolving as ossified, senseless artifact.

Flaubert's reading of culture intersects here with the poststructuralist interrogation of language as we find it in Jacques Derrida's *Of Grammatology* (esp. 27–73), where attention to writing, to the meaningless and arbitrarily instituted trace, instigates a crisis of meaning in terms of the crisis of difference between origin and copy, first and second, or presence and representation. The letter no more imitates or naturally represents a sound than a sound or phoneme imitates or conforms to the meaning(s) that we conventionally invest in it or its combinations. The arbitrariness of meaning is accordingly analogous to and symbolized by the witless materiality of the letter, which therefore—and here is the paradox, the logical scandal—truly represents organized meaning in its untraceable origin, its unfounded career.

Deconstruction, as it questions the oppositions between signifier and signified at the level of the sign, between writing and speech at the level of language, between speech and phenomena or representation and reality at the level of experience, is not an arcane puzzle machine. Rather, it functions significantly as a critique of difference and of the hierarchical levels inspired and legitimized by conventional oppositions: spiritual versus material, ideal versus real, depth versus surface, true versus false—in short, all the differences so dear to Emma (and her readers). Flaubert's critique of romantic difference is properly deconstructive when it traces difference to a selfsame and irrepressible *bêtise*, to undifferentiated repetition. In this sense, as Naomi Schor points out (*Breaking* 12), Homais is much more the symbolic foil, the antithetical double of Emma, even down to the symmetry of their names: Emma/Homais, by contrast with the consonantal density of Charles, who can barely pronounce his name at the beginning of the novel, while Homais "avait toujours des expressions congruentes à toutes les circonstances imaginables" 'always found expressions that filled all imaginable circumstances' (201; 96).

Though Flaubert is neither a linguist nor an anthropologist (except perhaps in a deeper, truer sense), he is party to this poststructuralist sense of language and meaning when he introduces Homais via a worship of letters, names, taxonomies. In his very garrulity, Homais personifies *bêtise* as a crisis of difference between meaning and nonmeaning, between signifying origin and inane repetition, between intelligence and stupidity. It is a crisis with which Flaubert identified all of bourgeois culture and with which poststructuralism has identified all of language itself. The contradiction of the new man, the neo-man—the self-made man embodied in Homais's devotion to books, to writing, to letters and their journalistic proliferation—corresponds to the self-contradiction of a trace without an origin (of which it is the trace), the anomaly of a copy without a source, an echo without an originating voice, a repetition without a beginning.

Paradoxically, it is mediation and repetition that constitute the deep structure, the profoundly hollow foundation of this novel. This is doubtless why it jumps in medias res, with Charles entering between the headmaster and a school servant. Charles's first words in the novel issue in a stuttering attempt to pronounce his name, which arouses the mocking hilarity of his schoolmates and is grasped by the teacher only when it is spelled out and written down—a chore that nets him the punitive assignment of copying *ridiculus sum* twenty times. (If we are in a Latin class, it is because of the author's burgeoning sense that French will come to share the fate of Latin as a dead language, destined to survive only in writing.) Charles's last words in the novel also amount to a stutter, the "grand mot" he utters to Rodolphe being a clumsy echo of his wife's amorous correspondence: "C'est la faute de la fatalité" 'Fate is to blame' (424; 255); trans. modified by eds.). The uncomely proximity of the two causes fatality to lose its grandeur in its approximation to inarticulate noise.

This obsession with repetition also explains why, as Michal Ginsburg points out, there is something secondhand about everything in *Madame Bovary* (*Flaubert Writing* 85). Emma is Charles's second wife; she has two love affairs; the first is followed by a near-fatal illness that foreshadows her ghastly demise, after which Homais and the curate Bournisien resume a dispute sparked by Homais after Emma's convalescence (2.14). Even her wake briefly evokes a micro-instance of the novel's problematic of difference:

—Lisez Voltaire! disait l'un; lisez d'Holbach, lisez l'*Encyclopédie*!
—Lisez les *Lettres de quelques juifs portugais*! disait l'autre; lisez la *Raison du Christianisme*, par Nicolas, ancient magistrat!   (405)

"Read Voltaire," said the one, "read D'Holbach, read the *Encyclopédie*!"
"Read the 'Letters of some Portuguese Jews,' " said the other; "read 'The Meaning of Christianity,' by the former magistrate Nicolas." (241)

Difference obtains at the level of content or substance—theological versus enlightenment-humanist authority—but it is submerged, vacated by the identical form of enunciation. Flaubert's use of indefinite pronouns ("the one," "the other") reinforces the strict nonentity of antagonists.

This dissolution of substance is in every sense spectacularly exercised in the scene at the agricultural fair—though in essence it is only an amplified reorchestration of Emma's first meeting with Léon at the inn at Yonville. In both scenes the exchange of romantic commonplaces is framed and punctuated by a discourse—Homais's at the inn, the orators' at the fair—that at once contradicts and complements the amorous dialogue. Everything in *Madame Bovary* is testimony to boundary collapse, to an erosion of difference that Albert Thibaudet describes as "le grotesque triste" 'the cheerless grotesque' pervading Flaubert's work (199).

At the agricultural fair Flaubert's play with structure is deliberate and thematic, and it may rightly be considered as the centerpiece of the novel (being located in chapter 8 of 15, in part 2). Ineptitude is the prevailing motif throughout. The national guard is borrowed from a neighboring community. There is a false alert of officialdom's arrival—in a rented landau. "The feast was long, noisy, ill-served"; the fireworks figuring a dragon, having been stowed for safety in a damp cellar, "failed completely" (219; 109). A difference of levels of discourse, in terms of high and low, soul and body or human and animal, is literalized by Rodolphe's leading Emma to a place in the town hall overlooking the public speeches and distribution of awards taking place below, and Rodolphe himself exploits this difference in denouncing "the morality of small men" (211; 104). But the thematic difference between amorous and agricultural discourse is complicated, compromised, and made problematic by the way the two levels echo and correspond to each other. Both are seduction scenes: the state woos and flatters the populace with metaphors no less trite and jumbled—"the chariot of the state amidst the incessant perils of a stormy sea" (208; 102)—than Rodolphe's blandishments about dreams, treasures, and "the blue heavens that give us light" (211; 104). Against the speaker's all-embracing praise of the government in "peace as well as war, industry, commerce, agriculture and the fine arts" (208; 102) reverberates Rodolphe's sweeping claim for the passions as "the source of heroism, of enthusiasm, of poetry, music, the arts, in a word, of everything" (211; 104). As the animals below move closer to the grandstand, mixing their lowing and bleating with audible fragments of the oration, Rodolphe moves closer to Emma, evoking their attraction "in some previous state of existence" (215; 107) while the second speaker cites examples of civilization from antiquity.

Beginning with this second speech, Flaubert eliminates the blank spaces separating ostensibly rival discourses, public and private, civic and sentimental. He further accelerates the counterpoint by casting this address entirely in free indirect discourse, which, here as elsewhere in the novel, is a means of evidencing the stale, derived nature of thought and speech. The absence of quotes and of attribution to a speaker connotes a more fundamental absence of subjective identity; it suggests that we do not speak for ourselves but, rather, are spoken for by the surrounding culture. The deconstructive word for this indeterminate "sourcery" is *undecidability*, which interests us not as a logical impasse but as a sociohistorical reality affecting so-called selves (see Perruchot 277). Indeterminacy is a rhetorical strategy that Dominick LaCapra, among others, ranks as one of Flaubert's most radical gestures in undermining bourgeois individualism, the illusion of a self-possessed ego as master of its own mind and wishes. It is to this archly modern delusion that Girard opposes his notion of "interdividuality," designating the nonlinear, mediated route of our ideas and desires (*Things* 283–91).

The erasure of individual identity reaches its formal and thematic climax in the ensuing syncopation, which interlaces the distribution of prizes with Rodolphe's fawning solicitations, where direct discourse without attribution has the same effect of isolating and alienating words from their speaking source (215; 107). The concatenation of numbers, which are pure signifiers, empty signs, binds indissolubly two discourses whose substance is recycled waste material, a notion that, as Flaubert's correspondence testifies insistently, epitomizes his view of his culture (*Correspondance*, ed. Bruneau, 1: 708; 2: 244, 517, 600).

And it goes on this way; a moment later we read:

> —Oh! non, n'est-ce pas, je serai quelque chose dans votre pensée, dans votre vie?
> —Race porcine, prix *ex aequo* . . .   (216)

> "—But no, tell me there can be a place for me in your thoughts, in your life, can't there?"
> "Hog! first prize equally divided . . ."   (107)

The Latinate dignity pursued by officialdom functions as an unconscious parody of romantic evasion, while *ex aequo* translates, in a dead language, as the substantial equivalence of competing levels—in sum, a loss of differences as comical as our culture's panicky efforts to mark and market them.

Teaching *Madame Bovary* through Film

Mary Donaldson-Evans

In *The Perpetual Orgy*, Mario Vargas Llosa's book-length ode to *Madame Bovary*, the author states that his first contact with Flaubert's famous novel was cinematographic:

> It was 1952, a stifling hot summer night. . . . James Mason appeared as Flaubert; Louis Jourdan, tall and svelte, was Rodolphe Boulanger; and Emma Bovary took on visible form by way of the nervous movements and gestures of Jennifer Jones. I couldn't have been terribly impressed because the film didn't cause me to rush out and hunt up a copy of the book, despite the fact that it was at precisely this period in my life that I'd begun to stay up nights devouring novels like a cannibal.
>
> (*L'orgie* 9; trans. mine)

The film version that served as Vargas Llosa's introduction to *Madame Bovary*—there have been eight in all—was directed by Vincente Minnelli in 1949. Along with Jean Renoir's 1934 adaptation, it was, until the Chabrol *Bovary* appeared in 1991, the best known of the adaptations, not because it was the most faithful to the text (quite the contrary) but because it was simply a good film. Today this black-and-white film stands as a period piece, offering modern viewers a revealing glimpse of American attitudes in the late 1940s (Wagner 253).

For several years now, I have been using the videotape of this film (widely available in video stores) to teach Flaubert's novel to undergraduates at the

University of Delaware. The idea of pairing films and novels was initially part of a literature-in-translation project that was not terribly successful. While the course never failed to "carry," it did not attract the large enrollments for which such courses aim, and I was forced to draw two conclusions: students do not as a rule like to see film adaptations of novels they have read, and most of today's students, spoiled by Hollywood's sophisticated special effects, are intolerant of earlier filming techniques. *Gervaise*, René Clément's 1956 adaptation of Zola's *L'assommoir*, seemed interminable to them. Subtitles added another element of frustration: students' reaction was not unlike that of Mallory on the TV sitcom *Family Ties*, who, on learning that her parents are taking her to see a foreign film, moans, "Oh no! You mean it's a movie we have to *read*?" The one notable exception to this disappointing state of affairs was Minnelli's adaptation of *Madame Bovary*. For whatever reason—that this adaptation was in English or that it betrayed Flaubert in countless ways—the film generated tremendous excitement, and the animated discussion that followed its viewing contributed to a deeper understanding of Flaubert's novel and a greater appreciation of his achievement.

Mario Vargas Llosa was right: the film does not measure up. Nevertheless, if the order of contact is reversed, its instructive value may be considerable. I have since decided to make the viewing of this film a requirement in the nineteenth-century French novel course, a double-listed course (i.e., open both to MA students and to advanced undergraduates) that is conducted entirely in French. Although a certain understanding of "what novels can do that films can't and vice versa" (to borrow the title of an article by Seymour Chatman) results from the discussion, and although I do present students with a bare-bones introduction to cinematographic techniques so that they have a basic vocabulary with which to discuss the film, the principal goal of this approach is to enhance students' esteem for and comprehension of Flaubert's novel.

Because my syllabus includes five novels (down from the six to seven taught by my predecessor but no doubt still too ambitious), I allocate only three weeks to a discussion of *Madame Bovary*. The class meets once weekly for two and a half hours; as for each of the works discussed, students are expected to have completed their reading of the novel for the first class in the segment. A ten-minute check quiz on the novel's plot and characters ensures that most of them will have done so. The first class begins with a brief (twenty-minute) introduction to Flaubert in which I emphasize those elements of his biography that seem particularly relevant to this novel (i.e., the medical environment of his youth, the *Madame Bovary* trial). This introduction, together with the quiz, leaves two hours for a general discussion of the novel. We start by discussing the title: Who is Mme Bovary? How many Mme Bovarys are there in the novel? Why did Flaubert choose this title rather than *Emma*, for example? Once we have established the heroine's problematic identity and the importance of the number three, we move on to the novel's structure: Why the tripartite division? What are the principal episodes in each part? To which of

Emma's three men does each part correspond? These questions in turn lead to a discussion of characters and character, of which the most animated part, of course, concerns Emma herself. We reflect on her illusions and their source in her youthful readings and convent education, we discuss the three B's (*Bovarysme, bêtise, bourgeoisie*), and, in this context, we also examine the bourgeois monarchy of Louis Philippe, which provides the temporal context for the novel. During this contextualization, I usually find it necessary to elucidate a few other matters: the status and function of the *officier de santé*; the practice, in certain milieus, of sending one's child to a wet nurse; and the prescribed role of women in nineteenth-century French provincial society. Following this introduction, we consider the novel's numerous oppositions and their figuration (religion versus science, illusion versus reality, Romanticism versus realism, etc.). We conclude by contemplating the various interpretations that have been accorded Flaubert's famous statement "Madame Bovary, c'est moi." Essentially, then, the initial discussion focuses on plot, setting, characters, principal themes, and, in a general sense, structure. We reserve discussion of symbols, individual scenes (such as the Vaubyessard ball or the agricultural fair), narrative technique, and style for the second class.

At the conclusion of the first class, a pre-viewing questionnaire is distributed. Students are asked to imagine that they are making a film of *Madame Bovary*. Whom would they cast in the principal roles? Since the only French actor with whom most American students are familiar is Gérard Depardieu, who, despite his versatility, is too well known and too charismatic for any of the male leads, they tend to select American or British actors and actresses. This is not a problem. The important thing is to get them to consider the dominant traits, whether physical or moral, of each of the major characters and to decide who, among contemporary screen stars, could best represent these traits. Students, amazed to discover how much they differ in the way they "see" the various characters, come to appreciate the reader's active role in creating meaning. I am not as interested in their final casting (although it sometimes occasions great merriment in the classroom) as I am in getting them to think about the various attributes of the novel's cast of characters. When I ask them to provide five adjectives to describe each of the major characters and then to justify their choice with specific reference to the text, students come quickly to the realization that, with the exception of Larivière, there is hardly a likable character in this novel and, moreover, that it is by showing, rather than telling, that Flaubert reveals character. The students have thus been exposed to one of the hallmarks of realistic technique, while at the same time encouraged to believe, as many have before them, that *Madame Bovary* literally (no pun!) begs to be adapted to the screen, where showing is telling.

I then ask them to consider another of the film director's tasks: editing. Since a novel of this magnitude will obviously have to be condensed for the demands of the screen, students must decide which of its episodes and characters may be eliminated with the least damage to its integrity. For each episode or character they propose to remove, they are to consider its function (symbolic, narrative, etc.) in the novel and then justify the ellipsis. Finally, I ask the students to identify the particular challenges in adapting this novel to film and to suggest how a director might meet them. To give them firsthand experience in dealing with these challenges, I ask them to write the scenario of a specific scene.

The questionnaire, distributed at the end of the first class and completed at home, provides the basis for discussion during the second class meeting. I invite two or three students to present their scenarios, an exercise that inevitably results in a discussion of how difficult it would be to render Emma's thoughts and dreams. We then proceed to analyze selected passages of the novel. The purpose of this exercise is to get students to appreciate the salient aspects of Flaubert's style, most notably his lexical precision, his predilection for the imperfect tense, his narrative technique, his use of irony. I generally choose paragraphs from the wedding, the ball scene, the agricultural fair, and the clubfoot operation. For example, the paragraph describing Emma's observation of the old duc de Laverdière at the Vaubyessard ball serves well as an introduction to Flaubert's use of free indirect style; the passage describing the discovery of Hippolyte's tumefied leg illustrates the author's ironic stance. This exercise is not unrelated to the previous one, since once students have understood the effects of these techniques (for example, the use of the imperfect to convey the idea of ennui), they must ask themselves how similar effects might be achieved visually. To solve such problems, they must have some familiarity with cinematographic techniques. Thus, the last half hour of this class meeting is spent on an introduction to film theory, an area in which I have little expertise but which can be adequately prepared for the needs of this course thanks to such excellent source materials as the works of Jean Mitry and Robert Withers. Here, the goal is to get students to reflect on the role of the camera (which has sometimes been likened to that of the narrator in the literary medium), on problems encountered by filmmakers who seek to adapt literary works to the screen, and on the techniques available to them. We discuss camera angle and distance, the sound track, use of light and shadow, the manipulation of time, and related topics. I distribute a glossary of cinematographic terms (an understanding of such terms as montage, cutting, cross-cutting, fade-out, establishing shot, close-up, flashback, and voice-over is helpful).

The assignment for the third class is to view the film. Again, I distribute a questionnaire and ask students to peruse it before the viewing and to complete it immediately afterward. The questions, which are designed so that "total recall" is not necessary, number about twenty and focus for the most part on points of divergence between novel and film. Students are asked to comment on the casting, on Minnelli's deletions of characters and scenes, on the ways in which he alters the basic facts and chronology of the novel, and on the techniques he uses to render Emma's thoughts. I single out a few scenes (e.g., the first meeting between Emma and Charles, the wedding, the Vaubyessard ball, the death scene) for closer attention.

We devote the last class to a discussion of the film, using the questionnaire as a guide, and to re-viewing certain scenes on videotape. Minnelli's adaptation, which takes great liberty with Flaubert's novel, frames Emma's story not with a "before" and "after" picture of Charles but with scenes from Flaubert's trial. After listening to the charges that his novel is immoral and his heroine "a disgrace to France and an insult to womanhood," Flaubert himself (played by James Mason) takes the stand to defend Emma (and thus himself), presenting her as a "kitchen drudge who dreamed of love and beauty," a description that seems more relevant to Cinderella than to Emma Bovary. In addition to considering the accuracy or inaccuracy of the epithet, students ponder why Minnelli may have wished to adopt this framing device. How does it alter the spectator's reception of the novel? Would Flaubert have approved? Why or why not? Did Flaubert frame Emma's story? If so, how? What is the effect of Flaubert's frame, as opposed to Minnelli's? It has been said that Minnelli's strategy was in fact intended to mollify the censors, still zealous in 1949 where tales of adultery were concerned (Harvey 200). Whether or not this is true, the device serves an important technical purpose, for when the courtroom scene fades and is replaced by the arrival of Charles at the Rouault farm, the voice-over has been firmly established: Flaubert thus becomes in this version an omniscient, highly subjective narrator. Students are invited to reflect on this narrative perspective and to compare it to that of the novel. The continual back-and-forth movement from novel to film does far more than to yield a bland "I liked the book better." Only after considering the effect of a narrative strategy such as that used by Minnelli do students come to a full realization of the indeterminacy bred by Flaubert's brilliantly composite narration. If they missed the significance of free indirect style when it was discussed earlier, they invariably reach an understanding of it at this point.

Students are positively indignant when it comes to Minnelli's casting and directing. If all the male leads are portrayed as "too nice," Charles in particular is seen as too handsome, too likable, and too lucid (he's fully aware not only of his wife's infidelities but also of his own limitations). His decision, in Minnelli's version, *not* to perform the clubfoot operation is seen as the ultimate betrayal. We then must examine why Minnelli made such a change. What is the function of the surgical fiasco in the novel? How does it reveal character? Does it alter the course of events? Is it symbolic? Does it bear a relation to other scenes? Another of Minnelli's alterations, collapsing the viscount and Rodolphe into one character, leads us to discuss the value of repetition in the novel and Emma's quest for love's incarnation, which takes her from Charles to the blind beggar (also missing from the film), that supremely ironic figure who replaces all the others and who follows (chronologically) an evocation of the crucified Christ, on whose effigy Emma plants her last kiss.

Discussion of Minnelli's ball scene, considered to be one of the greatest set pieces in the history of film, provides an opportunity to discuss ways in which the visual medium can successfully render mood and feeling with little dialogue.

The use of camera angle, the sound track, and the panning to represent Emma's dizziness are particularly noteworthy. Although students tend to find this scene a bit long, they readily admit that Emma's enthrallment and Charles's discomfiture are artfully revealed. This observation paves the way for a more general consideration of the role of contrast in the novel and the ways in which the film does or does not succeed in representing it. We turn then to a consideration of the scene of Emma's agony and death, heavily romanticized by Minnelli. Concluding remarks emphasize Flaubert's achievement and his place in the history of the novel.

Had Mario Vargas Llosa read *Madame Bovary* before viewing the film, he would probably have been even more unimpressed by the latter. It is a truism that novels possess more authority than their film adaptations. It has also been said that great novels make mediocre films (although such successes as *Dangerous Liaisons* suggest that this is no longer necessarily true). Still, the eternally seductive *Madame Bovary* continues to tempt filmmakers, and 1991 saw the appearance of a new cinematographic adaptation, that of Claude Chabrol. Widely acclaimed as the most faithful of the adaptations to date (Desmond Ryan contrasts Chabrol's fidelity to Flaubert with "Emma Bovary's flexible loyalty to her cloddish husband"), it is also, in the view of many reviewers, suffocatingly literal. The following contribution to the "Metropolitan Diary" feature of the *New York Times* offers amusing (if somewhat disturbing) testimony to what I regard as the film's failure to do justice to the novel:

> The scene: the Angelika movie theater, where the feature is the new French language version of "Madame Bovary." As the lights go down, neighbors hear two female voices in the row behind them.
>
> "I remember reading the book even before I knew what adultery was," one of the women said. "Maybe even before I knew what passion was."
>
> The house lights dim; the movie begins. Some 130 minutes later, the film is over. The woman speaks again.
>
> "I'd also forgotten how boring the book was," she said.   (Alexander)

I have taught *Madame Bovary* many times. Students who must read it in French often remark on the tedium of the reading process itself, which necessitates constant use of a dictionary. Occasionally, they also complain about the unrelenting pessimism of Flaubert's view of humanity, and they do not always relate well to the heroine. But boring? This is not a criticism that one hears often.

Chabrol's film has become readily available for the classroom since its recent release on videotape. Having seen the film twice in the theater, I have taken careful note of its strengths and weaknesses, its fidelities and betrayals, and I am prepared—experimentally—to substitute this film for the Minnelli version. Here, too, we would begin with a discussion of the casting. The choice of Isabelle Huppert to play Emma has proved controversial, despite Chabrol's ardent conviction that Huppert was Emma's "incarnation idéale" ("ideal incarnation") (Boddaert, Biasi, et al. 25). Movie critics, especially on this side of the Atlantic, have been less enthusiastic, not only because she is fair (one might ask students to locate a physical description of Emma in the novel and to discuss whether or not conformity to such descriptions is important), but because her own reading of the heroine as a protofeminist (Boddaert, Biasi, et al. 127) colors her interpretation. Characterized by Vincent Canby as "imperious and . . . frosty, so level-headed and so in command that it seems impossible that she could mess up her life with such wanton and short-sighted thoroughness," Huppert's Emma tends to leave the spectator cold. Would Flaubert have approved? To what extent is the reader invited to identify with the heroine—or with any other character, for that matter? What steps did he take to ensure the reader's noninvolvement? Is Huppert's characterization of Emma as a feminist valid?

Like Minnelli, Chabrol regards *Madame Bovary* as Emma's story; his adaptation begins with Charles's arrival at the farm and draws to a close almost immediately after her death. All the details of the health officer's youth and education are hence suppressed, as is his reading of Rodolphe's letters and his meeting with his wife's first lover. Chabrol manages to salvage a few of the most famous moments from the deleted passages; for example, it is when Emma says, "Je voudrais savoir votre nom, docteur" ("I would like to know your name, doctor"), that Charles replies, "Charbovari," and it is to those assembled around Emma's bed that he laments, "C'est la fatalité" ("It's fate!"). One might ask students why Chabrol may have felt it necessary to include these comments and to what extent the decontextualization is or is not successful. In this connection, since Chabrol's attention to detail is remarkable, students may well notice things in the film that they failed to retain from their reading of the novel. As in the novel, Emma pricks her finger twice in the film; black liquid oozes from Hippolyte's gangrenous leg and from the dead Emma's mouth; the mirror is evoked in countless scenes. Such details are part of the novel's symbolic structure, and students should be asked to interpret them. This exercise inevitably leads back and forth between novel and film: for example, the ink-black bile issuing from Emma's mouth has been interpreted as part of a complex network of images linking Emma to the writer (Wing 41), but Chabrol fails to emphasize this aspect of her role (just as he neglects to insist on Emma as a reader: a far more egregious omission, in my view). Again, students must return to the novel to find the relevant passages.

One of the most famous of *Madame Bovary*'s episodes is that of the agricultural fair. Indeed, Flaubert's technique in this scene—the cross-cutting from one level of action to another—has been described as cinematographic, an early example of "the spatialization of form in a novel" (Frank 15). Students who fail to seize the irony of this incident on a first reading of the novel (as many do) could hardly miss it in the film, where its lack of subtlety makes it almost ludicrous. Nevertheless, a replay of this scene, along with the scene in the Lion d'Or when Emma first meets Léon, could serve to illustrate the link between the motifs of love and commerce, as well as Flaubert's use of irony through contrast and repetition.

If Chabrol makes even more extensive use of voice-over than Minnelli does (the French film includes approximately a dozen interventions of this nature), the words we hear are those of the text itself, drawn from the novel's most celebrated passages. In addition to highlighting and discussing the passages that Chabrol felt compelled to include, one could ask students to consider the purpose of these narrative interventions in the film and their effect. By what other means does Chabrol render Emma's thoughts? Minnelli (and Flaubert) used flashback to present Emma's background, whereas Chabrol observes a strict linear progression. What is the effect of this decision? Other subjects for discussion might be the representation of Yonville (critics find it too picturesque), the reduction of the opera scene to a mere pretext for the encounter with Léon, the elimination of the highly sexualized sacrament of extreme unction, and the diminished importance of the religion-versus-science dispute between Homais and Bournisien.

I am far from certain that Chabrol's interpretation will awaken as much interest as Minnelli's does. Because it remains so close to the text, because it relies so heavily on language to convey Emma's boredom and the mediocrity of provincial life, it may simply bore students. Conversely, with Minnelli's highly unfaithful version, there is always the danger that they will recall the film rather than the novel. Perhaps, as my colleague Barbara Cooper has suggested, one could make judicious use of both films by showing excerpts from each one in the classroom and then asking students to compare them and to discuss their effectiveness. Clearly, the availability of Chabrol's film on videotape will modify my approach, and I may well substitute it for the Minnelli version as the definitive film for this class, showing only excerpts of the earlier film. But whichever version I use, I will continue to teach *Madame Bovary* through film, not only because it brings students to a deeper appreciation of the subtleties of Flaubert's art but because it awakens them to the evocative powers of the written word. To persuade members of this visually oriented (some would say "vidiot") generation of literature's value is not the least achievement of such an approach.

Reading Realist Literature: *Madame Bovary* in a Great Books or World Literature Course

Monika Brown

"It's like real life," our students say of *Madame Bovary*. Flaubert's masterpiece still rings true, from Emma's sentimental scheming and Charles's passive acceptance to the atmosphere of provincial isolation and limited choices, of dreams pursued and crushing disappointments. Familiarity of milieu engages students with Flaubert's text as printed (in Paul de Man's or, as of the 1992 edition, Francis Steegmuller's translation) in the *Norton Anthology of World Masterpieces*, volume 2 (Mack et al.). At Pembroke State University, founded as a normal school for Native Americans and now a triracial branch of the University of North Carolina, *Madame Bovary* is taught in World Literature 2 as the center of a four-week unit on nineteenth-century realism. In this course sophomores and juniors read great books mainly of the Western tradition, deepen their appreciation of literary art, relate readings to other areas of knowledge, and examine what Mortimer J. Adler terms "persistent unanswerable questions" and "basic ideas and issues" (333) in post-Renaissance cultures and in their lives. Early units on the Enlightenment and Romanticism introduce classics of comedy, tragedy, fiction, and lyric poetry. In the unit on realism, *Madame Bovary* is compared with works of contemporary autobiography, drama, and poetry to reveal special features of nineteenth-century realism, including its relation to democratic pluralism.

Class activities in World Literature 2 are adapted to a student population of whom half are in the first generation to attend college, one-quarter are nontraditional (that is, older) students, and one-third are minorities. A typical class of twenty-five to thirty includes a high proportion of prospective teachers and a majority that finds literature intimidating. As students engage with literary classics, they practice four approaches to reading: for personal and aesthetic responses, for literal and thematic understanding, for critical analysis and interpretation, and for evaluation and applying wider contexts (see Hart; Milner). Open-ended assignments, supplemented by audiovisual materials and research reports, prepare both inexperienced readers and English majors to appreciate literature on their own.

Before we begin the unit on realism that *Madame Bovary* dominates, World Literature 2 has exposed students to two broad varieties of realism. Realism as mimesis, representation in artistic form of human experiences, informs the entire course. Along with Robert Alter, I affirm that "at a time when several schools of criticism have come to regard mimesis as a sham or an impossibility, the persuasive representation of reality in an artistic medium answers a deep human need and provides profound and abiding delight in itself" (92). Literary theories that explode representation are saved for the unit on modernism. When literature reflects Adler's persistent unanswerable questions, literary study involves realism as mimesis; in Harry Levin's words, "all great writers, in so far as they are committed to a searching and scrupulous critique of life as they know it, may be reckoned among the realists" (83). Many class assignments connect literature and experience.

Realism is also an artistic mode that creates for viewers or readers an impression of lived experience. Among its literary variations, which Erich Auerbach traces from the Bible to *Ulysses*, are common features worth introducing in class. As George Levine explains, realism "always implies an attempt to use language to get beyond language, to discover some nonverbal truth out there" (6). Realist fiction thus achieves, according to David Lodge's definition, "the representation of experience in a manner which approximates closely to descriptions of similar experience in nonliterary texts of the same culture" (qtd. in Levine 8). The philosopher Nelson Goodman's *Of Mind and Other Matters* helps students understand that several characteristics make fiction realistic: a fiction can be a "real-object story," whose characters and events could exist; a story (even with fantastic subjects) may exhibit "metaphorical truth," a connection with "real objects" at a deeper level of shared characteristics or themes; or a fiction may suggest reality by a "familiar mode of representation": chronological sequence, logic of cause and effect, and consistency of characters (123–30, 59–65). The critic Marshall Brown, using similar categories (minute particulars, recognizable universals, and cause-effect connections), points out that these "realities" may contradict one another (228–30). For Brown, realism balances oppositions by "silhouetting," a shifting of foreground and background that also shapes realist plots (which interweave description and action, individuals and groups) as well as realist form and style (which juxtapose specification and the indefinite, "symbolisms and literalisms," universals and particulars) (230–33). And in the post-Renaissance literature we study, the dialectic of realism ultimately affirms the value of individual human lives—by recognizing, in Terrence Doody's words, "the essentially equal but contending claims that issue from, and yet also bind together, the self and the world, the author and his work, one character and another, the narrator and the reader, readers and their experiences" (92–93).

The four-week unit on nineteenth-century realism is designed for two seventy-five-minute classes per week but also works well with three fifty-minute periods.

Week 1: Autobiography as facts, truths, and literary art. Frederick Douglass, *Narrative of the Life of a Slave*. Realistic novel: Gustave Flaubert, *Madame Bovary*. Major characters, background, relationship: part 1, chapters 1–7.

Week 2: Environment and character: part 1, chapter 8–part 2, chapter 8. Character development and symbolism: part 2, chapter 9–part 3, chapter 5.

Week 3: Themes and literary art: whole novel. Realist tragedy: Henrik Ibsen, *Hedda Gabler* (film and text).

Week 4: Lyric poetry and the mid-nineteenth-century worldview. Matthew Arnold, "Dover Beach," and Alfred Tennyson, *In Memoriam*, stanzas 27, 54–56. Realism in other contexts: oral reports on authors, works, period, related arts.

The unit begins with an autobiography, Douglass's *Narrative of the Life of a Slave*. For the basic facts of Douglass's life, we look to a biography, as found in the textbook introduction. While reading *Narrative*, each student focuses on Douglass's life story, the main character, or the settings (including secondary characters). In class, we classify observations into facts about Douglass's life and themes based on his experiences (resembling Goodman's metaphorical truths and Brown's universals). In the close reading activity that follows, small groups analyze a paragraph or two, identifying facts, thematic insights, and stylistic features. Students find that in Douglass's most affecting descriptions—of his aunt's whipping, his white mistress's corruption by the institution of slavery, and his struggle to become a reader—factual details and insights on the human condition are expressed by powerful words and images as well as crafted sentences whose parallelism and antitheses echo the King James Bible. We discuss how Douglass's thematic intentions and literary strategies may distort his facts and how religious and literary conventions of European American culture may undermine his African American identity. Had he written for court testimony or a news story, he might have remained more faithful to the facts, but only at great sacrifice of the dramatic impact and deeper truths that make this classic literary autobiography resemble imaginative literature.

To introduce *Madame Bovary* and the nineteenth century's special variant of the realist mode, I use Goodman's and Brown's categories to remind students that fiction, like autobiography, embodies truths about human experience. If all novelists invent characters, conflicts, and settings, the nineteenth-century realist attempts to create not only what could exist (Goodman's real-object stories and Brown's particulars) but also what could occur in an average, unexceptional life among the lower and middle classes. These fictional truths express insights (Goodman's metaphorical truth and Brown's universals) that recall Douglass's themes. Moreover, nineteenth-century novelists integrate all varieties of realism as identified by Goodman and Brown. Willing to risk, in the service of verisimilitude and a richer texture of reality, contradictions identified by Brown and Levine, realist writers conflate high and low subjects, modes, and styles, creating a medley of particulars, universal symbols, and techniques that evoke lived experience for readers (from Dickens's poetic sympathy to Flaubert's objective craftsmanship). This eclectic realism exhibits the oppositions identified by Brown and Doody as well as the implicit, if not always intended, connection between realism and democratic values that even Flaubert's reviewers recognized.

Our four classes on *Madame Bovary* begin with the fictional but real-object world of story (as distinguished from plot), characters, and setting, move to themes and symbols and then to the literary art with which Flaubert struggled to achieve his effects, so evident in de Man's translations. Using Brown's concept of silhouetting, I alert students not only to features of Flaubert's art but also to the shape our discussions will take, as we by turn foreground and background characters, setting, themes, and artistic choices. If possible, we read aloud the opening pages in class before the first assignment is due; students notice the dense detail, symbolic resonances, ironies, and shifting points of view that will shape their understanding of characters, action, and setting. A brief scene from the 1991 Claude Chabrol film adaptation, showing Emma (Isabelle Huppert) and Charles (Jean-François Balmer) at her father's house, raises the students' curiosity about these characters.

Characters are central to the first session on *Madame Bovary*, which covers most of part 1. As students read, they pay attention to Charles, Emma, and their relationship. After reminding them that realist fiction resembles biography, I ask what sorts of things we notice and learn when we get to know a person as a friend. Students will suggest appearance, dress, voice, personality, likes and dislikes, family background, and education; these particulars lead us to list what we learn about Charles and Emma. We notice that each has qualities to admire and to criticize. We also recognize that, though Emma is more complex, the young hero and heroine have traits in common: if the romantic Emma demands far more from life than Charles, he too has brief episodes of rebellion; if she goes to extremes in pursuing goals, he too makes special efforts. We also discuss early influences—of parents and education—that shaped each character's psychology: Charles's humiliation in school, his domineering mother and first wife, the appreciation of his patients; Emma's loss of her mother, her superficial religious education, and her fascination with sentimental fiction and the lives of social superiors. Next students debate the question "Can this marriage be saved?" They comment on what attracts the couple to each other, why the marriage disappoints Emma, what problems lie at the heart of their difficulties (neither understands the other's desires), and what options were available in that era to an unhappily married woman. Married female students expect Emma to adjust; younger students find that suggestion hard to accept. A look ahead at the bouquet-burning episode (1.9) hints at the likely future of this relationship and allows us to reflect on Flaubert's themes: some fit the novel's place and time; others recall our unit on Romanticism or suggest enduring human problems.

The second session (1.8–2.8) is devoted to the environment, as suggested by the novel's subtitle *Moeurs de province*: the physical and social settings for Emma and Charles's married life. Students select one aspect of provincial life to focus on as they read: the town of Yonville, a symbolic secondary character (Homais as learning and science, Léon as culture, Bournisien as religion, Rodolphe as petty gentry), or a social scene or event (the ball, the Yonville inn, the agricultural fair). Impressions, descriptive details, key passages, and effects on Emma and Charles are shared in small groups. As each group presents findings and reads passages aloud, we reflect on symbolic truths: how constricting and superficial French provincial life appears as Flaubert describes it; how Flaubert illuminates enduring features of petit bourgeois life and ways of thinking, including the population's "stupidity" and attachment to "idées reçues" (Kundera 162–63). Students recognize that Emma's idealized society is shown at the ball to be superficial and corrupt; that Yonville is a town where everything is mediocre; that the pharmacist's vaunted intellect muddles Enlightenment and Romantic clichés and the priest has no interest in souls; that though Emma protests against restrictions in women's lives, a rigid moral code initially protects her from adultery; and that the agricultural fair equates the empty rhetoric of politicians with that of the seducer Rodolphe.

In this class, I talk about French society and politics under the July Monarchy and, using slides, show paintings by Millais and Courbet as well as photographs and nineteenth-century prints of Rouen and the nearby village Ry (possible site of the fictional Yonville). As time allows, I present excerpts from the 1949 Vincente Minnelli film (the ball scene), the Globe Radio Repertory dramatization (the agricultural prizes in polyphony with Rodolphe's wooing), and the 1991 Chabrol film.

Our third class is devoted to character development and symbolic activities during Emma's two love affairs. After reviewing Emma's early friendship with Léon as an illustration of her patterns of behavior, I ask each group of students to discuss one later relationship—the early phase of the Rodolphe affair, the relationship with Charles in connection with his clubfoot operation, the Rodolphe affair after the operation, or the involvement with Léon—noticing aspects such as what activities occur and in what settings, what roles each lover plays, what each gains from the relationship, what problems arise, and what effects the experience has on Emma. Groups also analyze a page or two from an early stage of each relationship, identifying images, metaphors, and allusions that symbolize the relationship and foreshadow its future course: the seduction and Emma's return to her home (2.9), Emma's response to her father's letter and her hopes from the operation (2.10–11), Emma's hopes for escape with Rodolphe (2.12), and the cathedral scene and cab ride (3.1). After group reports, we compare personal qualities Emma exhibits with our first impressions of her character. Through Flaubert's characterization, she remains the romantic pursuer of dreams, even as the new experiences enhance her maturity, her influence over husband and lover, her indulgence in sensuality and deceit, her materialism and selfish greed. Our image of Emma becomes more complex and less sympathetic.

Our class on the whole novel begins with discussion of its major themes. As students finish reading, they reflect on possible answers to the novel's central question, marking passages in the late chapters to support their conclusions. Why does Emma's life take the course it does? Why does she kill herself? Is Emma a victim of circumstances or of a particular character flaw? Is she a tragic heroine or merely a pathetic fool, or, in Jonathan Culler's formulation, "is she foolish woman made tragic heroine or tragic heroine revealed as foolish woman?" (*Flaubert* 140). Students who read most attentively often prefer not to commit themselves, a reaction that Culler attributes to Flaubert's deliberate indeterminacy (138–46). Those who condemn Emma point out that she fails to use wisely those opportunities she is given for improving her life, from friendship with Léon and raising a child to her control over Charles's financial affairs, and that she selfishly abandons husband and child. Emma's sympathizers, often adult women, view her as superior to her surroundings, recognize the severe constraints that society placed on women of her class, applaud her indefatigable efforts to make life fit her ideals, and point to the irony that Charles becomes romantic only after her death. By introducing related contexts—Flaubert's trial for writing an immoral novel, the debate about whether he turned himself into a woman to create Emma or made Emma masculine, and his statement "Madame Bovary, c'est moi"—I help students recognize parallels, in a society dominated by middle-class (male) values, between a discontented woman and an artist who tries, as Flaubert did, to transcend conventions. This parallel is reinforced by the novel's ending, which awards the final sentence to the triumph of Homais.

Finally, we address directly a few features of Flaubert's literary craft. By now students recognize that, as Lilian R. Furst reminds us, the realist novelist is no mere reporter of experiences but an artist who must struggle with "complexities, constraints, and artifices" to make a fictional world believable (21). I explain how seriously Flaubert took his writing, quote from letters about his objectives and struggles to achieve them, show multiple revisions in his printed manuscripts (a passage from the agricultural fair), and display a transparency that shows, in English translation, how carefully Flaubert sketched out, expanded, and then streamlined the paragraph describing the administration of extreme unction (3.8) through four drafts (Maurice 222–25). I introduce Flaubert's varying perspectives on Emma's experiences and emotions, especially the limited omniscient point of view and free indirect speech that create what Alter calls "experiential realism." Here readers follow "the character's pulse beats and perceptions and shifting emotions . . . in the full tide of living from moment to moment" while the narrator retains his own vocabulary, sentence structure, imagery, and "the freedom to ironize, analyze, and judge what is going on in the character" (Alter 185). I comment briefly on Flaubert's techniques for evoking Emma's consciousness, using as examples the dinner table paragraph (1.9) analyzed in Auerbach (482–86), in which the narrator sympathizes with his heroine, and the ironically presented paragraphs (2.9) in which Emma romanticizes her first extramarital encounter. Then students divide into groups to analyze two later sections (both in 3.8). In Emma's emotional trauma after Rodolphe refuses to help with her debts, they find empathic evocation of madness through style, images, similes, and free indirect speech; in her death scene, they notice how direct narration, objective perspective, sound images, similes, and the ironic symbolism of the blind man and his song heighten the horror of Emma's fate even as they distance it from the reader. If time remains, we return to the novel's themes, commenting on the suitability of Flaubert's techniques and on whether close reading has modified our conclusions.

In our next class, students view substantial sections of Ibsen's *Hedda Gabler* in a 1987 Canadian film adaptation starring Susan Clark and a brief excerpt from a 1975 production with Glenda Jackson. As an introduction, I explain that here a fictional heroine's destructive manipulations and descent to despair take an elapsed time of fewer than forty-eight hours, a mere two hours onstage, splendidly illustrating Ibsen's challenges and achievements as the founder of realist drama. In this brief space, Ibsen creates a realist's feel of lived experience: fully formed adult characters and the family background that shaped them, the constraints and opportunities of a social milieu, the dynamics of a lifetime of interaction among five diverse characters, image patterns and symbols that deepen significance, and a believable sequence of dramatically effective events. Ibsen succeeds because he confronts characters with problems that bring out their most powerful personality traits and motives. Groups of students are asked to watch for specific realist features and to notice choices made in casting, staging, and directing; after about twenty minutes, I stop the film to allow comments. Another discussion takes place after we view the film. Hedda, like Emma Bovary, is frustrated by her limitations; an apparently strong character in manipulating the weaknesses of others, Hedda emerges as more repressed than her friend Thea. We also notice that a realist play cannot reproduce the novel's complex interactions between character and society.

We return to *Madame Bovary* in two classes devoted to wider contexts. One session reviews the historical and intellectual situation of nineteenth-century Europe: social and political reforms and imperialism; an expanding scientific worldview; and, in particular, the triumph of such middle-class values as hard work, individualism, the separation of public and private spheres, and ambivalence toward the arts. Drawing on recollections of *Madame Bovary*, we recognize how tenuous "progress" can be and discuss why critics connect the flowering of artistic realism with science, philosophical positivism, and such values as democracy and pluralism. Lyric poems introduce additional themes: "Dover Beach" and selections from *In Memoriam* dramatize the impact of declining religious faith and the fragility of the human bonds and creative efforts that are offered as substitutes.

The unit on realism ends with a class session in which ten to fifteen students present oral reports on aspects of *Narrative of the Life of a Slave, Madame Bovary,* or *Hedda Gabler.* I can organize these reports effectively since students submit written reports in advance. The research report, which I adapted from an assignment used by my colleague Patricia D. Valenti, gives students two options for presenting one or two library sources. The first is a three-hundred-word summary of a critical essay or chapter, followed by a three-hundred-word response to the literary work and the criticism. In oral reports based on this option, students have introduced their classmates to relevant biographical information, to fresh perspectives on major and minor characters, and to sociological, feminist, and structuralist approaches to all three major works. The second option is a three-hundred-word description of a related artwork, film scene, music selection, translation, or other literary work, followed by a three-hundred-word comparison with a related aspect of the work discussed in class. This approach has brought into class reviews of different translations of the novel, realist paintings, and scenes from the films of *Madame Bovary*.

Realism in its nineteenth-century richness still attracts novelists and remains a rewarding topic for literature classes, as Raymond Tallis explains:

> [M]otivated by an unflashy radicalism . . . it takes up the challenge of all literary art most directly and most compendiously: to discover a significant order (or disorder) in common experience; to deepen and shape our sense of reality; and, ultimately, to mediate between the small facts that engage us and the great facts—that we are unoccasioned, that we are transient, that we nonetheless make sense of the world—that enclose us. The writer who faces that challenge does so, as Flaubert did, in solitude, alone with his sense of astonishment, his terror, his joy.   (215)

Facing these challenges, Flaubert's masterpiece draws students into Emma's fictional life and his fictional world. Careful readers recognize that *Madame Bovary* is a "great book" whose characters and experiences express enduring themes even as its art struggles against romanticism, carries realism to one of its climactic realizations, and anticipates modern fiction. And I am gratified as a teacher of humanities when once-intimidated students comment that they now feel confident about reading novels on their own; when a former student uses questions from our handouts to lead informal book-group discussions at home; or when, with local teachers, I attend a library discussion series that includes *Madame Bovary*. After many rereadings it remains for me the classic novel, a delight to rediscover with each new class.

NOTE

This essay draws on a decade of student responses, the writings of Hart and Milner, and much support from colleagues and friends, especially Thomas Leach, Dennis Sigmon, Patricia Valenti, Dana Washington, Sue Fidler, Linda Baker, and Robert Brown. In summer 1992, in the NEH seminar Rereading Realist Fiction under the wise guidance of Lilian Furst, I encountered readings and insights from participants that will inform further development of my unit on realism.

Teaching *Madame Bovary* through Writing
Carol de Dobay Rifelj

> Bad week. Work didn't go; I had reached a point where
> I didn't know what to say. It was all shadings and
> refinements; I was completely in the dark: it is very
> difficult to clarify by means of words what is still obscure
> in your thoughts. I made outlines, spoiled a lot of paper,
> floundered and fumbled. Now I shall perhaps find my
> way again.

No, my epigraph is not the journal entry of a student writing a paper on *Madame Bovary*; it is Flaubert himself on writing *Madame Bovary* (letter to Louise Colet, *Madame Bovary*, ed. de Man, 310). What better model for writing than Flaubert? And what better way to teach Flaubert than through the writing process? Flaubert integrated into his novel the difficulty of putting experience into words: part of Emma's problem is her incapacity to bring language into congruence with reality. She is both a flawed reader and a failed writer: "Les mots lui manquaient donc, l'occasion, la hardiesse" 'Words failed her and, by the same token, the opportunity, the courage' (100; 29). In both writing-intensive courses and general courses on the novel, whether in French or English, writing can provide an effective means of access to *Madame Bovary*. First, it encourages careful reading by concentrating attention on particular aspects of the text; second, it stimulates the conceptual effort necessary to produce a good paper. By integrating into our syllabi the various stages of writing Flaubert alludes to in his letter—clarifying thoughts, preparing outlines, working with drafts, and making "refinements"—we can help our students find their way in *Madame Bovary*.

Writing to Discuss

One way to encourage careful reading before class and to stimulate good discussion during class is to hand out several discussion questions in advance and ask students to prepare a paragraph in response to one of them. Depending on the size of the class and the organization of the course, questions may be assigned for each class, once a week, or once during the sessions on *Madame Bovary*. If students need to work on written French or on paragraph construction, they can hand in their responses for the instructor's comments and corrections, perhaps for a grade, perhaps in preparation for a rewrite. However responses are handled, I have found it useful for students to read them aloud, using them as a means to organize and stimulate class discussion.

Questions may be based on particular sections of the novel, such as the following:

Why does Flaubert begin the novel with the scene of Charles's first day at school?

When do we first have access to Emma's thoughts? What indications do we have of her feelings before that? What is the effect of this delay?

What does the wedding scene show us about the relationship between Emma and Charles? How does Flaubert present it?

What does the ball at Vaubyessard represent in Emma's life?

Does Emma's affair with Léon follow the pattern we have seen in her earlier experiences?

Questions based on the novel as a whole can elicit various points of view:

Flaubert claimed that his poor Madame Bovary, "without a doubt, is suffering and weeping at this very instant in twenty villages of France" (316). To what extent are Emma's problems those of women of her time, place, and social class?

How would you defend Flaubert against the charges of immorality that were brought against the novel?

I also find it useful to suggest as paragraph topics passages to study in detail: for example, the arrival at Yonville, parts of the chapter on the agricultural fair, Emma writing to Léon, passages that use the free indirect style. Another subject to propose is tracing a theme through the novel or the section assigned for a particular day, such as the importance of clothing, reading and writing, or confinement versus movement.

I find it helpful to use the paragraphs as a way to organize class discussions, focusing on several issues each time, guided by the responses students give. For example, in writing on the wedding scene, students will pick up links with many different themes, indications of the relationship between Emma and Charles, and stylistic elements. Some will note the contrast between the wedding Emma had wanted (at midnight, by torchlight) and the one she gets; others study the procession through the field where Emma picks burrs off her gown, the description of the wedding cake, the contrast between Emma's and Charles's reactions the morning after and what it tells us about their sexual relationship, or the indirect way their reactions are presented. Discussion of these observations, in turn, alerts the students to textual clues they will notice as they continue reading the novel: the emphasis on what the characters wear or eat; other scenes in which Emma's clothing is caught when she is with a man; further evidence of Charles's inaction; the parallel but reversed contrast between Emma and Rodolphe after their first sexual encounter.

A side benefit of using paragraphs to stimulate discussion is that all students have the chance to present their views, even those who usually hang back. More of them, in fact, are likely to participate actively when the discussion opens up, because they have staked out a position to defend or have noticed elements in the novel that support or undermine a particular argument. Different students will emphasize different aspects of a question so that, rather than guessing what the instructor has in mind, they themselves can lead the discussion to a constellation of related issues in the novel. In this way, frequent writing helps students concentrate their attention on the text and learn to talk about it.

Discussing to Write: Paper Topics

Writing to discuss also provides a start for writing papers, not only because the experience of writing about novels becomes more familiar but also because the paragraphs may form the basis of a paper or suggest related paper topics. Rather than assign a particular topic, I prefer to let my students develop their own subjects, although I suggest general areas for papers (for example, comparing analogous scenes in *Madame Bovary* and in another novel they've read for the course, studying an element of the setting, tracing imagery through the novel, or reacting to a critical article). Devoting part of a class session to articulating paper topics also has proved successful for generating ideas. Two sessions before the paper is due, I ask students to come to class with either a thesis statement or an idea for a paper. It does not have to be definitive (they haven't finished the novel yet); a topic might well change or even be abandoned altogether. In class, we spend time on each student's topic. For those who have brought in thesis statements, we try to imagine what kinds of issues the reader would expect to encounter in the paper and what examples from the novel would be effective in supporting a thesis. For those with ideas not yet fully formulated, we collaborate on developing a thesis statement to fit the ideas and examples the student has in mind. I have found that this class session, while geared to questions of writing, in fact becomes an excellent discussion of the novel.

For instance, one of my students, Paul, presented his topic as an analysis of Flaubert's use of details that take on symbolic significance. He was going to study rivers, food, and several other elements. Other students saw immediately that the topic was too broad and suggested that he limit his paper to one of these aspects. But how, he rejoined, was he to come up with a paper that was more than just a list of appearances of an element of the setting? This is a good question, and it led to a discussion of the role imagery and leitmotiv play in novels in general and in *Madame Bovary* in particular, where the indirectness of the narration means that the reader must be especially attentive to pick up small but significant details. Another student in the class, Vanessa, had chosen to study food, and a discussion of her idea clarified, not only for Paul but for us all, ways to approach such a topic. She had noted many telling details: that Rodolphe Boulanger (i.e., "baker") was the first man to satisfy Emma sexually, that she is nauseated or unable to eat when she is frustrated, that she is compared to a carp, that certain foods at the ball are those traditionally associated with sexuality (e.g., truffles, pomegranates). In class, we were able to sketch an outline that put these elements into a conceptual framework: first, the contrast between

Charles (satisfied) and Emma (either hungry or rejecting food); then the symbolic significance of food (foods linked with sexuality; the contrast between pure and toxic foods); and, finally, the use of food in similes describing the characters. Not surprisingly, her paper turned out to be excellent, although the subject proved still too large.

These discussions provide an opportunity for us to show students how to go beyond plot summary and questions of personality and verisimilitude, heading off common problems students make in writing about the novel. For instance, both Ellen and Steffen decided to write on Emma's relationships with men. Not only is this subject too vast, but it has the obvious pitfall of leading to plot summary and simplistic character analysis. Fortunately, other students also saw the danger. In my own interventions, I try to be supportive while encouraging the students and others in the class to suggest solutions to potential problems.

Through class discussions and individual conferences, students develop a variety of topics. Some of my students' papers have expanded on topics that I had proposed for discussion paragraphs:

> A Comparison of the Ball Scenes in *Le Père Goriot* and *Madame Bovary*
> (what they represent for Eugène de Rastignac and Emma)
> Ideal Love and Blindness: The Agricultural Fair
> Madame Bovary's Window: Theater in the Provinces

Others have expanded on the readings of passages we worked on in class:

> Two Seductions: A Comparison of the Waltz at Vaubyessard and the Day
> on Horseback with Rodolphe
> The Waltz and Some Central Themes in *Madame Bovary*
> Velvet in *Madame Bovary*

Some have been refined through our discussion of paper topics in class:

> The Role of Food in *Madame Bovary*
> Symbolism of Food in *Madame Bovary*
> The Influence of Books on Emma and Léon
> Reading in *Madame Bovary* and *François le champi*
> Madame Bovary as an Artist (her creation of an artificial life)

Others have been worked out later in paper conferences with me:

> A Comparison of the Suicide of Emma Bovary and the Crucifixion of
> Jesus Christ
> Monsieur Lheureux and the Ruin of Emma Bovary
> Monsieur Emma Bovary (Emma's masculine traits)
> Two Madame Bovarys (parallels between Emma and Charles's energetic
> but frustrated mother)

Still another possibility is a reaction to a critical essay. Because students often get lost in the maze of critical work on this novel, I prefer to direct them to specific articles or books, especially those with a stance that can provoke a response. The Norton edition includes essays that may serve as a point of departure. Assigning a particular critical approach or theme is another way to help students concentrate their own critical energies. In my course Will and Desire in the Nineteenth-Century French Novel, I ask that they choose one of three chapters from critical works that center on questions of desire: Leo Bersani's "*Madame Bovary* and the Sense of Sex," the beginning of René Girard's *Deceit, Desire, and the Novel* (which takes *Madame Bovary* as a major example), and chapter 6 of Eric Gans's Madame Bovary: *The End of Romance*. The day the papers are due, our discussion focuses in large measure on students' responses to these works. Here, discussion follows rather than precedes writing about the novel.

Shadings and Refinements

As Flaubert makes clear in the passage quoted above, the writing process, if it is to be successful, is a long and often painful one. Students are impressed and also rather taken aback to learn that Flaubert spent five years writing *Madame Bovary* and that he produced some three thousand pages of notes and drafts. Reading Flaubert's letters in the de Man edition may help students take the measure of the novel's complexity and denseness and, at the same time, encourage them in their own efforts. His repeated allusions to the difficulty, even the agony, of writing show them that they are not alone in confronting the pain of composition. They, too, have "bad weeks" when the work "doesn't go." These letters also give them a sense of Flaubert's passionate belief that the right word matters, based on a profound conviction that language is uniquely powerful and that his efforts, whatever the cost, will be justified in the completed work.

Students do not have five years to perfect their papers, but time must be built into the schedule so that they have the time to work on outlines and drafts, the "shadings and refinements" Flaubert describes. They should not compress this process into a few hours the night before the paper is due. Having students read drafts to each other in class, exchange drafts with a writing partner, or come in for a paper conference may stimulate both rewriting and rereading of the novel.

In writing courses, a system of peer review is especially important. Learning to be a critical reader of others' work helps students learn to find ways to revise their own. First, one can set aside fifteen or twenty minutes of a penultimate session on the novel for students to read their introductory paragraphs to one another in groups of three or four. I encourage them to look for clear statements of the topic and a sense of how the argument will develop. The instructor moves from group to group, offering suggestions to the questioners and the students reading from their work. Second, one can establish a system of peer review of drafts, either through a computer network or by asking each student to give a copy of a draft to his or her writing partner. The partner then writes a brief reader's report (perhaps on a one-page form), to be taken into account in revisions and turned in with the paper.

The writing partners will need guidelines indicating what to look for and pitfalls to avoid. I warn students against organizing their papers along the lines of the story ("first . . . , then . . . , at the end . . ."). Simply eliminating this kind of structure makes students think more abstractly, in terms of concepts rather than plot. I also point out that they should try to make "Flaubert," not "Emma," the subject of their sentences. I encourage them to use quotes and examples to support their arguments but not to give long quotes without commentary. The conclusion (and there should be a conclusion) should emphasize what they have discovered: what does their paper show us about *Madame Bovary*? about Emma or Monsieur Lheureux? about Flaubert or the differences between Flaubert and Balzac?

Articulating the point of the paper is especially important in comparative papers, which students seem to have difficulty structuring. Susan, for instance, planned to discuss reading in *François le champi* and *Madame Bovary*. She had seen that it provided a link between François and Madeleine and between Emma and Léon. But her plan was to divide her paper into two parts: the first on Sand, the second on Flaubert. Such a structure would have led to two plot summaries with a conclusion in which she would have had to do all the work of comparison. After drawing out the elements she had noted in both novels, we were able to come up with several aspects that she could choose to examine, treating both novels in each section: how books bring the characters together, how the characters model their lives on books, how reading sets these characters apart from others in their social circles, and how the way their reading is described echoes other themes in each novel (as "a constant *exchange* of books and of romances" in *Madame Bovary* [164; 71; emphasis added], implying a link with money; as simple and pure, like peasant life, in *François le champi*).

Such a discussion requires an individual conference with the student. Conferences can take big chunks of time, but they often prove especially rewarding, improving papers and allowing for productive interchange with students. There are ways, too, to reduce the time commitment. One is to have students read their papers aloud in the conference. This technique not only eliminates the necessity to read a draft ahead of time but also allows the teacher to become a live audience, making the students aware that they are always writing for an audience, one who experiences the written word in a temporal dimension. (Remember, too, how Flaubert would read revisions of *Madame Bovary* to Louis Bouilhet every Sunday [Steegmuller 241–42, 262].) Or one can have them bring their introductions or outlines rather than a whole draft to the conference, to read aloud or just to discuss.

These conferences need not be lengthy, and they can lead to work on both organization and content. For example, Drew had noticed a series of parallels between Emma's death agony and the crucifixion of Christ and wondered whether that comparison might be a good topic for a paper. Needless to say, I encouraged him to pursue it. In the course of a brief conversation, I was able to help him to organize the paper (until then, it was just a series of observations) and, through its organization, to see differences as well as parallels, differences that become more marked after the moment in the novel when the two death agonies come together, as Emma kisses the crucifix.

Conferences also provide the time to have real conversations with students. Katherine, an excellent reader, was writing a paper on Emma's masculine traits and needed no guidance from me. She had noted the examples of cross-dressing, the appearance of phallic objects (whips, pipes, cigarettes), and the association of masculinity with liberty, and she was ready to discuss their implications in terms of Emma's conflicting desires to dominate men and to be the love object of a virile man. All I had to provide was encouragement. I also pointed out work that had been done on the topic, from Baudelaire (in the de Man edition) to Mario Vargas Llosa. Our conversation was a pleasure, moving from Flaubert to Yeats's "Adam's Curse," which she was studying in her English class, to the larger problems of men writing in the voice or from the point of view of women. In talking with students like Drew and Katherine and in reading their papers, I find that not only do my students learn from our work together, but I learn from them, too.

Because Flaubert is so insistent on questions of form, and because the text is so rich, working with *Madame Bovary* may show students how reading a novel is a process of discovery. Teaching the novel through writing can provide the means to structure and enhance this experience, helping students to be not only better writers but also better critical readers of *Madame Bovary*.

Teaching Reading Tactics in *Madame Bovary*

William J. Berg and Laurey K. Martin

Students tend to read literally and linearly, much as one reads a newspaper, a textbook, or a potboiler. The best read with considerable pace, good retention of detail, and a firm grasp of the plot—skills one might learn in a standard speed-reading course. Teaching students to read literarily, however, means supplementing their literal and linear habits with creative techniques and tactics, ten of which we illustrate here. Each of these tactics involves two underlying principles: first, seeing textual elements not as isolated data but in terms of their relations with other elements of the text and, second, formulating questions, since the reading of literature is an active process of questioning the text, not a passive, albeit rapid and accurate, digestion of inert matter. We are convinced that, of all nineteenth-century novels, *Madame Bovary* is the richest proving ground for these reading tactics, warranting as much as a third of a semester course, since during that time students are not just studying Flaubert but learning to read literature.

Reading deductively. This tactic is the simplest; it involves approaching the text as one might read a mystery story or, indeed, as a detective might analyze clues to solve a mystery. In literature, details are assumed to be meaningful, not gratuitous, and connected, not randomly, as they often are in life, but causally. By asking why, for example, Flaubert describes Charles's hat in such detail early in the novel, students can follow a deductive path that leads to conclusions about Charles's background (country bumpkin), his current situation (out of it), and his personality (heteroclite) and thus to a forecast of Emma's future with him.

Reading alternatively. We find it productive to have students assess the effect of a given expression by asking them to imagine an alternative way of saying the same thing. They have no difficulty doing so, even in a foreign language, since they generally express things in a relatively standard or literal way. The difference between their expression and Flaubert's is a difference in style, which amounts to a choice between possible forms of expression. For example, the figurative "toute l'amertume de l'existence lui semblait servie sur son assiette" 'all the bitterness of life seemed served up on her plate' (126; 47) may be compared to a more literal expression like "elle était amère" 'she was bitter.' By focusing on the differences between the two expressions, the student comes to appreciate Flaubert's phrasing, which suggests the impact of the mundane through the metaphor involving eating and gives Emma's feelings a sense of material weight, reinforced by the repetition of *s*, further suggesting, perhaps, the sizzling of her stove.

The same process may be implemented in larger textual segments, as when Léon seduces Emma in a carriage careening around Rouen (316–18; 176–77). By asking students to imagine the scene registered through Emma's viewpoint rather than from outside the coach, as Flaubert depicts it, the teacher helps them appreciate the value of Flaubert's choice in creating a certain distance and detachment that invariably lead to irony and humor.

Through both of the above examples, instructors may convey to students the significance of style in Flaubert's work by asking why he chose his particular form of expression. Students are, of course, resistant to the notion of "literary style"; the worst of them are thoroughly indifferent, the best impatient to get to the work's "meaning." *Madame Bovary* is, perhaps, the best novel for demonstrating that style organizes the formless, meaningless matter of human experience into a coherent, significant whole. Style accompanies meaning, underscores meaning, generates meaning; in fact, style *is* meaning or, as Flaubert put it, "an absolute manner of seeing things" (*Correspondance*, ed. Bruneau, 2: 70).

Reading backward. In addition to reading forward for plot, students must learn to read backward for structure. Thus, when "the plaster curé" is broken during the Bovarys' trip from Tostes to Yonville (152; 62), the use of the definite article causes one to ask when the statue was previously mentioned, engendering a return to Emma's garden in Tostes for a detailed description: "Dans les sapinettes, près de la haie, le curé en tricorne qui lisait son bréviaire avait perdu le pied droit, et même le plâtre, s'écaillant à la gelée, avait fait des gales blanches sur sa figure" 'Under the spruce by the hedgerow, the curé in the three-cornered hat reading his breviary had lost his right foot, and the very plaster, scaling off with the frost, had left white scabs on his face' (125; 46). Here, yet another definite article sends us farther back along a trail leading next to the day after the ball at the Vaubyessard château (116; 40) and finally to Emma's first day in her new home in Tostes, where the use of the indefinite article to qualify the statue allows us to end our pursuit and read the object as a symbol of marital sanctity and promise (92; 23). At this point, its crumbling appearance and breaking acquire their full meaning as a symbol of marital disintegration and destruction. In similar fashion, one will return to the statue's lost foot when Hippolyte loses his leg and to the flaking scabs when the blind man shows his.

Reading sideways. Whereas the previous reading tactic involves repetition or "reprise" of the same textual element in different contexts, two different objects in the same context may acquire meaning by virtue of their contiguity, as when the statue and the disintegrating wedding bouquet burned by Emma combine near the end of part 1, chapter 9, to constitute a pattern symbolizing the dissolution of her marriage and of her dreams.

Reading analogously. Two different objects in different contexts may also be connected by analogy, as when the organ-grinder appears at Emma's window in the chapter following the ball (1.9):

> Dans l'après-midi, quelquefois, une tête d'homme apparaissait derrière les vitres de la salle, tête hâlée, à favoris noirs, et qui souriait lentement, d'un large sourire doux à dents blanches. Une valse aussitôt commençait, et, sur l'orgue, dans un petit salon, des danseurs hauts comme le doigt, femmes en turban rose, Tyroliens en jaquette, singes en habit noir, messieurs en culotte courte, tournaient, tournaient entre les fauteuils, les canapés, les consoles, se répétant dans les morceaux de miroir que raccordait à leurs angles un filet de papier doré.　(125–26)

> Sometimes in the afternoon outside the window of her room, the head of a man appeared, a swarthy head with black whiskers, smiling slowly, with a broad, gentle smile that showed his white teeth. A waltz began, and on the barrel-organ, in a little drawing-room, dancers the size of a finger, women in pink turbans, Tyrolians in jackets, monkeys in frock-coats, gentlemen in knee britches, turned and turned between the armchairs, the sofas and the tables, reflected in small pieces of mirror that strips of [gold] paper held together at the corners.　(46)

The waltz recalls the ball, as does the repetition of the verb *tourner* (see 113; 38); here, however, the characters are grotesque (monkeys in evening dress), the scene is miniaturized, and Emma is on the outside looking in, yet another symbol of her failing romantic outlook and aspirations.

Reading contrapuntally. In the famous scene of the country fair in part 2, chapter 8, Flaubert interweaves two "speeches": the councillor's, celebrating agricultural progress, and Rodolphe's, seducing Emma. Below, in the town square, the councillor's rhetoric is all too mundane, while above, in the council room, Rodolphe musters all the romantic clichés already associated with Emma's dreams in order to win her favors. By interweaving the two speeches, by juxtaposing them rather than presenting them in separate contexts, Flaubert creates a double irony that cuts in both directions: the political rhetoric of the councillor is seen as a seduction of the populace, while Rodolphe's romantic discourse takes on the banality of agricultural parlance. Flaubert reinforces the reader's association of the two speeches by further relating them in several ways, notably parallelism (a theme or word, such as *duty*, occurs in both), word games (*bovine* recalls Bovary), and continuation (as Rodolphe states, "I followed you and stayed . . . ," an award is made "[f]or manures!" [107]). The obvious contrapuntal structure of this famous scene suggests ways of reading other elements of the text, even if they are not always juxtaposed within the same context, such as the sustained contrast between the characters Homais and Bournisien. A great work like *Madame Bovary* thus contains the keys for deciphering its messages and, indeed, its coding mechanisms.

Reading emblematically. An individual object or scene may stand as an emblem of the entire story, such as Emma's wedding cake (88; 20), whose various layers suggest the stages of her life: first her wedding, symbolized by a "temple"; then her marriage, denoted by a "dungeon"; and finally her escape into adultery, suggested by "a small Cupid." Here the part (the cake) contains the whole (Emma's life), an operation like that of the rhetorical figure of synecdoche.

Reading figuratively. Indeed, it can be noted that the relations underlying the four preceding categories of reading tactics correspond to those governing the four major forms of rhetorical figure: metonymy (contiguity or causality), metaphor (analogy), irony (contrast), and synecdoche (inclusion). If students tend to read literally, then *Madame Bovary*, with its heavy dosage of figurative language, provides the appropriate antidote. By examining occurrences of each type of trope in short textual segments, students learn to identify figurative language, and more important, to evaluate its function within the text.

Metaphor (we use the term generically to describe all figures based on analogy) is no doubt the easiest form of figure to identify, since it involves the intrusion of an alien contrast (a comparing term) into the scene at hand (the phenomenon compared) and since in *Madame Bovary* it often takes the form of a simile with an identifiable modulating term (*like* or *as*). Less apparent, however, is the function of such figures in developing the characters, creating the atmosphere, and shaping the work. Take, for example, the phrase "ses rêves tombant dans la boue comme des hirondelles blessés" 'her dreams sinking into the mire like wounded swallows' (252; 133). Although the swallows are clearly figurative, they not only belong to the provincial landscape weighing on Emma but also recall the name of the coach (the *Hirondelle*) that departs from Yonville and thus symbolizes her desire for escape. Flaubert's comparisons, usually generated by the surroundings and mediated by the characters, are often overdetermined and constitute a main structuring feature of his novels.

Synecdoche involves not the combination of analogous elements from different contexts but a shift within the same context from a whole entity to one of its parts, as in the following example: "Les pieds retombaient en mesure, les jupes se bouffaient et frôlaient, les mains se donnaient, se quittaient; les mêmes yeux, s'abaissant devant vous, revenaient se fixer sur les vôtres" 'feet marked time, skirts swelled and rustled, hands touched and parted; the same eyes that had been lowered returned to gaze at you again' (111; 36). In this description of a waltz at the Vaubyessard château, disembodied parts—feet, skirts, hands, eyes—seem to detach themselves and move independently, merely hinting at the persons to whom they belong. The technique not only underscores the movement of the dance but also suggests a fragmenting of human beings and thus a dehumanizing of human experience that permeates much of the novel.

Metonymy also involves a shift within the same context, but it is based on contiguity or causality rather than on inclusion. Flaubert's passages often begin with a series of effects whose cause is revealed only later in the passage. For example, the following sentence describes Emma's perception as she leaves Rodolphe's château, just before poisoning herself: "Il lui sembla tout à coup que des globules couleur de feu éclataient dans l'air" 'Suddenly it seemed to her that fiery spheres were exploding in the air' (388; 228). The identity or cause of these fiery phenomena is not revealed for a full three sentences, when they turn out to be merely "the lights of the houses that shone through the fog" (388; 228). By insisting on the effects, Flaubert is able to heighten not only the haziness (and indeed madness) of Emma's perception but also the sense of suspense for the reader.

Irony involves the combination of two contrasting elements within the same context, as in the sentence describing the effect of Charles's student life on his studies: "Grâce à ces travaux préparatoires, il échoua complètement à son examen d'officier de santé" 'Thanks to these preparatory labors, he failed completely in his examination for his degree of *officier de santé*' (69; 7). Not only is the term "preparatory labors" an ironic description of Charles's carousing, but the positive statement beginning the sentence is undercut by the negative result ending it, bringing us back to harsh reality, as Flaubert is wont to do. By examining the mechanisms governing rhetorical figures in minute detail, students come to see that such figures are far from ornaments tacked onto the text but, rather, constitute ways of organizing the text and indeed of conceiving relations in a nonlinear manner.

Reading polyvalently. An individual textual element may acquire layers of meaning, as does the blind beggar, whose grotesque appearance in part 3 of the novel serves as a counterpoint to Emma's fantasies and a symbol of her moral decay, just as his blindness, a conventional symbol of justice, reflects her inability to see reality. At the same time, his song recalls Emma's dreams, his tapping cane makes the same haunting sound as Hippolyte's wooden leg (a reminder of failure), and his grotesque gestures foreshadow those of Emma during her death throes (see 3.8). In short, on top of the blind man's denotation as a person who cannot see and conventional connotations involving justice and social ostracism, the figure acquires layers of meaning produced within the text itself. Indeed, a masterpiece like *Madame Bovary* writes its own dictionary.

Reading metaliterarily. Ultimately, any great literary work is also about literature itself, as we are reminded by Flaubert's preoccupation with types of speech and statements about language and communication. For example, in summarizing Rodolphe's opinion that Emma's words are trite, the narrator moves from her situation to a generalization about the limitations of human expression:

> . . . comme si la plénitude de l'âme ne débordait pas quelquefois par les métaphores les plus vides, puisque personne, jamais, ne peut donner l'exacte mesure de ses besoins, ni de ses conceptions ni de ses douleurs, et que la parole humaine est comme un chaudron fêlé où nous battons des mélodies à faire danser les ours, quand on voudrait attendrir les étoiles.   (259)

> . . . as though the abundance of one's soul did not sometimes overflow with empty metaphors, since no one ever has been able to give the exact measure of his needs, his concepts, or his sorrows. The human tongue is like a cracked cauldron on which we beat out tunes to set a bear to dancing when we would make the stars weep with our melodies.   (138)

Here, the rare use of the first-person plural implies that Flaubert is talking as much about the difficulties of writing as about Emma's failure to communicate the elements of her dream. The example goes far in justifying Flaubert's reputed (and oft-disputed) dictum "Madame Bovary, c'est moi" and in encouraging students to read literarily.

All the reading techniques outlined above involve approaching a given textual element (a word, a character, a scene, etc.) not linearly and literally but in terms of the relations constituted by that textual element and other textual elements, either within the same microcontext (textual segment) or within different contexts (other textual segments, other texts, general conventions, reality, the reader, the author, etc.). The abstraction of the previous sentence, however, may well make our efforts at synthesis—the very purpose of this approach—somewhat inaccessible to the student. As an antidote to such abstraction, we suggest the use of a chart like the one opposite, perhaps the most effective way of synthesizing complex relations, however imperfect its drawing or tentative its conclusions.

Students can use such a chart as a reference point for further class activities, two of which we suggest briefly in conclusion. As a pièce de résistance, we combine the various reading tactics, emphasizing the role of the signifiers (sounds, rhythm, syntax, etc.), and introduce students to the dreaded *explication de texte*, itself a reading tactic far too complicated to describe here in passing. We also use the techniques derived from *Madame Bovary* to approach other texts often reputed to be less "literary," where the students can apply their newly acquired tactics.

In Zola's *Germinal*, for example, as students tackle the final figure, which foreshadows the miners as a germinating army, they can read it as emblematic of the entire novel, reflected in its title (itself polyvalent, suggesting both growth and revolution), and as an extension of textual elements encountered earlier (the network of botanical metaphors, the collective actions of the miners, the growth of class consciousness). Furthermore, Etienne's decision to abandon grassroots activism and attack the system from within, as an intellectual, points to Zola's own position as a writer engaged in consciousness-raising activity. The students may come to appreciate the importance of style in any approach—ideological, sociocritical, psychocritical, visual (all of which we attempt to introduce in an undergraduate course on the novel)—and, especially, the uniqueness of *Madame Bovary* in helping them uncover the multifarious tools of textual analysis.

READING TACTICS AND TEXTUAL RELATIONS

Reading tactic	Textual elements	Context	Relation
1. Deductive	different	same	causality
2. Alternative	different	different (reader)	contrast
3. Backward	same	different (textual)	similarity
4. Sideways	different	same	contiguity
5. Analogous	different	different (textual)	similarity
6. Contrapuntal	different	same	contrast
7. Emblematic	different	different (textual)	inclusion
8. Figurative			
metaphor	different	different (textual)	similarity
synecdoche	different	same	inclusion
metonymy	different	same	causality
irony	different	same	contrast
9. Polyvalent	same	different (multiple)	similarity
10. Metaliterary	different	different (author)	similarity

Relevance, Meaning, and Reading

Ross Chambers

I sometimes ask my students to keep informal journals of their reading. Not long ago, one of them, a reader of *Madame Bovary*, wrote, "Emma is right to want to get out of Yonville and go to Paris. I was in Paris last summer and it was wonderful. . . . Every morning when I wake up, I wish I was in Paris, like Emma." Here is a student from whom we teachers can learn something, about relevance and about reading.

My impulse was, of course, to throw the word *irony* at "Jane" (yes, this reader was a woman) and to enforce the orthodox view that, as a victim of unrealizable desire, Emma would be unhappy wherever she was. But there is obviously a sense in which she might have been happier, òr at least unhappy in a different way, had she lived in Paris rather than Yonville: some of her boredom arises from the constraints of the village, which would not apply in the capital. So I raised some questions, inviting Jane to specify Emma's situation more closely and to differentiate it from her own:

Why *can't* Emma go to Paris? (We discussed the marriage laws in nineteenth-century France and the fact that Emma could move only if Charles were also to move.) Could Charles practice medicine in the capital? (He is not a doctor but an *officier de santé*.) And anyway, what would Paris with Charles be like for Emma (who does not include Charles in her daydreams)?

Supposing she could move to Paris, what chance would a poor doctor's wife (or, worse, a woman separated from her husband) have of finding happiness on Emma's terms (i.e., access to the gilded life of the upper-class heroes and heroines she has read about)? Doesn't the episode at Vaubyessard suggest that it is life in the country that occasionally offers her the chance to mix with the beautiful people?

My intention was to get Jane to see the impracticality of Emma's desires and daydreams (in the course, I heavily emphasized the idea that *Madame Bovary* analyzes the vulnerability of upwardly mobile people, and of women in particular, to having desires produced for them that are not in their own interests but in those of commercial and financial powers). But, as a first step, it was necessary to get her to dissociate Emma from herself and her own desires, to see the difference between Emma's situation and her own. Once that goal was accomplished, she might be able to think about not the similarity but the relevance of Emma's situation to her own; that is, she might begin to consider the way in which her own desires were being produced. As long as she identified with Emma (as the novel itself partly encourages, in its deployment of free indirect style), she could not, any more than Emma, distance herself from Emma's desires sufficiently to understand them. The strength of Jane's own desire was making her an Emma-like reader (an "identificatory" reader) and preventing her from becoming a reader of Emma.

One has to learn to be a reader in that second sense; reading in the first, identificatory sense—the text becomes a simple mirror in which the reading subject merely recognizes the already familiar—is intellectually unproductive (although it may be pleasurable). Yet some of the most cherished practices of literary education in the liberal arts curriculum actually encourage identificatory reading: teachers tend to de-emphasize historical and cultural difference and to foster naive conceptions of relevance by asking students to "relate" to texts they have had to read at great speed and have had little time to think about—that is, interpret. Naturally enough, they relate to what seems familiar to them. An essential component of the experience of reading—a certain distance between reader and text—is thereby slighted. In reading, one does not recognize what one already knew to be the case so much as one gains "new" knowledge, knowledge that one certainly recognizes as relevant to oneself but did not, in any simple sense, already know. And this mediated acquisition of knowledge can occur only if there is an initial degree of difference (which cannot be so great, however, as simply to discourage interest). It is from the experience of discovering how the apparently remote and alien proves, on reflection, to be unexpectedly germane to oneself and one's own situation that important insights emerge. Giving the lie to the phrase "of direct relevance," reading then instructs us that self-knowledge is a matter of indirect experience and that it depends therefore on a certain connectedness with the other—with other selves and other lives, including fictional ones. A teacher of literature can take an initial step in the direction of mediated relevance by teaching reading in terms of a couple of simple rules of thumb: if the text is familiar, look for what is strange in it; if the text is strange, look for the ways in which it is familiar. (Wonderfully enough, there is always something familiar in the strange and something strange in the familiar, when one looks hard enough.)

Another way of putting my point would be to say that relevance does not reside in the literal: as teachers, we have to break the grip of the literal so that texts can become meaningful to our students. I was close to twenty and the bulk of my college education was behind me when a thoughtful teacher, hearing my learned but superficial prattle, revealed to me something that made dazzling sense as soon as he pointed it out but that I had not been able to formulate for myself: texts "mean" other than they "say," and it is that space of otherness between their saying and their meaning that makes them texts. Texts, then, are the products of interpretive reading; the "strangeness" of a text that is in its literality familiar and the "familiarity" of a text that is in its literality strange are names that can be given to what we are able to recognize, in the text, as meanings that are potentially of value to us. I want to record that teacher's name. It was Ron Jackson.

Meaning, however, is a tricky concept, and it is hard to think of a text better suited than *Madame Bovary* to teaching some of that trickiness.

For one thing, there is meaning as signification (what is the meaning of this sentence?) and meaning as intention (does the speaker mean what he or she says?), these two meanings of *meaning* being distinct but interrelated (does the speaker mean or intend what the sentence means or signifies?). It is the interrelation of two kinds of meaning (the degree of correlation between a speaker's intention and a statement's signification) that characterizes discourse as "utterance" (*énonciation* as opposed to *énoncé*); consequently, an early task of teaching is to draw students' attention to the fact that language never occurs except in some context (i.e., as utterance) and that it is because of the difficulty of knowing the context that hesitation over meaning occurs. Such hesitation can be over signification (the meaning is obscure, as when a speaker uses a "hard" word), or it can be over intention (is the speaker "kidding" or not?), or it can be over the degree of correlation between signification and intention (does the use of a hard word indicate pompousness, technical accuracy, or irony on the speaker's part?). Only a certain construal of the context will determine such matters and produce a meaning.

An example is Emma's passionate correspondence with Rodolphe, Rodolphe's misinterpretation of her love letters as standard stuff, and the textual commentary in the famous interpolated passage—"Il s'était tant de fois entendu dire ces choses" 'He had so often heard these things'—that attributes the gap between what one says and what one means to a metaphysical deficiency of language, a failure of its expressivity: "nous battons des mélodies à faire danser les ours, quand on voudrait attendrir les étoiles" 'we beat out tunes to set a bear dancing when we would make the stars weep with our melodies' (259; 138). Reading fast and reading literally, students will often miss some of the complexity of this episode, catching only the most obvious point: that through indifference and habit, Rodolphe fails to realize the intensity of Emma's feelings. But in discussion they can be led to see that both characters are caught in a more general problematics of meaning to which all speakers are subject. I ask them questions like the following:

Have you ever found yourself saying "I love you" and then later regretting it? In what kind of circumstances? Did you mean what you said at the time?

Has anyone ever said "I love you" to you, leaving you disturbed, distressed, or hesitant ("confused") about what it meant? In what circumstances?

How many phrases can you think of that are appropriate to say in certain circumstances but of which it would be ridiculous to ask whether they are sincerely meant (e.g., "Howya doin'?" "Nice talking to you!")? Does "I love you" (sometimes? always? never?) belong to that category? If it sometimes does and sometimes doesn't, how can one tell the difference?

Is Rodolphe completely wrong in his estimation of Emma? Is it possible (and, if so, how is it possible) for a passion that is real and sincerely felt to be expressed in clichés and conventional expressions? (Is "I love you" a cliché?) Have you ever found yourself quoting a song or a movie at some highly emotional moment when your sincerity was not in doubt? Has anyone ever done the same to you (and were you sure of that person's sincerity)?

What is Rodolphe's context for interpreting Emma's letters? (What has his experience of women been to this point?) What is Emma's context for understanding her own letters? What happens when a playboy meets a woman who has had a sheltered upbringing? Is this situation in any way characteristic of men's relations with women and women's relations with men? (Then? Now?) Are men and women brought up to misunderstand one another? Why should that be?

The kinds of discussions that are likely to be sparked by such questions can in turn be good starting points for examining the two major rhetorical features of the novel's writing, both of which complicate its reading and complexify the notion of meaning. They are its deployment of free indirect style and its pervasively ironic tone. Free indirect style unsettles the idea that discourse has a single, autonomous subject capable of controlling (intending) its meaning: it shows that subjective experience and the expression thereof do not necessarily mean what the subject thinks (intends). Take the episode of Emma and Rodolphe's riding excursion, with its lyrical description of the countryside that begins, "On était aux premiers jours d'octobre" 'It was early in October' (225; 114). Who is responsible for the way in which the landscape is presented? (Compare "on apercevait au loin les toits d'Yonville" 'gleamed from afar the roofs of Yonville' with, a sentence later, "Emma fermait à demi les paupières . . . et jamais ce pauvre village où elle vivait ne lui avait semblé si petit" 'Emma half closed her eyes . . . and never had this poor village where she lived appeared so small.' If Emma is clearly responsible for "petit," who is responsible for "pauvre"?) What does it mean to turn a Norman landscape into a lake? What kind of landscape might Emma particularly like? (Why? How do we know?) What does the insight into her subjective consciousness that we seem to get here tell us about her mood? What is likely to happen as a result of this mood? Can one be sure of any of these interpretations? (If so, why? If not, why not?)

At this point, it ought to be possible to widen the discussion of discursive multisubjectivity. I might ask students, Can you think of circumstances when something like free indirect style occurs in "real life" (the minutes of a committee meeting? a term paper in which you simultaneously summarize and analyze an argument drawn from a book?)? Quotation, plagiarism, and other forms of discursive appropriation may suggest themselves (teachers should be prepared to work hard to neutralize moralistic interpretations of such phenomena). Is anyone in the class prepared to argue that something like free indirect style happens all the time, that what we say is never fully "ours"? Back to Emma's love letters: Who decides what they mean? Why and how does the novel lead us to favor Emma's understanding of them over Rodolphe's? How, in real life, do we know what we mean? Who decides, for example, the meaning of our lives?

As for irony, it has a close affinity with free indirect style (see Ramazani). Both have a citational or mentioning structure: the discourse produced acquires its significance (meaning) by mentioning, and so distancing itself from, a discourse whose intention is judged deficient, naive, impoverished, or limited, so that it does not mean what it seems to mean. In free indirect style, there are at least grammatical markers (shifters, verb tense) that actualize the mentioning discourse, but irony is even trickier because there are not necessarily any formal markers at all. An inference is required of the receiver (addressee or reader), who must "read" the irony—that is, determine that the discourse is not a "use" but a "mentioning" of what is being said (see Sperber and Wilson). In an undergraduate class one does not need to wax technical to push the problematics of meaning further by adding the evidence irony offers to the evidence of multisubjectivity: to wit, the subject as controller (intender) of meaning is ultimately a construction resulting from a discursive relation (neither in the text nor in the reader but a product of their dialogue). Because of its rhetorical status as a mentioning, not a use of discourse, we may never be certain whether an irony is meant (intended); further, the meaning (signification) of an irony is always an implicit or "negative" quantity (one knows only that what is said is what is not meant). To the extent that it becomes explicit or "positive," such a meaning is necessarily furnished, as a matter of interpretation, by a reader.

These facts make irony difficult to teach, if only because, when students miss the irony (as often happens), teachers are put in a doubly coercive position: they must, first, identify the discourse as ironic and, second, suggest or propose—in support of the claim that the irony is meant (intended)—an explicit interpretation of its meaning (signification). A helpful device in the first case is to emend the punctuation. Take the last sentence of the novel: what differences are there among the following three versions?

> "Il vient de recevoir la croix d'honneur!"
> "Il vient de recevoir la croix d'honneur (!)"
> "Il vient de recevoir la croix d'honneur."

When (if) students more or less agree that a period can be deadpan (implying but not employing an exclamation point or a parenthetical exclamation point) and that the deadpan effect is inferable from an unacknowledged anomaly, discussion can proceed to the second problem. What is anomalous about the award of an honor to M. Homais? Are prizes and awards generally anomalous in *Madame Bovary*? (Consider the scene at the agricultural fair, particularly the medal awarded to Catherine Leroux for "un demi-siècle de servitude" 'a half century of servitude' [217; 108]. Is it significant that both Catherine Leroux and Homais are timeservers?) Notice that the strategy of interpreting the irony shifts the focus from the individual, M. Homais, as an unworthy recipient of an honor, to a whole social system that makes use of prizes as a way of controlling behavior. It is at this second stage of interpretation that the irony against M. Homais, with whom few readers are likely to identify, becomes readable as relevant to the students' own experience. (What kind of student gets to be the high school valedictorian? Why is there a valedictorian? Why do students work hard—or, alternatively, scheme—to get a good grade? What exactly is a grade "worth"? etc.)

But a second difficulty in teaching irony is that students (who frequently and understandably conflate irony with satire and with sarcasm) tend to assume that irony is necessarily hostile toward its butt. Consequently, they may have little difficulty in identifying the ironic treatment of Homais but fail—especially because of the identificatory effect of free indirect style—to notice that Emma is also subject to ironic treatment. (That was my student Jane's case.) That it is possible for a reader to sympathize with a character while that character's perspective is ironized is not a straightforward proposition to many students. Sometimes it may be helpful to begin by discussing cases, like wry humor, in which complicity is sought while deficiencies or limitations are acknowledged. The effect of the writing in the riding excursion episode is perhaps similarly describable as wry in the sense that we are encouraged to sympathize with Emma's happiness while our attention is drawn to her ironic obliviousness to the gulf between her perspective and Rodolphe's more matter-of-fact approach to the business of seduction (cf., after their lovemaking: "Rodolphe, le cigare aux dents, raccommodait avec son canif une des deux brides cassée" 'Rodolphe, a cigar between his lips, was mending with his penknife a broken bridle' [228; 116; trans. modified by eds.]). Why does the novel allow us to share Emma's perspective, silly and sentimental as it may be? Why does it not encourage similar identification with Rodolphe's vision? Can it be that there is a set of implicit values operating here whereby, although it is not good to be silly and sentimental, it is still better to be silly and sentimental (or maybe it is more understandable that a woman should be silly and sentimental) than to be, like Rodolphe, calculating, exploitive, and cynical? Does our sympathy for Emma work as a device to strengthen the irony against Rodolphe (and the other exploitive figures in the novel)? Or does the opposite occur? And, finally, does the irony that accompanies this sympathy identify her as a victim, whom we should understand but not identify with?

The novel's partiality toward a character who is simultaneously ironized may lead to a discussion of a more general feature of irony: its involvement with what it takes as its butt (where *involvement* designates a combination of understanding with a refusal of identification). How and why does one choose (?) to be ironic about certain people, attitudes, ways of speaking and being, and not about others? Is irony perhaps a matter of "It takes one to know one" (see Sedgwick 147–54 for a discussion of the sentimental in relation to this maxim)? of "the pot calling the kettle black"? Can it be that irony always indicates complicity with, as well as distance from, what is ironized? Does one ironize only that with which one does not wish to be, or to be thought, complicitous? If so, is there a sense in which a novel such as *Madame Bovary* is more like the male seducers and exploiters of Emma (who are most heavily ironized) than like Emma (whose ironization is tempered by manifest sympathy)? If we can make that argument, then the problem of meaning is doubly complexified by irony: in irony, the meaning of *discourse* is not controlled by its subject but produced—how? why? with what assurance of accuracy?—by readers, and the meaning of *irony* itself may well be the reverse of what it appears (i.e., it is an involuntary avowal of complicity with the butt, albeit an avowal that is made by producing signs of distance, aversion, and even hostility).

Madame Bovary's ironic complicity with the sentimental Emma, its combination of identificatory and detached treatment of the character, leads me to a final circumstance in which matters of meaning and issues of relevance are intertwined. Relevance, I have suggested, is a matter not of direct or literal reference but of meaning, and meaning, in turn, is not given but must be constructed, dialogically, through reading. Further, reading is a function of contexts that are themselves uncertain and indeed must be constructed in their turn. One obvious context of reading, in which the meaning of a text such as *Madame Bovary* is constructed, is that of education itself. What does it mean to "teach" *Madame Bovary*? What does it mean to "read" the novel in class? These questions are implicitly asked in the opening scene of the novel, Charles's induction into the classroom, which may be understood as a figuration (through Charles) of the novel's own relation to social institutions in general and to the institution of class in particular (remember that "la classe," in French, refers not only to the classroom but also to social class).

Madame Bovary is frequently taught in courses of the "great books" or "survey" type: it has the status of an institutionally approved classic. Yet in 1857 its author was brought to trial on the charge of having committed an offense against public morals. It was once a text sufficiently outrageous that the authorities of the day sought to repress it. What, then, has happened? By what paradox of history does a text that was once officially suspect become a text officially authorized and recommended? However one may interpret or explain the matter, if Dominick LaCapra is correct in thinking that the trial was provoked more by the undecidability of the novel's writing and the elusiveness of its meaning than by the alleged scandalousness of its content, I am demonstrating exactly that paradox of history when I advocate that the novel be used to teach, in our own age, the issues that gave it, at the time of publication, its socially disturbing character (i.e., its questioning of the nature of meaning). To say, as one is tempted, that modernism itself, as a movement, has undergone the same historical shift—from social oppositionality to a position of aesthetic and educational orthodoxy—does not really resolve the paradox but simply repeats it.

Having helped students see why *Madame Bovary* should make us feel uncomfortable, we must ask, then, how we can now feel comfortable enough with it to use it as standard classroom reading. My own analysis of this question has to do with the observation that it is not possible to oppose a dominant ideology except from an ideological position that is necessarily related to the dominant form of ideology and may therefore readily become dominant in turn. In its desire to distinguish itself from the values of middle-class "common sense" (utilitarianism, mercantilism, industrialism, etc.), modernism was itself in accord with a major bourgeois value, the desire not to be bourgeois, the desire for distinction (see Bourdieu). But *Madame Bovary*, I think, is more particularly committed to a special form of this desire for distinction, and that is the value of "concern." Where so many of the male characters in the novel are shown to be indifferent toward Emma, the readerly attitude implied by its combination of identificatory and ironic techniques toward her is one that could well be described as an attitude of caring. But such concern, I submit, is itself the distinguished form of indifference. To express concern for the plight of a woman such as Emma in the 1850s was perhaps to record a salutary disagreement with prevailing attitudes of indifference. But concern has now become—and was already becoming, helped along by novels like *Madame Bovary*—a staple of bourgeois sensibility and certainly a value thought to be worth teaching.

Concern is the great alibi of bourgeois liberalism and perhaps the particular predilection of middle-class intellectuals. To identify a problem or an injustice and to show oneself sensitive to the plight it reduces people to is thought to be enough. To care does not necessarily imply that one plans to act. There are so many problems that need attention, some of them more urgent than this particular one (and to remedy matters, would one not need to change the existing order of things, possibly to the detriment of the individual expressing concern?). Concern, in short, is the ideological device of those who are made uncomfortable by social problems and would like to see them resolved but without making an effort in that direction themselves or consenting to any other personal sacrifice. Consequently, this attitude is widespread in contemporary culture. I ask students to watch the network news for a few evenings and to count expressions of concern by politicians and others, substituting for policies and programs, and manifestations of concern as the value (the "attitude to the news") projected by the reporting itself.[1] Many are shocked at the results, and I then ask whether they plan to do something about what they have discovered or whether they will simply remain concerned about it. Teachers who follow my example should be prepared, however, for someone to detect concern in their own attitudes (is not a liberal education conceived, in large part, as the teaching of concern?).

In characters like Charles, Léon, Rodolphe, Homais, Lheureux, Binet, *Madame Bovary* diagnoses indifference as the inability to empathize with Emma. The empathy for her that it fosters in the reader through rhetorical devices like free indirect style is itself accompanied, however, by distancing irony that produces the awareness of Emma's limitations and deficiencies as an alibi for dissociating oneself from her situation. This combination of distance and empathy is exactly the structure of concern, and if it can be thought to have represented an ideological advance on the prevailing indifference in 1857, this structure is now easily integrated into the values of a certain dominant sensibility that is too rarely examined: that of the nightly television viewer who, confronted with famine in Ethiopia, violence and homelessness in cities in the United States, the plight of disempowered populations everywhere, thinks, "It is awful, but what can I do about it?" So powerful is this attitude in contemporary culture that I doubt one can teach *Madame Bovary* without in some degree feeding into it; that relation to concern is indubitably an aspect of the novel's relevance that we cannot afford to ignore.

We should not allow ourselves to be paralyzed by it, either, of course. An ideological position of some kind is the condition of any meaningful social practice, and the problem—a difficult one—is not to escape ideology but to practice a pedagogy that moves in social directions which are generally empowering and liberating, rather than obfuscating and mystifying, for our students (and ourselves). What those directions will be at any given moment is likely to be a matter of debate, but it is difficult not to conclude that they must entail, as a precondition, a degree of lucidity with respect to the social (con-) "text" in which our lives, as teachers and as students, are entwined.

Having begun by advocating the teaching of reading as that which demonstrates the split between saying and meaning, I am now in a position to conclude, therefore, that reading is the necessary instrument of such social lucidity. Seeking the strange in the familiar, the familiar in the strange, reading makes a text like *Madame Bovary* relevant by producing meanings that inevitably bring into view and make available for examination the social context in which the reading itself is pursued. For meaning, as we have seen, is not inherent "in" or transmitted "by" a text so much as it is produced in conjunction with a text, which means that the meaning of a text must always be recognizable to—because it is part of the context of—a reader who is the agent of production through whom that meaning is able to emerge. The meaning is recognizable, then, but simultaneously—by virtue of the detour through the mediation of the text—estranged and newly visible: available for examination. "Direct relevance" is a lie; there is nothing to be learned from it. Only when it is obtained obliquely, through reading, is relevance truly relevant, for only then is it an instrument of lucidity.

NOTE

[1] Reading this, Ali Behdad points out that the great device of concern is personalization (in the late 1980s, for example, a fitting object of presidential concern was Ryan White, in whom the general category of persons with AIDS was simultaneously subsumed and elided). The novel's generic interest in the lives of fictional individuals, perfectly illustrated by the focus on Emma in *Madame Bovary*, may well have been one of the historical determinants of this ideological device.

I am grateful, too, to Raymonde Carroll for the stimulus of a conversation we had some years ago about concern.

CONTRIBUTORS AND SURVEY PARTICIPANTS

Listed below are the names and affiliations of the contributors to this volume and the scholars and teachers who generously agreed to participate in the survey of approaches to teaching *Madame Bovary*. Without their assistance, this volume would not have been possible.

Starr Ackley, *College of Idaho*
Edward J. Ahearn, *Brown University*
Benjamin F. Bart, *University of Pittsburgh*, emeritus
Benedict Beit-Ishoo, *Los Angeles City College*
William J. Berg, *University of Wisconsin, Madison*
Frank Paul Bowman, *University of Pennsylvania*
Patrick Brady, *University of Tennessee, Knoxville*
Monika Brown, *Pembroke State University*
Ross Chambers, *University of Michigan, Ann Arbor*
Grant Crichfield, *University of Vermont*
Jonathan Culler, *Cornell University*
Dean de la Motte, *Guilford College*
Muriel Dominguez, *Marymount University*
Mary Donaldson-Evans, *University of Delaware, Newark*
Priscilla Parkhurst Ferguson, *Columbia University*
Edna C. Fredrick, *Westfield, MA*
Lilian R. Furst, *University of North Carolina, Chapel Hill*
Michal Peled Ginsburg, *Northwestern University*
Irene Gnarra, *Kean College of New Jersey*
Thomas Goetz, *State University of New York, Fredonia*
Michel Grimaud, *Wellesley College*
Evelyn Haller, *Doane College*
James Hamilton, *University of Cincinnati*
Melanie Hawthorne, *Texas A&M University, College Station*
Aimée Israel-Pelletier, *University of Rochester*
Michael Issacharoff, *University of Western Ontario*
Dorothy Kelly, *Boston University*
Elisabeth Ladenson, *Columbia University*
Anna Lambros, *Georgia State University*
Eric Le Calvez, *University of Dundee*
Laurey K. Martin, *University of Wisconsin, Madison*
Andrew McKenna, *Loyola University, Chicago*
William Nelles, *University of Massachusetts, Dartmouth*
Marshall Olds, *University of Nebraska, Lincoln*
Linda Orr, *Duke University*
Linda Paige, *Georgia Southern University*

Lauren Pinzka, *Connecticut College*
Gerald Prince, *University of Pennsylvania*
Patricia Reynaud, *Miami University, Oxford*
Carol de Dobay Rifelj, *Middlebury College*
Denise Rochat, *Smith College*
Monique Saigal, *Pomona College*
Beryl Schlossman, *Emory University*
Kathleen Smith, *Kalamazoo College*
Frank Triplett, *Muskingum College*
James Winchell, *Stanford University*
Susan L. Wolf, *Colgate University*
Anthony Zielonka, *Temple University*

WORKS CITED

Books and Articles

Abcarian, Richard, and Marvin Klotz, eds. *Literature: The Human Experience*. 3rd ed. New York: St. Martin's, 1994.

Adler, Mortimer J. *Reforming Education: The Opening of the American Mind*. Ed. Geraldine Van Doren. New York: Macmillan, 1989.

Adorno, Theodor W. *Aesthetic Theory*. Trans. C. Lenhardt. Ed. Gretel Adorno and Rolf Tiedemann. London: Routledge, 1984.

Alexander, Ron. "Metropolitan Diary." *New York Times* 15 Jan. 1992: C2.

Alter, Robert. *The Pleasures of Reading in an Ideological Age*. New York: Simon, 1989.

Amossy, Ruth, and Elisheva Rosen. "Le cliché ou l'envers de la 'représentation': *Madame Bovary*." *Les discours du cliché*. Paris: SEDES, 1982. 6–82.

Auerbach, Erich. *Mimesis: The Representation of Reality in Western Literature*. Trans. Willard R. Trask. Princeton: Princeton UP, 1953.

Bal, Mieke. *Narratologie: Essais sur la signification narrative dans quatre romans modernes*. Paris: Klincksieck, 1977.

Bally, Charles. "Le style indirect libre en français moderne." *Germanisch-Romanische Monatsschrift* 4 (1912): 549–56, 597–606.

Barnes, Hazel E. *Sartre and Flaubert*. Chicago: U of Chicago P, 1981.

Barnes, Julian. *Flaubert's Parrot*. New York: Knopf, 1985.

Bart, Benjamin F. *Flaubert*. Syracuse: Syracuse UP, 1967.

Barthes, Roland. "L'artisanat du style." *Le degré zéro de la littérature*. Paris: Seuil, 1953. 89–94. Trans. as *Writing Degree Zero*. London: Cape, 1967. 68–72.

———. "The Reality Effect." *French Literary Theory Today: A Reader*. Ed. Tzvetan Todorov. Cambridge: Cambridge UP; Paris: Editions de la Maison des Sciences de l'Homme, 1982. 11–17.

Baudelaire, Charles. "*Madame Bovary*." *Art Poétique*. Paris: Conard, 1925. 393–408. Vol. 3 of *Œuvres complètes*. Trans. in Flaubert, *Madame Bovary*, ed. de Man, 336–43.

———. "Le reniement de saint Pierre." *Œuvres complètes*. Paris: Gallimard, 1961. 114–15.

Becker, George Joseph. "Modern Realism as a Literary Movement." *Documents of Modern Literary Realism*. Princeton: Princeton UP, 1963. 3–38.

Beeton, Isabella Mary. *Mrs. Beeton's Book of Household Management*. 1867. New York: Exeter, 1986.

Bellemin-Noël, Jean. *Psychanalyse et littérature*. Paris: PUF, 1978.

Bersani, Leo. "Flaubert and the Threats of Imagination." *Balzac to Beckett: Center and Circumference in French Fiction*. New York: Oxford UP, 1970. 140–91.

————. "*Madame Bovary* and the Sense of Sex." *A Future for Astyanax: Character and Desire in Literature*. Boston: Little, 1976. 89–105.

Boddaert, François, Pierre-Marc de Biasi, et al. *Autour d'Emma*. Paris: Hatier, 1991.

Bollème, Geneviève, ed. *Extraits de la correspondance ou préface à la vie d'écrivain*. Paris: Seuil, 1963.

————. *La leçon de Flaubert*. Paris: Julliard, 1964.

Booth, Wayne C. *A Rhetoric of Irony*. Chicago: U of Chicago P, 1974.

Bourdieu, Pierre. *La distinction: Critique social du jugement*. Paris: Minuit, 1979. Trans. as *Distinction: A Social Critique of the Judgement of Taste*. Cambridge: Harvard UP, 1984.

Branca, Patricia. "Image and Reality: The Myth of the Idle Victorian Woman." *Clio's Consciousness Raised: New Perspectives on the History of Women*. Ed. Lois Banner and Mary S. Hartman. New York: Harper, 1974. 179–91.

Briggs, Asa, ed. *The Nineteenth Century: The Contradictions of Progress*. New York: McGraw, 1970.

Brombert, Victor. "Flaubert and the Status of the Subject." Schor and Majewski 100–15.

————. *Flaubert par lui-même*. Paris: Seuil, 1971.

————. *The Novels of Flaubert: A Study of Themes and Techniques*. Princeton: Princeton UP, 1966.

Brontë, Charlotte. *Jane Eyre*. Oxford: Oxford UP, 1980.

Brown, Marshall. "The Logic of Realism: A Hegelian Approach." *PMLA* 96 (1981): 224–41.

Bruneau, Charles. *L'époque réaliste*. Part 2. Vol. 13 of *Histoire de la langue française: Des origines à 1900*. Ed. Ferdinand Brunot. Paris: Colin, 1972.

Brunetière, Ferdinand. "Le naturalisme français: Etude sur Gustabe Flaubert." *Le roman naturaliste*. 1883. Paris: Calmann-Lévy, 1896. 149–203.

Canby, Vincent. "From Claude Chabrol, a *Madame Bovary* with Isabelle Huppert." *New York Times* 25 Dec. 1991: 13–14.

Carlut, Charles. *La correspondance de Flaubert: Etude et répertoire critique*. Columbus: Ohio State UP, 1968.

Carlut, Charles, Pierre H. Dubé, and J. Raymond Dugan. *A Concordance to Flaubert's Madame Bovary*. 2 vols. New York: Garland, 1978.

Chambers, Ross. "Répétition et ironie." *Mélancolie et opposition: Les débuts du modernisme en France*. Paris: Corti, 1987. 187–222.

Chatman, Seymour. "What Novels Can Do That Films Can't and Vice Versa." *Critical Inquiry* 7 (1980): 121–40.

Chodorow, Nancy. *The Reproduction of Mothering: Psychoanalysis and the Sociology of Gender*. Berkeley: U of California P, 1978.

Collas, Ion K. Madame Bovary: *A Psychoanalytic Reading*. Geneva: Droz, 1985.

Colwell, David J. *Bibliographie des études sur G. Flaubert*. 4 vols. Egham, Surrey: Runnymede, 1988–90.

Culler, Jonathan. *Flaubert: The Uses of Uncertainty*. 1974. Rev. ed. Ithaca: Cornell UP, 1985.

———. "The Uses of *Madame Bovary*." *Diacritics* 11 (1981): 74–81. Rpt. in Schor and Majewski 1–12.

Dällenbach, Lucien. "Du fragment au cosmos (La comédie humaine et l'opération de lecture I)." *Poétique* 40 (1979): 420–31.

Debray-Genette, Raymonde, ed. *Flaubert*. Paris: Didot, 1970.

Derrida, Jacques. *La dissémination*. Paris: Seuil, 1972.

———. *Of Grammatology*. Trans. Gayatri Spivak. Baltimore: Johns Hopkins UP, 1976.

Descharmes, René. *Flaubert: Sa vie, son caractère et ses idées avant 1857*. Paris: Ferroud, 1909.

Doody, Terrence. "Don Quixote, Ulysses, and the Idea of Realism." *Why the Novel Matters: A Postmodern Perplex*. Ed. Mark Spilka and Caroline McCracken-Flesher. Bloomington: Indiana UP, 1990. 76–93.

Du Camp, Maxime. *Souvenirs littéraires*. 2 vols. Paris: Hachette, 1906.

Duchet, Claude. "Discours social et texte italique dans *Madame Bovary*." *Langages de Flaubert*. Ed. Michael Issacharoff. Paris: Lettres Modernes, 1976. 143–63.

———. "Roman et objets: L'exemple de *Madame Bovary*." *Europe* 485–87 (1969): 171–201.

Felman, Shoshana. *Jacques Lacan and the Adventure of Insight*. Cambridge: Harvard UP, 1987.

———. "Modernité du lieu commun—en marge de Flaubert: *Novembre*." *Littérature* 20 (1975): 32–48.

Flaubert, Gustave. *Les comices agricoles de* Madame Bovary *de Flaubert*. Ed. Jeanne Goldin. 2 vols. Geneva: Droz, 1984.

———. *Correspondance*. Enl. ed. 9 vols. Paris: Conard, 1926–33.

———. *Correspondance*. Ed. Jean Bruneau. 3 vols. Paris: Gallimard, 1973–91.

———. *Correspondance: Supplément*. 4 vols. Paris: Conard, 1954. Supp. to Conard ed.

———. *The Dictionary of Accepted Ideas*. Trans. and introd. Jacques Barzun. Norfolk: New Directions, 1954.

———. *Dictionnaire des idées reçues*. Ed. Lea Caminiti. Diplomatic ed. of the Rouen mss. Paris: Nizet, 1966.

———. *The Letters of Gustave Flaubert*. Ed. and trans. Francis Steegmuller. Cambridge: Harvard UP, 1980.

———. *Madame Bovary*. Nouveaux Classiques Larousse. Paris: Larousse, 1971.

———. *Madame Bovary*. Ed. Bernard Ajac. Paris: Garnier-Flammarion, 1986.

———. *Madame Bovary*. Trans. Lowell Bair. New York: Bantam, 1987.

———. *Madame Bovary*. Ed. Claudine Gothot-Mersch. Classiques Garnier. Paris: Garnier, 1971.

———. *Madame Bovary*. Ed. Maurice Nadeau. Folio. Paris: Gallimard, 1972.

———. *Madame Bovary*. Trans. Alan Russell. New York: Viking Penguin, 1951.

———. *Madame Bovary*. Trans. and introd. Francis Steegmuller. New York: Random, 1981.

———. Madame Bovary; *Backgrounds and Sources; Essays in Criticism*. Ed. Paul de Man. Trans. Eleanor Marx Aveling and Paul de Man. New York: Norton, 1965.

————. *Madame Bovary: Life in a Country Town*. Trans. Gerard Manley Hopkins. Ed. Terence Cave. World's Classics. New York: Oxford UP, 1989.

————. *Œuvres*. Ed. Maurice Nadeau. 18 vols. Lausanne: Rencontre, 1964–65.

————. *Œuvres complètes*. Ed. Maurice Bardèche et al. 16 vols. Paris: Club de l'Honnête Homme, 1971–76.

————. *Œuvres complètes*. Ed. Bernard Masson. 2 vols. Paris: Seuil, 1964.

Frank, Joseph. *The Widening Gyre: Crisis and Mastery in Modern Literature*. New Brunswick: Rutgers UP, 1963.

Frappier-Mazur, Lucienne. "Desire, Writing, and Identity in the Romantic Mystical Novel: Notes for a Definition of the Feminine." *Style* 18.3 (1984): 328–68.

Freud, Sigmund. "A Child Is Being Beaten." *Standard Edition* 17: 170–204.

————. "The Ego and the Id." *Standard Edition* 19: 3–66.

————. "Female Sexuality." 1931. *Standard Edition* 21: 223–43.

————. "Instincts and Their Vicissitudes." *Standard Edition* 14: 117–40.

————. *The Interpretation of Dreams*. Trans. and ed. James Strachey. New York: Avon, 1965.

————. *The Standard Edition of the Complete Psychological Works of Sigmund Freud*. Ed. James Strachey. 24 vols. London: Hogarth, 1953–74.

————. "The Uncanny." 1919. *Collected Papers*. Ed. Ernest Jones. Trans. Joan Rivière. Vol. 4. London: Hogarth and Inst. of Psychoanalysis, 1953. 368–407.

Furst, Lilian R., ed. *Realism*. Modern Literatures in Perspective. New York: Longman, 1992.

Gaillard, Françoise. "L'en-signement du réel (ou la nécessaire écriture de la répétition)." Gothot-Mersch, *La production* 197–220.

Gallop, Jane. *The Daughter's Seduction: Feminism and Psychoanalysis*. Ithaca: Cornell UP, 1982.

Gans, Eric. Madame Bovary: *The End of Romance*. Boston: Twayne, 1989.

Gaultier, Jules de. *Le Bovarysme*. Paris: Mercure de France, 1902.

Gay, Peter. *The Bourgeois Experience: Victoria to Freud*. New York: Oxford UP, 1984. Vol. 1 of *Education of the Senses*. 2 vols.

Genette, Gérard. *Narrative Discourse: An Essay in Method*. Ithaca: Cornell UP, 1980. In French in *Figures III*. Paris: Seuil, 1972. 65–282.

————. *Narrative Discourse Revisited*. Ithaca: Cornell UP, 1988.

Gengembre, Gérard. *Gustave Flaubert: Madame Bovary*. Paris: PUF, 1990.

Gilbert, Sandra M., and Susan Gubar. *The Madwoman in the Attic: The Woman Writer and the Nineteenth-Century Literary Imagination*. New Haven: Yale UP, 1984.

Gilligan, Carol. *In a Different Voice: Psychological Theory and Women's Development*. Cambridge: Harvard UP, 1982.

Ginsburg, Michal Peled. *Flaubert Writing: A Study in Narrative Strategies*. Stanford: Stanford UP, 1986.

————. "Free Indirect Discourse: A Reconsideration." *Language and Style* 15 (1982): 133–49.

Girard, René. *Deceit, Desire, and the Novel: Self and Other in Literary Structure*. Trans. Yvonne Freccero. Baltimore: Johns Hopkins UP, 1965.

————. *Mensonge romantique et vérité romanesque*. Paris: Grasset, 1961.

———. *Things Hidden since the Foundation of the World*. Trans. Stephen Bann and Michael Metteer. Stanford: Stanford UP, 1987.

Goodman, Nelson. *Of Mind and Other Matters*. Cambridge: Harvard UP, 1984.

Gordon, Ruth. *Adam's Rib*. New York: Viking, 1972.

Gothot-Mersch, Claudine. "Aspects de la temporalité dans les romans de Flaubert." *Flaubert: La dimension du texte*. Ed. P. M. Wetherill. Manchester: Manchester UP, 1982. 6–55.

———. *La genèse de* Madame Bovary." Paris: Corti, 1966.

———. Introduction. *Madame Bovary*. Ed. Gothot-Mersch. v–lxiii.

———. "Le point de vue dans *Madame Bovary*." *Cahiers de l'Association Internationale des Etudes Françaises* 23 (1971): 243–59.

Graff, Gerald. *Professing Literature*. Chicago: U of Chicago P, 1987.

Grana, Cesar. *Bohemian versus Bourgeois: French Society and the French Man of Letters in the Nineteenth Century*. New York: Basic, 1964.

Gray, Eugene F., and Laurence M. Porter. "Gustave Flaubert." *The Nineteenth Century*. Ed. David Baguley. Vol. 5 of *A Critical Bibliography of French Literature*. Syracuse: Syracuse UP, 1994. 801–66.

Haig, Stirling. *Flaubert and the Gift of Speech: Dialogue and Discourse in Four Modern Novels*. Cambridge: Cambridge UP, 1986.

———. "The Madame Bovary Blues." *The Madame Bovary Blues: The Pursuit of Illusion in Nineteenth-Century French Fiction*. Baton Rouge: Louisiana State UP, 1987. 79–93.

Hart, Francis Russell. *Beyond the Books: Reflections on Teaching and Learning*. Columbus: Ohio State UP, 1989.

Harvey, Paul, and J. E. Heseltine. *The Oxford Companion to French Literature*. Oxford: Clarendon–Oxford UP, 1959.

Harvey, Stephen. *Directed by Vincente Minnelli*. New York: Harper, 1989.

Hellerstein, Erna Olafson. "Women, Social Order, and the City: Rules for French Ladies, 1830–1870." Diss. U of California, Berkeley, 1980.

Hemmings, F. W. J. *The Age of Realism*. Baltimore: Penguin, 1974.

———. *Culture and Society in France, 1789–1848*. Leicester: Leicester UP, 1987.

———. *Culture and Society in France, 1848–1898: Dissidents and Philistines*. London: Batsford, 1971.

Homans, Margaret. *Bearing the Word: Language and Female Experience in Nineteenth-Century Women's Writing*. Chicago: U of Chicago P, 1986.

Houston, John Porter. "Flaubert." *The Traditions of French Prose Style: A Rhetorical Study*. Baton Rouge: Louisiana State UP, 1981. 204–31.

Irigaray, Luce. *Speculum of the Other Woman*. Trans. Gillian C. Gill. Ithaca: Cornell UP, 1985.

Jameson, Fredric. *The Political Unconscious: Narrative as a Socially Symbolic Act*. Ithaca: Cornell UP, 1981.

Janet, Paul. *La famille: Leçons de philosophie morale*. Paris: Levy, 1855.

Joyce, James. *Ulysses*. Ed. Hans Walter Gabler. New York: Vintage, 1986.

Kaplan, Louise. *Female Perversions: The Temptations of Madame Bovary*. New York: Doubleday, 1991.

Kelly, Dorothy. *Fictional Genders: Role and Representation in Nineteenth-Century French Narrative*. Lincoln: U of Nebraska P, 1989.

Klapp, Otto. *Bibliographie der französischen Literaturwissenschaft*. Frankfurt: Klostermann, 1960– .

Knight, Diana. *Flaubert's Characters: The Language of Illusion*. Cambridge: Cambridge UP, 1985.

Kovel, Joel. "On Reading *Madame Bovary* Psychoanalytically." *The Radical Spirit: Essays on Psychoanalysis and Society*. London: Free Assn., 1988. 33–52.

Kundera, Milan. *The Art of the Novel*. Trans. Linda Asher. New York: Grove, 1988.

Lacan, Jacques. *Ecrits: A Selection*. Trans. Alan Sheridan. New York: Norton, 1977.

LaCapra, Dominick. Madame Bovary *on Trial*. Ithaca: Cornell UP, 1982.

Lafay, Jean-Claude. *Le réel et la critique dans* Madame Bovary *de Flaubert*. Paris: Lettres Modernes, 1986.

Lagarde, André, and Laurent Michard. *La littérature française*. 5 vols. Paris: Bordas, 1970–72.

Lanson, Gustave. *L'art de la prose*. 1909. Paris: Nizet, 1968.

Laplanche, Jean, and J.-B. Pontalis. "Fantasme originaire, fantasmes des origines, origine du fantasme." *Les temps modernes* 19 (1964): 1833–68.

———. *The Language of Psychoanalysis*. Trans. Donald Nicholson-Smith. New York: Norton, 1973.

Larousse, Pierre. *Grand dictionnaire universel du dix-neuvième siècle*. Paris: Administration du Grand Dictionnaire Universel, 1866–90.

Leggewie, Robert, ed. "Gustave Flaubert." *Anthologie de la littérature française*. 3rd ed. Vol. 2. New York: Oxford UP, 1990. 177–83.

Levin, Harry. *The Gates of Horn: A Study of Five French Realists*. New York: Oxford UP, 1963.

Levine, George. *The Realistic Imagination: English Fiction from* Frankenstein *to* Lady Chatterley. Chicago: U of Chicago P, 1981.

Lloyd, Rosemary. *Madame Bovary*. London: Unwin, 1990.

Lombard, Alf. *Les constructions nominales dans le français moderne*. Uppsala: Almqvist, 1930.

Lottman, Herbert R. *Flaubert: A Biography*. New York: Fromm, 1990.

Lubbock, Percy. *The Craft of Fiction*. New York: Viking, 1957. Excerpts rpt. in Flaubert, *Madame Bovary*, ed. de Man, 349–57.

Lyotard, Jean-François. *Discours, figure*. Paris: Klincksieck, 1985.

Macauley, Robie, and George Lanning. *Technique in Fiction*. New York: Harper, 1964.

Mack, Maynard, et al., eds. *Madame Bovary*. *The Norton Anthology of World Masterpieces*. 4th ed. Vol. 2. New York: Norton, 1979. 740–995.

Malory, Thomas. *Works*. Ed. Eugene Vinaver. 2nd ed. New York: Oxford UP, 1977.

Martin, William. *Recent Theories of Narrative*. Ithaca: Cornell UP, 1986.

Marx, Karl. *Capital*. Vol. 1. Trans. Eden Paul and Cedar Paul. London: Dent, 1957.

——. *The Class Struggles in France, 1848–1850.* New York: International, 1964.

——. *A Contribution to the Critique of Political Economy.* Trans. S. W. Ryazanskaya. New York: International, 1970.

——. *Economic and Philosophic Manuscripts, 1844.* Trans. Martin Milligan. Ed. Dirk Struik. New York: International, 1964.

——. *The Eighteenth Brumaire of Louis Bonaparte.* New York: International, 1964.

——. *Foundations of the Critique of Political Economy.* Trans. Martin Nicolaus. New York: Vintage, 1973. 100–11.

Marx, Karl, and Friedrich Engels. *The Marx-Engels Reader.* Ed. Robert C. Tucker. 2nd ed. New York: Norton, 1978.

Marx, Karl, and V. I. Lenin. *The Civil War in France. The Paris Commune.* New York: International, 1968.

Mathet, Marie-Thérèse. "Madame (Bovary)." *Poétique* 11 (1980): 346–53.

Maurice, Arthur Bartlett. *The Paris of the Novelists.* Garden City: Doubleday, 1919.

Millet-Robinet, Cora-Elisabeth. *Maison rustique des dames.* 5 vols. Paris: Librairie Agricole de la Maison Rustique, 1844–45.

Milner, Joseph O. "A Developmental Approach to Literature Instruction." *Passages to Literature: Essays on Teaching in Australia, Canada, England, the United States, and Wales.* Ed. Joseph O'Beirne Milner and Lucy Floyd Morcock Milner. Urbana: NCTE, 1989. 106–15.

Mitry, Jean. *Dictionnaire du cinéma.* Paris: Larousse, 1963.

Muecke, Douglas C. *The Compass of Irony.* London: Methuen, 1969.

Nadeau, Maurice. *Gustave Flaubert écrivain.* Paris: Lettres Nouvelles, 1969. Trans. as *The Greatness of Flaubert.* New York: Library, 1972.

Ostriker, Alicia. *Stealing the Language: The Emergence of Women's Poetry in America.* Boston: Beacon, 1986.

Patmore, Coventry. "The Angel in the House." Excerpts rpt. in *Victorian Women.* Ed. Erna Olafson Hellerstein, Leslie Parker Hume, and Karen Offen. Stanford: Stanford UP, 1981. 134–40.

——. "The Social Position of Women." *North British Review* 14 (1851): 514–40.

Perruchot, Claude. "Le style indirect libre et la question du sujet dans *Madame Bovary.*" *La production* 253–86.

Pichois, Claude. *Le romantisme.* Vol. 2: 1843–69. Paris: Arthaud, 1979.

Plato. *Phaedrus. The Dialogues of Plato.* Ed. and trans. B. Jowett. 4th ed. Vol. 3. Oxford: Clarendon–Oxford UP, 1953. 133–89. 4 vols.

Porter, Laurence M., ed. *Critical Essays on Gustave Flaubert.* Boston: Hall, 1986.

Poulet, Georges. "Flaubert." *Studies in Human Time.* Trans. Elliott Coleman. Baltimore: Johns Hopkins UP, 1956. 248–62.

Prince, Gerald. *A Dictionary of Narratology.* Lincoln: U of Nebraska P, 1987.

——. *Narrative as Theme: Studies in French Fiction.* Lincoln: U of Nebraska P, 1992.

——. *Narratology: The Form and Functioning of Narrative.* New York: Mouton, 1982.

——. "On Attributive Discourse in *Madame Bovary.*" *Pre-text, Text, Context.* Ed. Robert L. Mitchell. Columbus: Ohio UP, 1980. 269–75.

————. *La production du sens chez Flaubert.* Ed. Claudine Gothot-Mersch. Actes du Colloque de Cérisy. Paris: UGE, 1975.

Proust, Marcel. "A propos du 'style' de Flaubert." *Contre Sainte-Beuve.* Paris: Gallimard, 1971. 586–600.

Raimond, Michel. *Le roman depuis la révolution.* Paris: Colin, 1981.

Raitt, Alan W. "Nous étions à l'étude." *Revue des lettres modernes* 777–81 (1986): 161–92.

Ramazani, Vaheed. *The Free Indirect Mode.* Charlottesville: UP of Virginia, 1988.

Ricardou, Jean. "Belligérance du texte." *La production* 85–124.

————. *Nouveaux problèmes du roman.* Paris: Seuil, 1978.

Richard, Jean-Pierre. "La création de la forme chez Flaubert." *Littérature et sensation.* Paris: Seuil, 1954. 119–219.

Riffaterre, Michael. "Flaubert's Presuppositions." *Diacritics* 11.4 (1981): 2–11.

Rothfield, Lawrence. "From Semiotic to Discursive Intertextuality: The Case of *Madame Bovary.*" *Novel* 19 (1985): 57–81.

Rousset, Jean. "*Madame Bovary* ou le livre sur rien." *Forme et signification: Essais sur les structures littéraires de Corneille à Claudel.* Paris: Corti, 1962. 109–33.

Ryan, Desmond. "Claude Chabrol Adapts Flaubert's Masterpiece for the Screen." *Philadelphia Inquirer* 25 Dec. 1991: 6D.

Said, Edward. *Beginnings: Intention and Method.* New York: Columbia UP, 1985.

Sainte-Beuve, Charles-Augustin. "*Madame Bovary* par Gustave Flaubert." *Causeries du lundi.* Vol. 13. Paris: Garnier, [1858]. 346–63. Trans. in Flaubert, *Madame Bovary,* ed. de Man, 325–36.

Sartre, Jean-Paul. *L'idiot de la famille.* 3 vols. Paris: Gallimard, 1971–72. Rev. ed. 1988. Trans. as *The Family Idiot.* Trans. Carol Cosman. Chicago: U of Chicago P, 1981–89.

Schor, Naomi. *Breaking the Chain: Women, Theory, and French Realist Fiction.* New York: Columbia UP, 1985.

————. "For a Restricted Thematics: Writing, Speech, and Difference in *Madame Bovary.*" *The Future of Difference.* Ed. Hester Eisenstein. Boston: Hall, 1980. 167–92. Rpt. in *Breaking the Chain* 3–28. In French in *Littérature* 22 (1976): 30–46.

————. "Triste Amérique: Atala and the Postrevolutionary Construction of Woman." *Rebel Daughters: Women and the French Revolution.* Ed. Sara E. Melzer and Leslie W. Rabine. New York: Oxford UP, 1992. 139–56.

Schor, Naomi, and Henry F. Majewski, eds. *Flaubert and Postmodernism.* Lincoln: U of Nebraska P, 1984.

Sedgwick, Eve Kosofsky. *Epistemology of the Closet.* Berkeley: U of California P, 1990.

Seymour-Smith, Martin. *An Introduction to Fifty European Novels.* London: Heinemann, 1980.

Sherrington, R. J. *Three Novels by Flaubert: A Study of Techniques.* Oxford: Clarendon–Oxford UP, 1970.

Smith, Bonnie G. *Ladies of the Leisure Class: The Bourgeoises of Northern France in the Nineteenth Century.* Princeton: Princeton UP, 1981.

Sperber, Dan, and Deirdre Wilson. "Les ironies comme mentions." *Poétique* 36 (1978): 399–412.

Starkie, Enid. *Flaubert: The Making of the Master*. New York: Atheneum, 1967.

———. *Flaubert, the Master*. New York: Atheneum, 1971.

Steegmuller, Francis. *Flaubert and* Madame Bovary: *A Double Portrait*. 1939. Rev. ed. Chicago: U of Chicago P, 1977.

Strauch, Gérard. "De quelques interprétations récentes du style indirect libre." *Recherches anglaises et américaines* 7 (1974): 40–73.

Tallis, Raymond. *In Defence of Realism*. London: Arnold, 1988.

Tanner, Tony. *Adultery in the Novel: Contract and Transgression*. Baltimore: Johns Hopkins UP, 1979.

Terdiman, Richard. *Discourse/Counter-discourse: The Theory and Practice of Symbolic Resistance in Nineteenth-Century France*. Ithaca: Cornell UP, 1985.

Thibaudet, Albert. *Gustave Flaubert*. Paris: Plon-Nourrit, 1922; Gallimard, 1935, 1963. Extracts trans. in Flaubert, *Madame Bovary*, ed. de Man, 371–83.

Thorlby, Anthony. *Gustave Flaubert and the Art of Realism*. New Haven: Yale UP, 1957.

Tillett, Margaret G. *On Reading Flaubert*. London: Oxford UP, 1961.

Ullmann, Stephen. "Reported Speech and Internal Monologue in Flaubert." *Style in the French Novel*. 1957. New York: Barnes, 1964. 94–120.

Uspenskii, Boris. *A Poetics of Composition*. Trans. Valentina Zavarin and Susan Wittig. Berkeley: U of California P, 1973.

Vargas Llosa, Mario. *L'orgie perpétuelle (Flaubert et* Madame Bovary). Paris: Gallimard, 1978.

———. *The Perpetual Orgy: Flaubert and* Madame Bovary. Trans. Helen Lane. New York: Farrar, 1986.

Wagner, Geoffrey. *The Novel and the Cinema*. Rutherford: Fairleigh Dickinson UP, 1975.

Weber, Eugen. *Peasants into Frenchmen*. Stanford: Stanford UP, 1976.

Weinberg, Bernard. *French Realism: The Critical Reaction, 1830–1870*. London: Oxford UP, 1937.

Wing, Nathaniel. *The Limits of Narrative: Essays on Baudelaire, Flaubert, Rimbaud, and Mallarmé*. Cambridge: Cambridge UP, 1986.

Withers, Robert. *Introduction to Film*. New York: Barnes, 1983.

Wolf, Susan L. "Possessing Emma: The 'Enigma of Woman' in *Madame Bovary*." Diss. U of Washington, 1989.

Wright, Gordon. *France in Modern Times, from the Enlightenment to the Present*. 1968. New York: Norton, 1988.

Zeldin, Theodore. *France, 1848–1945*. 2 vols. Oxford: Clarendon–Oxford UP, 1973–1977. Vol. 2. Rev. Oxford: Oxford UP, 1980.

Audiovisual Aids

Album Flaubert [iconography]. Ed. Jean Bruneau, and Jean-A. Ducourneau. Paris: Gallimard, 1972.

Clark, Kenneth. "The Fallacies of Hope." Pt. 12 of *Civilisation*. BBC, 1970. Distr. Time-Life Films, 100 Eisenhower Dr., Paramus, NJ 07652.

Hedda. Dir. Trevor Nunn. With Glenda Jackson. Royal Shakespeare Co. Bret Productions, 1975.

Hedda Gabler. Dir. George Bloomfield. Adapt. Jack Ludwig. With Susan Clark. Canadian Broadcasting Co., 1987.

Lang, K. D. "Pullin' Back the Reins." *Absolute Torch and Twang.* Sire, 4-25877, 1989.

Madame Bovary. Dir. Claude Chabrol. With Isabelle Huppert, Jean-François Balmer, Christophe Malavoy, Jean Yanne, and Lucas Belvaux. MK2 Productions, 1991.

Madame Bovary. Dir. Vincente Minnelli. With James Mason, Louis Jourdan, Jennifer Jones, Van Heflin, Christopher Kent. MGM, 1949.

Madame Bovary. Dir. Jean Renoir. With Pierre Renoir, Robert LeVigan, Max Dearly, and Valentine Tessier. Editions Gallimard, 1934.

Madame Bovary. Dir. Jean Sherrard. Adapt. Jean Sherrard and John Siscoe. Based on the Francis Steegmuller trans. National Public Radio Playhouse. Globe Radio Repertory Theatre, Seattle, 1986.

INDEX

Modern Language Association of America
Approaches to Teaching World Literature
Joseph Gibaldi, series editor

Momaday's The Way to Rainy Mountain. Ed. Kenneth M. Roemer. 1988.

Montaigne's Essays. Ed. Patrick Henry. 1994.

Murasaki Shikibu's The Tale of Genji. Ed. Edward Kamens. 1993.

Pope's Poetry. Ed. Wallace Jackson and R. Paul Yoder. 1993.

Shakespeare's King Lear. Ed. Robert H. Ray. 1986.

Shakespeare's The Tempest *and Other Late Romances.* Ed. Maurice Hunt. 1992.

Shelley's Frankenstein. Ed. Stephen C. Behrendt. 1990.

Shelley's Poetry. Ed. Spencer Hall. 1990.

Sir Gawain and the Green Knight. Ed. Miriam Youngerman Miller and Jane Chance. 1986.

Spenser's Faerie Queene. Ed. David Lee Miller and Alexander Dunlop. 1994.

Sterne's Tristram Shandy. Ed. Melvyn New. 1989.

Swift's Gulliver's Travels. Ed. Edward J. Rielly. 1988.

Voltaire's Candide. Ed. Renée Waldinger. 1987.

Whitman's Leaves of Grass. Ed. Donald D. Kummings. 1990.

Wordsworth's Poetry. Ed. Spencer Hall, with Jonathan Ramsey. 1986.